To

_____

From

_____

Date

_____

ONE YEAR WITH JESUS

NEW LIVING TRANSLATION®

Selected and Edited by
James C. Galvin, Ed.D.
Linda Chaffee Taylor
David R. Veerman, M.Div.

Tyndale House Publishers, Inc.
Carol Stream, Illinois

Visit Tyndale's exciting Web site at www.tyndale.com

TYNDALE is a registered trademark of Tyndale House Publishers, Inc.

Tyndale's quill logo is a trademark of Tyndale House Publishers, Inc.

One Year is a registered trademark of Tyndale House Publishers, Inc.

One Year with Jesus

Produced for Tyndale House with the assistance of The Livingstone Corporation. James C. Galvin, Linda Chaffee Taylor, David R. Veerman, project staff.

Library of Congress Cataloging-in-Publication Data

One year with Jesus : New Living Translation / selected and edited by James C. Galvin, Linda Chaffee Taylor, David R. Veerman.
    p. cm.
    ISBN-13: 978-0-8423-3461-7
    ISBN-10: 0-8423-3461-0 (sc : alk. paper)
    1. Jesus, Christ—Biography—Sources, Biblical. 2. Jesus, Christ—Biography—Meditations.
3. Bible. N.T. Gospels—Meditations. 4. Bible. N.T. Gospels—Harmonies, English 5.Devotional
calendars. I. Galvin, James C. II. Taylor, Linda Chaffee, date. III. Veerman, David. IV. Bible. N.T.
Gospels. English. New Living Translation. 1999.
BT299.2.053 1999
232.9'01—dc21   99-26276
[B]

Printed in the United States of America

08   07   06   05
7   6   5   4

INTRODUCTION

One Year with Jesus has been prepared especially for those who want to learn more about Jesus and grow closer to him through the year. Each day contains a selection from the four Gospels, a Life Application note, and an information note.

The readings for each day are arranged according to the Harmony of the Gospels found in the back of this book. A harmony is a useful tool for studying the life of Christ. It simply arranges the events in the four Gospels in chronological order and makes it easier for you to compare parallel accounts. Each day's reading includes a number that guides you to the correct location in the harmony. Referring to the harmony helps you see what happened before and after any particular event. You can deepen your study by looking up any parallel passages noted for a particular reading. The Life Application notes provide insight and encouragement to take action. The information notes provide interesting background and helpful explanations.

Although these daily readings begin January 1, you can easily begin with today's date. Alternatively, you can read this book from cover to cover—no matter what today's date is—and use a bookmark to keep your place. The structure of the one-year format is not meant to confine you. It is simply there to help you if you enjoy this approach. Either way, you will finish this book in one year and meet your goal of learning more about Jesus and growing closer to him.

January 1

Luke's purpose in writing
Luke 1:1-4 *(Harmony 1)*

*M*ost honorable Theophilus:
Many people have written accounts about the events that took place among us. They used as their source material the reports circulating among us from the early disciples and other eyewitnesses of what God has done in fulfillment of his promises. Having carefully investigated all of these accounts from the beginning, I have decided to write a careful summary for you, to reassure you of the truth of all you were taught.

GOD'S TRUTH
As a medical doctor Luke knew the importance of being thorough. He used his skills in observation and analysis to thoroughly investigate the stories about Jesus. His diagnosis? The gospel of Jesus Christ is true! You can read the accounts of Jesus' life with confidence that they are true and reliable. Because the gospel is founded on historical truth, our spiritual growth must involve careful, disciplined, and thorough

The Gospel of Luke tells Jesus' story from Luke's unique perspective as a Gentile, a physician, and the first historian of the early church. Though not an eyewitness of Jesus' ministry, Luke nevertheless was concerned that eyewitness accounts be preserved accurately.

investigation of the truth of God's Word so that we can understand how God has acted in history. Christianity doesn't say, "Close your eyes and believe," but rather, "Check it out for yourself." The Bible encourages you to investigate its claims thoroughly (John 1:46; 21:24; Acts 17:11-12) because your conclusion about Jesus is a life-and-death matter. Check out the evidence.

January 2

God became a human being
John 1:1-5 *(Harmony 2a)*

*I*n the beginning the Word already existed. He was with God, and he was God. He was in the beginning with God. He created everything there is. Nothing exists that he didn't make. Life itself was in him, and this life gives light to everyone. The light shines through the darkness, and the darkness can never extinguish it.

Christ created the world, but the people he created didn't recognize him (1:10). Even the Jews rejected him although they had been chosen by God to prepare the rest of the world for the Messiah (1:11) and although the entire Old Testament pointed to his coming.

READ AND BELIEVE

What Jesus taught and what he did are tied inseparably to who he is. John shows Jesus as fully human and fully God. Although Jesus took upon himself full humanity and lived as a man, he never ceased to be the eternal God who has always existed, the Creator and Sustainer of all things, and the source of eternal life. This is the truth about Jesus and the foundation of all truth. If we cannot or do not believe this basic truth, we will not have enough faith to trust our eternal destiny to him. That is why John wrote this Gospel—to build faith and confidence in Jesus Christ so that we may believe that he truly was and is the Son of God (20:30-31). You can trust John, an eyewitness to what Jesus said and did. You can believe in Christ, God's Son.

January 3

God became a human being
John 1:6-13 *(Harmony 2b)*

*G*od sent John the Baptist to tell everyone about the light so that everyone might believe because of his testimony. John himself was not the light; he was only a witness to the light. The one who is the true light, who gives light to everyone, was going to come into the world.

But although the world was made through him, the world didn't recognize him when he came. Even in his own land and among his own people, he was not accepted. But to all who believed him and accepted him, he gave the right to become children of God. They are reborn! This is not a physical birth resulting from human passion or plan—this rebirth comes from God.

John wrote to believers everywhere, both Jews and non-Jews (Gentiles). As one of Jesus' twelve disciples, John was an eyewitness to Jesus' ministry. His book is not a biography (like the book of Luke); it is a thematic presentation of Jesus' life.

A NEW PERSON

All who welcome Jesus Christ as Lord of their lives are reborn spiritually, receiving new life from God. Through faith in Christ, we are changed from the inside out—rearranging our attitudes, desires, and motives. Being born makes you physically alive and places you in your parents' family (1:13). Being born of God makes you spiritually alive and puts you in God's family (1:12). Have you asked Christ to make you a new person? This fresh start in life is available to all who believe in Christ.

January 4

God became a human being
John 1:14-18 *(Harmony 2c)*

*S*o the Word became human and lived here on earth among us. He was full of unfailing love and faithfulness. And we have seen his glory, the glory of the only Son of the Father.

John pointed him out to the people. He shouted to the crowds, "This is the one I was talking about when I said, 'Someone is coming who is far greater than I am, for he existed long before I did.'"

We have all benefited from the rich blessings he brought to us—one gracious blessing after another. For the law was given through Moses; God's unfailing love and faithfulness came through Jesus Christ. No one has ever seen God. But his only Son, who is himself God, is near to the Father's heart; he has told us about him.

When Christ was conceived and born, God became a man. He was not part man and part God; he was completely human and completely divine. Christ is the perfect expression of God in human form. The two most common errors people make about Jesus are to minimize his humanity or to minimize his divinity. Jesus is both God and man.

GOD AND MAN
When Christ "became human and lived here on earth among us," he became (1) *the perfect teacher*—in Jesus' life we see how God thinks and therefore how we should think (Philippians 2:5-11); (2) *the perfect example*—as a model of what we are to become, he shows us how to live and gives us the power to live that way (1 Peter 2:21); (3) *the perfect sacrifice*—Jesus came as a sacrifice for all sins, and his death satisfied God's requirements for the removal of sin (Colossians 1:15-23). Keep your focus on Christ.

The ancestors of Jesus

Luke 3:23-38 (also in Matthew 1:1-17) *(Harmony 3)*

*J*esus was about thirty years old when he began his public ministry. Jesus was known as the son of Joseph. Joseph was the son of Heli. Heli was the son of Matthat. Matthat was the son of Levi. Levi was the son of Melki. Melki was the son of Jannai. Jannai was the son of Joseph. Joseph was the son of Mattathias. Mattathias was the son of Amos. Amos was the son of Nahum. Nahum was the son of Esli. Esli was the son of Naggai. Naggai was the son of Maath. Maath was the son of Mattathias. Mattathias was the son of Semein. Semein was the son of Josech. Josech was the son of Joda. Joda was the son of Joanan. Joanan was the son of Rhesa. Rhesa was the son of Zerubbabel. Zerubbabel was the son of Shealtiel. Shealtiel was the son of Neri. Neri was the son of Melki.

Matthew's genealogy goes back to Abraham and shows that Jesus was related to all Jews. Luke's genealogy goes back to Adam, showing that Jesus is related to all human beings. This is consistent with Luke's picture of Jesus as the Savior of the whole world.

Melki was the son of Addi. Addi was the son of Cosam. Cosam was the son of Elmadam. Elmadam was the son of Er. Er was the son of Joshua. Joshua was the son of Eliezer. Eliezer was the son of Jorim. Jorim was the son of Matthat. Matthat was the son of Levi. Levi was the son of Simeon. Simeon was the son of Judah. Judah was the son of Joseph. Joseph was the son of Jonam. Jonam was the son of Eliakim. Eliakim was the son of Melea. Melea was the son of Menna. Menna was the son of Mattatha. Mattatha was the son of Nathan. Nathan was the son of David. David was the son of Jesse. Jesse was the son of Obed. Obed was the son of Boaz. Boaz was the son of Salmon. Salmon was the son of Nahshon. Nahshon was the son of Amminadab. Amminadab was the son of Admin. Admin was the son of Arni. Arni was the son of Hezron. Hezron was the son of Perez. Perez was the son of Judah. Judah was the son of Jacob. Jacob was the son of Isaac. Isaac was the son of Abraham. Abraham was the son of Terah. Terah was the son of Nahor. Nahor was the son of Serug. Serug was the son of Reu. Reu was the son of Peleg. Peleg was the son of Eber. Eber was the son of Shelah. Shelah was the son of Cainan. Cainan was the son of Arphaxad. Arphaxad was the son of Shem. Shem was the son of Noah. Noah was the son of Lamech. Lamech was the son of Methuselah. Methuselah was the son of Enoch. Enoch was the son of Jared. Jared was the son of Mahalalel. Mahalalel was the son of Kenan. Kenan was the son of Enosh. Enosh was the son of Seth. Seth was the son of Adam. Adam was the son of God.

GOD'S TIMING

Imagine the Savior of the world working in a small-town carpenter's shop until he was thirty years old! It seems incredible that Jesus would have been content to remain in Nazareth all that time, but he patiently trusted the Father's timing for his life and ministry. Priests began their ministry at thirty (Numbers 4:3). Joseph began serving the king of Egypt at thirty (Genesis 41:46), and David was thirty years old when he began to reign over Judah (2 Samuel 5:4). Age thirty, then, was a good time to begin an important task in the Jewish culture. Like Jesus, we need to resist the temptation to jump ahead before receiving the Spirit's direction. Are you waiting and wondering what your next step should be? Don't jump ahead—trust God's timing.

January 6

An angel promises the birth of John to Zechariah
Luke 1:5-20 *(Harmony 4a)*

*I*t all begins with a Jewish priest, Zechariah, who lived when Herod was king of Judea. Zechariah was a member of the priestly order of Abijah. His wife, Elizabeth, was also from the priestly line of Aaron. Zechariah and Elizabeth were righteous in God's eyes, careful to obey all of the Lord's commandments and regulations. They had no children because Elizabeth was barren, and now they were both very old.

One day Zechariah was serving God in the Temple, for his order was on duty that week. As was the custom of the priests, he was chosen by lot to enter the sanctuary and burn incense in the Lord's presence. While the incense was being burned, a great crowd stood outside, praying.

Zechariah was in the sanctuary when an angel of the Lord appeared, standing to the right of the incense altar. Zechariah was overwhelmed with fear. But the angel said, "Don't be afraid, Zechariah! For God has heard your prayer, and your wife, Elizabeth, will bear you a son! And you are to name him John. You will have great joy and gladness, and many will rejoice with you at his birth, for he will be great in the eyes of the Lord. He must never touch wine or hard liquor, and he will be filled with the Holy Spirit, even before his birth. And he will persuade many Israelites to turn to the Lord their God. He will be a man with the spirit and power of Elijah, the prophet of old. He will precede the coming of the Lord, preparing the people for his arrival. He will turn the hearts of the fathers to their children, and he will change disobedient minds to accept godly wisdom."

Zechariah said to the angel, "How can I know this will happen? I'm an old man now, and my wife is also well along in years."

Then the angel said, "I am Gabriel! I stand in the very presence of God. It was he who sent me to bring you this good news! And now, since you didn't believe what I said, you won't be able to speak until the child is born. For my words will certainly come true at the proper time."

A Jewish priest was a minister of God who worked at the Temple. The priests were divided into twenty-four separate groups of about one thousand men each, according to David's directions (as described in 1 Chronicles 24:3-19). Zechariah was a member of the Abijah division, on duty this particular week. Each morning a priest was to enter the Holy Place in the Temple and burn incense. Lots were cast to decide who would enter the sacred room. One day the lot fell to Zechariah.

LET GOD DO THE IMPOSSIBLE
While Zechariah was burning incense on the altar, he was also praying, perhaps for a son or for the coming of the Messiah. In either case, God answered his prayer. He would soon have a son, who would prepare the way for the Messiah. God answers prayer in his own way and in his own time. He worked in an "impossible" situation—Zechariah's wife was barren—to bring about the fulfillment of all the prophecies concerning the Messiah. If you want to have your prayers answered, you must be open to what God can do in impossible situations. And you must wait for God to work in his way, in his time.

January 7

An angel promises the birth of John to Zechariah
Luke 1:21-25 *(Harmony 4b)*

*M*eanwhile, the people were waiting for Zechariah to come out, wondering why he was taking so long. When he finally did come out, he couldn't speak to them. Then they realized from his gestures that he must have seen a vision in the Temple sanctuary.

He stayed at the Temple until his term of service was over, and then he returned home. Soon afterward his wife, Elizabeth, became pregnant and went into seclusion for five months. "How kind the Lord is!" she exclaimed. "He has taken away my disgrace of having no children!"

FAITHFULNESS
Zechariah and Elizabeth were faithful people, yet they were suffering. At that time some Jews did not believe in a bodily resurrection, so their hope of immortality rested on their children. In addition, children would care for their elderly parents, and they added to the family's financial security and social status. Children were considered a blessing, and childlessness was seen as a

curse. Zechariah and Elizabeth had been childless for many years, and at this time they were too old to expect any change in their situation. They felt humiliated and hopeless. But God was waiting for the right time to encourage them and take away their disgrace. If you are facing difficult times, remain faithful to God. One day, in this world or in the world to come, God will take away your pain and replace it with his glory and peace!

The people were waiting outside for Zechariah to come out and pronounce the customary blessing upon them as found in Numbers 6:24-26.

January 8

An angel promises the birth of Jesus to Mary
Luke 1:26-33 *(Harmony 5a)*

In the sixth month of Elizabeth's pregnancy, God sent the angel Gabriel to Nazareth, a village in Galilee, to a virgin named Mary. She was engaged to be married to a man named Joseph, a descendant of King David. Gabriel appeared to her and said, "Greetings, favored woman! The Lord is with you!"

Confused and disturbed, Mary tried to think what the angel could mean. "Don't be frightened, Mary," the angel told her, "for God has decided to bless you! You will become pregnant and have a son, and you are to name him Jesus. He will be very great and will be called the Son of the Most High. And the Lord God will give him the throne of his ancestor David. And he will reign over Israel forever; his Kingdom will never end!"

FEELING INADEQUATE
Mary was young, poor, female—all characteristics that, to the people of her day, would make her seem unusable by God for any major task. But God chose Mary for one of the most important acts of obedience he has ever demanded of anyone. You may feel that your ability, experience, or education makes you an unlikely candidate for God's service. Don't limit God's choices. He can use you if you trust him.

Nazareth, Joseph and Mary's hometown, was a long way from Jerusalem, the center of Jewish life and worship. Located on a major trade route, Nazareth was frequently visited by Gentile merchants and Roman soldiers. Jesus was born in Bethlehem but grew up in Nazareth. Nevertheless, the people of Nazareth would reject him as the Messiah (Luke 4:22-30).

January 9

An angel promises the birth of Jesus to Mary
Luke 1:34-38 *(Harmony 5b)*

*M*ary asked the angel, "But how can I have a baby? I am a virgin." The angel replied, "The Holy Spirit will come upon you, and the power of the Most High will overshadow you. So the baby born to you will be holy, and he will be called the Son of God. What's more, your relative Elizabeth has become pregnant in her old age! People used to say she was barren, but she's already in her sixth month. For nothing is impossible with God."

Mary responded, "I am the Lord's servant, and I am willing to accept whatever he wants. May everything you have said come true." And then the angel left.

Jesus was born without the sin that entered the world through Adam. He was born holy, just as Adam was created sinless. In contrast to Adam, who disobeyed God, Jesus obeyed God and was thus able to face sin's consequences in our place and make us acceptable to God (Romans 5:14-19).

WILLING OBEDIENCE
A young unmarried girl who became pregnant risked disaster. Unless the father of the child agreed to marry her, she would probably remain unmarried for life. If her own father rejected her, she could be forced into begging or prostitution in order to earn her living. Mary, with her story about being made pregnant by the Holy Spirit, also risked being considered crazy. Still Mary said, despite the possible risks, "May everything you have said come true." When Mary made that statement, she didn't know about the tremendous opportunity she would have. She only knew that God was asking her to serve him, and she willingly obeyed. Don't wait to see the bottom line before offering your life to God. Offer yourself willingly, even when the outcome seems difficult.

January 10

Mary visits Elizabeth
Luke 1:39-45 *(Harmony 6a)*

A few days later Mary hurried to the hill country of Judea, to the town where Zechariah lived. She entered the house and greeted Elizabeth. At the sound of Mary's greeting, Elizabeth's child leaped within her, and Elizabeth was filled with the Holy Spirit.

Elizabeth gave a glad cry and exclaimed to Mary, "You are blessed by God above all other women, and your child is blessed. What an honor this is, that the mother of my Lord should visit me! When you came in and greeted me, my baby jumped for joy the instant I heard your voice! You are blessed, because you believed that the Lord would do what he said."

Apparently the Holy Spirit told Elizabeth that Mary's child was the Messiah because Elizabeth called her young relative "the mother of my Lord" as she greeted her. Elizabeth's greeting must have strengthened Mary's faith. Mary's pregnancy may have seemed impossible, but her wise relative believed in the Lord's faithfulness and rejoiced in Mary's blessed condition.

GOD DELIVERS
When told he would have a son, Zechariah had doubted the angel's word. From his human perspective, his doubt had been understandable—but with God, anything is possible. Although Zechariah and Elizabeth seemed long past the age of childbearing, God gave them a child! It is easy to doubt or misunderstand what God wants to do in our life. Even God's people sometimes make the mistake of trusting their intellect or experience rather than God. When you are tempted to think that one of God's promises is impossible, remember his work throughout history. God's power is not confined by narrow perspective or bound by human limitations. Trust him completely.

January 11

Mary visits Elizabeth
Luke 1:46-56 *(Harmony 6b)*

*M*ary responded, "Oh, how I praise the Lord. How I rejoice in God my Savior! For he took notice of his lowly servant girl, and now generation after generation will call me blessed. For he, the Mighty One, is holy, and he has done great things for me. His mercy goes on from generation to generation, to all who fear him. His mighty arm does tremendous things! How he scatters the proud and haughty ones! He has taken princes from their thrones and exalted the lowly. He has satisfied the hungry with good things and sent the rich away with empty hands. And how he has helped his servant Israel! He has not forgotten his promise to be merciful. For he promised our ancestors—Abraham and his children—to be merciful to them forever." Mary stayed with

This song is often called the Magnificat, the first word in the Latin translation of this passage. Mary's song has often been used as the basis for choral music and hymns. Like Hannah, the mother of Samuel (1 Samuel 2:1-10), Mary praised God in song for what he was going to do for the world through her.

Elizabeth about three months and then went back to her own home.

GOD'S GOOD GIFTS
When Mary said, "Now generation after generation will call me blessed," was she being proud? No, she was recognizing and accepting the gift God had given her. If Mary had denied her incredible position, she would have been throwing God's blessing back at him. Pride is refusing to accept God's gifts or taking credit for what God has done; humility is accepting the gifts and using them to praise and serve God. Don't deny, belittle, or ignore your gifts. Thank God for them and use them to his glory.

January 12

John the Baptist is born
Luke 1:57-66 *(Harmony 7a)*

Now it was time for Elizabeth's baby to be born, and it was a boy. The word spread quickly to her neighbors and relatives that the Lord had been very kind to her, and everyone rejoiced with her. When the baby was eight days old, all the relatives and friends came for the circumcision ceremony. They wanted to name him Zechariah, after his father. But Elizabeth said, "No! His name is John!"

"What?" they exclaimed. "There is no one in all your family by that name." So they asked the baby's father, communicating to him by making gestures. He motioned for a writing tablet, and to everyone's surprise he wrote, "His name is John!" Instantly Zechariah could speak again, and he began praising God.

Wonder fell upon the whole neighborhood, and the news of what had happened spread throughout the Judean hills. Everyone who heard about it reflected on these events and asked, "I wonder what this child will turn out to be? For the hand of the Lord is surely upon him in a special way."

Family lines and family names were important to the Jews. The people naturally assumed that the child would receive Zechariah's name, or at least a family name. Thus they were surprised that both Elizabeth and Zechariah wanted to name the boy John, as the angel had told them to do (see Luke 1:13).

GOD'S FAMILY
The circumcision ceremony was an important event in the family of a Jewish baby boy. God commanded circumcision when he was beginning to form his holy nation (Genesis 17:4-14), and he reaffirmed it through Moses (Leviticus 12:1-3). This ceremony was a time of joy when friends and family members celebrated the baby's becoming part of God's covenant

nation. Today there is also great joy when a baby is born, and some churches have special ceremonies to commemorate the blessed event. You were born into a human family, but to become a part of God's family, you must accept Jesus as your Savior. Are you a part of God's family?

January 13

John the Baptist is born
Luke 1:67-80 *(Harmony 7b)*

*T*hen his father, Zechariah, was filled with the Holy Spirit and gave this prophecy: "Praise the Lord, the God of Israel, because he has visited his people and redeemed them. He has sent us a mighty Savior from the royal line of his servant David, just as he promised through his holy prophets long ago. Now we will be saved from our enemies and from all who hate us. He has been merciful to our ancestors by remembering his sacred covenant with them, the covenant he gave to our ancestor Abraham. We have been rescued from our enemies, so we can serve God without fear, in holiness and righteousness forever.

"And you, my little son, will be called the prophet of the Most High, because you will prepare the way for the Lord. You will tell his people how to find salvation through forgiveness of their sins. Because of God's tender mercy, the light from heaven is about to break upon us, to give light to those who sit in darkness and in the shadow of death, and to guide us to the path of peace."

John grew up and became strong in spirit. Then he lived out in the wilderness until he began his public ministry to Israel.

GOD'S POWER AND FAITHFUL PEOPLE

Zechariah had just recalled hundreds of years of God's sovereign work in history, beginning with Abraham and going on into eternity. Then, in tender contrast, he personalized the story. His son had been chosen for a key role in the drama of the ages. Although God has unlimited power, he chooses to work through frail humans who begin as helpless babies. Don't minimize what God can do through those who are faithful to him. You may not feel as though you can do much for God, but all he requires is faith and a willing spirit. Let God do his work in and through you!

Zechariah prophesied the coming of a Savior who would redeem his people, and he predicted that his son, John, would prepare the Messiah's way. All the Old Testament prophecies were coming true. The Jews were eagerly awaiting the Messiah, but they thought he would come to save them from the powerful Roman Empire. They were ready for a military Savior but not a peaceful Messiah who would conquer sin.

January 14

An angel appears to Joseph
Matthew 1:18-19 *(Harmony 8a)*

N ow this is how Jesus the Messiah was born. His mother, Mary, was engaged to be married to Joseph. But while she was still a virgin, she became pregnant by the Holy Spirit. Joseph, her fiancé, being a just man, decided to break the engagement quietly, so as not to disgrace her publicly.

BORN OF A VIRGIN
Why is the Virgin Birth important to the Christian faith? Jesus Christ, God's Son, had to be free from the sinful nature passed on to all other human beings by Adam. Because Jesus was born of a woman, he was a human being; but as the Son of God, Jesus was born without any trace of human sin. Jesus is both fully human and fully divine.

Because Jesus lived as a man, we know that he fully understands our experiences and struggles (Hebrews 4:15-16). Because he is God, he has the power and authority to deliver us from sin (Colossians 2:13-15). We can tell Jesus all our thoughts, feelings, and needs. He has been where we are now, and he has the ability to help.

An engaged couple in our culture may call off a wedding at any time. But for the Jews, engagement was more permanent and could be broken only through death or divorce (even though sexual relations were not yet permitted). Because Mary and Joseph were engaged, Mary's apparent unfaithfulness carried a severe social stigma. According to Jewish civil law, Joseph had a right to divorce her, and the Jewish authorities could have had her stoned to death (Deuteronomy 22:23-24).

January 15

An angel appears to Joseph
Matthew 1:20-25 *(Harmony 8b)*

A s he considered this, he fell asleep, and an angel of the Lord appeared to him in a dream. "Joseph, son of David," the angel said, "do not be afraid to go ahead with your marriage to Mary. For the child within her has been conceived by the Holy Spirit. And she will have a son, and you are to name him Jesus, for he will save his people from their sins." All of this happened to fulfill the Lord's message through his prophet: "Look! The virgin will conceive a child! She will give birth to a son, and he will be called Immanuel (meaning, God is with us)."

When Joseph woke up, he did what the angel of the Lord commanded. He brought Mary home to be his wife, but she remained a virgin until her son was born. And Joseph named him Jesus.

A CHANGE OF PLANS

Perhaps Joseph thought he had only two options: divorce Mary quietly, or have her stoned. But God had a third option—marry her. In view of the circumstances, this had not occurred to Joseph. But God often shows us that there are more options available than we think. Joseph changed his plans quickly after learning that Mary had not been unfaithful to him. He obeyed God and proceeded with the marriage plans. Although others may have disapproved of his decision, Joseph went ahead with what he knew was right. Sometimes we avoid doing what is right because of what others might think. Like Joseph, we must choose to obey God rather than seek the approval of others.

The angel declared to Joseph that Mary's child was conceived by the Holy Spirit and would be a son. This reveals an important truth about Jesus—he is both God and human. The infinite, unlimited God took on the limitations of humanity so he could live and die for the salvation of all who would believe in him.

January 16

Jesus Is born in Bethlehem
Luke 2:1-5 *(Harmony 9a)*

*A*t that time the Roman emperor, Augustus, decreed that a census should be taken throughout the Roman Empire. (This was the first census taken when Quirinius was governor of Syria.) All returned to their own towns to register for this census. And because Joseph was a descendant of King David, he had to go to Bethlehem in Judea, David's ancient home. He traveled there from the village of Nazareth in Galilee. He took with him Mary, his fiancée, who was obviously pregnant by this time.

Augustus's decree went out in God's perfect timing and according to God's perfect plan to bring his Son into the world. God controls all history. By the decree of Emperor Augustus, Jesus was born in the very town prophesied for his birth (Micah 5:2), even though his parents did not live there.

GOD'S PLAN

The government forced Joseph to make a long trip just to pay his taxes. His fiancée, who had to go with him, was about to have a baby. Joseph and Mary were both descendants of David. (The Old Testament is filled with prophecies that the Messiah would be born in David's royal line [see, for example, Isaiah 11:1; Jeremiah 33:15; Ezekiel 37:24; Hosea 3:5]). But when they arrived in Bethlehem, they couldn't find a place to stay. When we do God's will, we are not guaranteed a comfortable life. But we are promised that everything, even our discomfort, has meaning in God's plan.

January 17

Jesus is born in Bethlehem
Luke 2:6-7 *(Harmony 9b)*

*A*nd while they were there, the time came for her baby to be born. She gave birth to her first child, a son. She wrapped him snugly in strips of cloth and laid him in a manger, because there was no room for them in the village inn.

MORE THAN A BABY
This mention of the manger is the basis for the traditional belief that Jesus was born in a stable. Stables were often caves with feeding troughs (mangers) carved into the rock walls. Although our first picture of Jesus is as a baby in a manger, it must not be our last. The Christ child in the manger has been made into a beautiful Christmas scene, but we cannot leave him there. This tiny, helpless baby lived an amazing life, died for us, rose from the dead, ascended to heaven, and will come back to this earth as King of kings. Christ will rule the world and judge all people according to their decisions about him. Do you still picture Jesus as a baby in a manger—or is he your Lord? Make sure you don't underestimate Jesus. Let him grow up in your life.

The blanket that Mary wrapped Jesus in actually was strips of cloth. These were used to keep a baby warm and give the baby a sense of security. The cloths were believed to protect the internal organs. The custom of wrapping infants this way continues to be practiced in many Mideastern countries.

Shepherds visit Jesus
Luke 2:8-14 *(Harmony 10a)*

*T*hat night some shepherds were in the fields outside the village, guarding their flocks of sheep. Suddenly, an angel of the Lord appeared among them, and the radiance of the Lord's glory surrounded them. They were terribly frightened, but the angel reassured them. "Don't be afraid!" he said. "I bring you good news of great joy for everyone! The Savior—yes, the Messiah, the Lord—has been born tonight in Bethlehem, the city of David! And this is how you will recognize him: You will find a baby lying in a manger, wrapped snugly in strips of cloth!"

Suddenly, the angel was joined by a vast host of others—the armies of heaven—praising God: "Glory to God in the highest heaven, and peace on earth to all whom God favors."

GREAT NEWS!

What a birth announcement! The shepherds were terrified, but their fear turned to joy as the angels announced the Messiah's birth. First the shepherds ran to see the baby; then they spread the word. The good news about Jesus is that he comes to all, including the plain and the ordinary. He comes to anyone with a heart humble enough to accept him. Whoever you are, whatever you do, you can have Jesus in your life. Don't think you need extraordinary qualifications—he accepts you as you are. Jesus is *your* Messiah, *your* Savior. Do you look forward to meeting him in prayer and in his Word each day? Discover a Lord so wonderful that you can't help sharing your joy with your friends!

Some of the Jews were waiting for a savior to deliver them from Roman rule; others hoped the Christ (Messiah) would deliver them from physical ailments. But Jesus, while healing their illnesses and establishing a spiritual kingdom, delivered them from sin. His work is more far-reaching than anyone could imagine. Christ paid the price for sin and opened the way to peace with God.

Shepherds visit Jesus
Luke 2:15-20 *(Harmony 10b)*

*W*hen the angels had returned to heaven, the shepherds said to each other, "Come on, let's go to Bethlehem! Let's see this wonderful thing that has happened, which the Lord has told us about." They ran to the village and found Mary and Joseph. And there was the baby, lying in the manger. Then the shepherds told everyone what had happened and what the angel had said to them about this child. All who heard the shepherds' story were astonished, but Mary quietly treasured these things in her heart and thought about them often. The shepherds went back to their fields and flocks, glorifying and praising God for what the angels had told them, and because they had seen the child, just as the angel had said.

SHEPHERDS AND THE LAMB OF GOD
God continued to reveal his Son, but not to those we might expect. Luke wrote that Jesus' birth was announced to shepherds in the fields. These may have been the shepherds who supplied many of the lambs that were sacrificed in the Temple for the forgiveness of sin. Here the angels invitekd these shepherds to greet the Lamb of God (John 1:36) who would take away the sins of the whole world forever. Christ paid the price for sin and opened the way to peace with God. He offers us more than temporary political or physical changes—he offers us new hearts that will last for eternity. God continues to invite men and women to discover the Savior. Have you found him?

The conception and birth of Jesus Christ are supernatural events beyond human logic or reasoning. Thus God sent angels to help certain people understand the significance of what was happening (see Luke 1:11, 26; 2:9, 13, 19). Angels are spiritual beings created by God who live in God's presence and help carry out his work on earth.

January 20

Mary and Joseph bring Jesus to the Temple
Luke 2:21-24 *(Harmony 11a)*

*E*ight days later, when the baby was circumcised, he was named Jesus, the name given him by the angel even before he was conceived. Then it was time for the purification offering, as required by the law of Moses after the birth of a child; so his parents took him to Jerusalem to present him to the Lord. The law of the Lord says, "If a woman's first child is a boy, he must be dedicated to the Lord." So they offered a sacrifice according to what was required in the law of the Lord—"either a pair of turtledoves or two young pigeons."

A BABY'S BIRTH

Why did Joseph and Mary have to return to the Temple? For forty days after the birth of a son and eighty days after the birth of a daughter, the mother was ceremonially unclean and could not enter the Temple. At the end of her time of separation, the parents were to bring a lamb for a burnt offering and a dove or pigeon for a sin offering. The priest would sacrifice these animals and declare her to be clean. If a lamb was too expensive, the parents could bring a second dove or pigeon instead. This is what Mary and Joseph did. Jesus was God's Son, but his family carried out all the specified ceremonies according to God's Law. Jesus was not born above the Law; instead, he fulfilled it perfectly. Mary and Joseph forthrightly obeyed God, fulfilling the requirements in the Law. What has God told you to do? Be obedient, be faithful.

Jewish families went through several ceremonies soon after a baby's birth: (1) Circumcision. Every boy was circumcised and named on the eighth day after birth (Leviticus 12:3; Luke 1:59-60). (2) Redemption of the firstborn. A firstborn son was presented to God one month after birth (Exodus 13:2, 11-16; Numbers 18:15-16). (3) Purification of the mother (Leviticus 12:4-8).

January 21

Mary and Joseph bring Jesus to the Temple
Luke 2:25-35 *(Harmony 11b)*

*N*ow there was a man named Simeon who lived in Jerusalem. He was a righteous man and very devout. He was filled with the Holy Spirit, and he eagerly expected the Messiah to come and rescue Israel. The Holy Spirit had revealed to him that he would not die until he had seen the Lord's Messiah. That day the Spirit led him to the Temple. So when Mary and Joseph came to present the baby Jesus to the Lord as the law required, Simeon was there. He took the child in his arms and praised God, saying, "Lord, now I can die in peace! As you promised me, I have seen the Savior you have given to all people. He is a light to reveal God to the nations, and he is the glory of your people Israel!"

Joseph and Mary were amazed at what was being said about Jesus. Then Simeon blessed them, and he said to Mary, "This child will be rejected by many in Israel, and it will be their undoing. But he will be the greatest joy to many others. Thus, the deepest thoughts of many hearts will be revealed. And a sword will pierce your very soul."

ALL WHO BELIEVE

The Jews were well acquainted with the Old Testament prophecies that spoke of the Messiah's blessings to their nation. They did not always give equal attention to the prophecies saying that he would bring salvation to the entire world, not just the Jews (see, for example, Isaiah 49:6). In the days following the Ascension, many thought that Christ had come to save only his own people. Luke made sure his Greek audience understood that Christ had come to save *all* who believe, Gentiles as well as Jews. Simeon prophesied that Jesus would have a paradoxical effect on Israel. Some would fall because of him (see Isaiah 8:14-15), while others would rise (see Malachi 4:2). With Jesus there would be no neutral ground: People would either joyfully accept him or totally reject him. What have you done with Jesus?

When Mary and Joseph brought Jesus to the Temple to be consecrated to God, they met an old man who told them what their child would become. Simeon's song is often called the Nunc Dimittis because these are the first words of its Latin translation. Simeon could die in peace because he had seen the Messiah.

January 22

Mary and Joseph bring Jesus to the Temple
Luke 2:36-40 *(Harmony 11c)*

*A*nna, a prophet, was also there in the Temple. She was the daughter of Phanuel, of the tribe of Asher, and was very old. She was a widow, for her husband had died when they had been married only seven years. She was now eighty-four years old. She never left the Temple but stayed there day and night, worshiping God with fasting and prayer. She came along just as Simeon was talking with Mary and Joseph, and she began praising God. She talked about Jesus to everyone who had been waiting for the promised King to come and deliver Jerusalem.

When Jesus' parents had fulfilled all the requirements of the law of the Lord, they returned home to Nazareth in Galilee. There the child grew up healthy and strong. He was filled with wisdom beyond his years, and God placed his special favor upon him.

NEVER TOO OLD

Although Simeon and Anna were very old, they had never lost their hope that they would see the Messiah. Led by the Holy Spirit, they were among the first to bear witness to Jesus. In the Jewish culture, elders were respected, so because of Simeon's and Anna's age, their prophecies carried extra weight. Our society, however, values youthfulness over wisdom, and potential contributions by the elderly are often ignored. As Christians, we should reverse those values whenever we can. Encourage older people to share their wisdom and experience. Listen carefully when they speak. Offer them your friendship and help them find ways to continue to serve God.

Did Mary and Joseph return immediately to Nazareth, or did they remain in Bethlehem for a time (as implied in Matthew 2)? Apparently there is a gap of several years between verses 38 and 39—ample time for them to find a place to live in Bethlehem, flee to Egypt to escape Herod's wrath, and return to Nazareth when it was safe to do so.

January 23

Visitors arrive from eastern lands
Matthew 2:1-8 *(Harmony 12a)*

*J*esus was born in the town of Bethlehem in Judea, during the reign of King Herod. About that time some wise men from eastern lands arrived in Jerusalem, asking, "Where is the newborn king of the Jews? We have seen his star as it arose, and we have come to worship him."

Herod was deeply disturbed by their question, as was all of Jerusalem. He called a meeting of the leading priests and teachers of religious law. "Where did the prophets say the Messiah would be born?" he asked them.

"In Bethlehem," they said, "for this is what the prophet wrote: 'O Bethlehem of Judah, you are not just a lowly village in Judah, for a ruler will come from you who will be the shepherd for my people Israel.'"

Then Herod sent a private message to the wise men, asking them to come see him. At this meeting he learned the exact time when they first saw the star. Then he told them, "Go to Bethlehem and search carefully for the child. And when you find him, come back and tell me so that I can go and worship him, too!"

Most Jews expected the Messiah to be a great military and political deliverer like Alexander the Great. Herod's counselors undoubtedly told this to Herod. No wonder this ruthless man took no chances and ordered all the baby boys in Bethlehem who were two years old and under killed (Matthew 2:16)!

WISE MEN
Not much is known about these astrologers (also known as wise men). We don't know where they came from or how many there were. Tradition says they were men of high position from Parthia, near the site of ancient Babylon. How did they know that the star

represented the Messiah? (1) They could have been Jews who had remained in Babylon after the Exile and knew the Old Testament predictions of the Messiah's coming. (2) They may have been eastern astrologers who studied ancient manuscripts from around the world. Because of the Jewish exile centuries earlier, they would have had copies of the Old Testament in their land. (3) They may have had a special message from God directing them to the Messiah. Some scholars say that each of these astrologers was from a different nation, representing the entire world bowing before Jesus. These men from faraway lands recognized Jesus as the Messiah when most of God's chosen people in Israel did not. Matthew pictures Jesus as King over the whole world, not just Judea. These men traveled thousands of miles to see the King of the Jews. When they finally found him, they responded with joy, worship, and gifts. This is quite different from the approach people often take today. We expect God to come looking for us, to explain himself, prove who he is, and give *us* gifts. But those who are wise still seek and worship Jesus, not for what they can get, but for who he is.

January 24

Visitors arrive from eastern lands
Matthew 2:9-12 *(Harmony 12b)*

*A*fter this interview the wise men went their way. Once again the star appeared to them, guiding them to Bethlehem. It went ahead of them and stopped over the place where the child was. When they saw the star, they were filled with joy! They entered the house where the child and his mother, Mary, were, and they fell down before him and worshiped him. Then they opened their treasure chests and gave him gifts of gold, frankincense, and myrrh. But when it was time to leave, they went home another way, because God had warned them in a dream not to return to Herod.

TRUE WORSHIP

The astrologers gave these expensive gifts because they were worthy presents for a future king. Bible students have seen in the gifts symbols of Christ's identity and what he would accomplish. Gold was a gift for a king; frankincense, a gift for deity; myrrh was a medicine and was also used as a burial spice. The astrologers brought gifts and worshiped Jesus for who he was. This is the essence of true worship—honoring Christ for who he is and being willing to give him what is valuable to you. Worship God because he is the perfect, just, and almighty Creator of the universe, worthy of the best you have to give.

Jesus was probably one or two years old when the astrologers found him. By this time Mary and Joseph were married, living in a house, and intending to stay in Bethlehem for a while.

January 25

The escape to Egypt
Matthew 2:13-15 *(Harmony 13a)*

*A*fter the wise men were gone, an angel of the Lord appeared to Joseph in a dream. "Get up and flee to Egypt with the child and his mother," the angel said. "Stay there until I tell you to return, because Herod is going to try to kill the child." That night Joseph left for Egypt with the child and Mary, his mother, and they stayed there until Herod's death. This fulfilled what the Lord had spoken through the prophet: "I called my Son out of Egypt."

FOLLOWING HIS LEAD
This was the second dream or vision that Joseph received from God. Joseph's first dream had revealed that Mary's child would be the Messiah (1:20-21). His second dream told him how to protect the child's life. Although Joseph was not Jesus' natural father, he was Jesus' legal father and was responsible for his safety and well-being.

Going to Egypt was not unusual because there were colonies of Jews in several major Egyptian cities. These colonies had developed during the time of the great captivity (see Jeremiah 43–44).

Divine guidance comes only to prepared hearts. Joseph remained receptive to God's guidance. How willing are you to listen to God? When you know what God wants, are you willing to follow his instructions?

January 26

The escape to Egypt
Matthew 2:16-18 *(Harmony 13b)*

*H*erod was furious when he learned that the wise men had outwitted him. He sent soldiers to kill all the boys in and around Bethlehem who were two years old and under, because the wise men had told him the star first appeared to them about two years earlier. Herod's brutal action fulfilled the prophecy of Jeremiah: "A cry of anguish is heard in Ramah—weeping and mourning unrestrained. Rachel weeps for her children, refusing to be comforted—for they are dead."

WHO'S ON THE THRONE?
Herod was afraid that this newborn king would one day take his throne. He completely misunderstood the reason for Christ's coming. Jesus didn't want

Herod's throne; he wanted to be king of Herod's life. Jesus wanted to give Herod eternal life, not take away his present life. Today people are often afraid that Christ wants to take things away when, in reality, he wants to give them real freedom, peace, and joy. Don't fear Christ— give him the throne of your life.

Herod, the king of the Jews, killed all the boys under two years of age in an obsessive attempt to kill Jesus, the newborn King. He stained his hands with blood, but he did not harm Jesus. Herod was king by a human appointment; Jesus was King by a divine appointment. No one can thwart God's plans.

January 27

The return to Nazareth
Matthew 2:19-23 *(Harmony 14)*

*W*hen Herod died, an angel of the Lord appeared in a dream to Joseph in Egypt and told him, "Get up and take the child and his mother back to the land of Israel, because those who were trying to kill the child are dead." So Joseph returned immediately to Israel with Jesus and his mother. But when he learned that the new ruler was Herod's son Archelaus, he was afraid. Then, in another dream, he was warned to go to Galilee. So they went and lived in a town called Nazareth. This fulfilled what was spoken by the prophets concerning the Messiah: "He will be called a Nazarene."

ANYTHING GOOD?
Nazareth sat in the hilly area of southern Galilee near the crossroads of great caravan trade routes. The Roman garrison in charge of Galilee was housed in this small town. The people of Nazareth had constant contact with people from all over the world, so world news reached them quickly. These people had an attitude of independence that many of the Jews despised. This may have been why Nathanael commented, "Nazareth! . . . Can anything good come from there?" (John 1:46). Obviously it was not wise for Nathanael to be prejudiced against the entire town, for someone truly good did live there: Jesus the Messiah. Be careful not to make quick or prejudicial judgments because of where people live or originate.

Herod the Great died in 4 B.C. of an incurable disease. Rome trusted him but didn't trust his sons. Herod knew that Rome wouldn't give his successor as much power, so he divided his kingdom into three parts, one for each son. Archelaus received Judea, Samaria, and Idumea; Herod Antipas received Galilee and Perea; Herod Philip II received Trachonitis.

Jesus speaks to the religious teachers
Luke 2:41-50 *(Harmony 15a)*

*E*very year Jesus' parents went to Jerusalem for the Passover festival. When Jesus was twelve years old, they attended the festival as usual. After the celebration was over, they started home to Nazareth, but Jesus stayed behind in Jerusalem. His parents didn't miss him at first, because they assumed he was with friends among the other travelers. But when he didn't show up that evening, they started to look for him among their relatives and friends. When they couldn't find him, they went back to Jerusalem to search for him there. Three days later they finally discovered him. He was in the Temple, sitting among the religious teachers, discussing deep questions with them. And all who heard him were amazed at his understanding and his answers.

His parents didn't know what to think. "Son!" his mother said to him. "Why have you done this to us? Your father and I have been frantic, searching for you everywhere."

"But why did you need to search?" he asked. "You should have known that I would be in my Father's house." But they didn't understand what he meant.

LETTING GO

Mary had to let go of her child and let him become a man. Fearful that she hadn't been careful enough with this God-given child, she searched frantically for him. But she was looking for a boy, not the young man who was in the Temple astounding the religious leaders with his questions. It is difficult to let go of people or projects that we have nurtured. It is both sweet and painful to see our children as adults, our students as teachers, our subordinates as managers, and our inspirations as institutions. But when the time comes to step back and let go, we must do so in spite of the hurt. Then our protégés can exercise their wings, take flight, and soar to the heights God intended for them.

According to God's Law, every male was required to go to Jerusalem three times a year for the great festivals (Deuteronomy 16:16). In the spring the Passover was celebrated, followed immediately by the weeklong Festival of Unleavened Bread. Passover commemorated the night of the Jews' escape from Egypt when God had killed all the firstborn sons and firstborn male animals in Egypt but had passed over Israelite homes (Exodus 12:21-36). Passover was the most important of the three annual festivals.

January 29

Jesus speaks with the religious teachers
Luke 2:51-52 (Harmony 15b)

*T*hen he returned to Nazareth with them and was obedient to them; and his mother stored all these things in her heart. So Jesus grew both in height and in wisdom, and he was loved by God and by all who knew him.

KEEPING IN BALANCE

The second chapter of Luke shows us that, although Jesus was unique, he had a normal childhood and adolescence. In terms of development, he went through the same progression that we do. He grew physically and mentally, he related to other people, and he was loved by God. A full human life is not unbalanced. It was important to Jesus—and it should be important to all believers—to develop fully and harmoniously in each of these key areas: physical, mental, social, and spiritual. Think about each area of your life. Work hard to stay physically fit, mentally sharp, socially adept, and spiritually in tune with God.

The Bible does not record any events of the next eighteen years of Jesus' life, but he undoubtedly was learning and maturing. As the oldest in a large family, he assisted Joseph in his carpentry work. Joseph may have died during this time, leaving Jesus to provide for the family. The normal routines of daily life gave Jesus a solid understanding of the Jewish people.

January 30

John the Baptist prepares the way for Jesus
Mark 1:1-6 (also in Matthew 3:1-6; Luke 3:1-6) (Harmony 16a)

*H*ere begins the Good News about Jesus the Messiah, the Son of God. In the book of the prophet Isaiah, God said, "Look, I am sending my messenger before you, and he will prepare your way. He is a voice shouting in the wilderness: 'Prepare a pathway for the Lord's coming! Make a straight road for him!'"

This messenger was John the Baptist. He lived in the wilderness and was preaching that people should be baptized to show that they had turned from their sins and turned to God to be forgiven. People from Jerusalem and from all over Judea traveled out into the wilderness to see and hear John. And when they confessed their sins, he baptized them in the Jordan River. His clothes were woven from camel hair, and he wore a leather belt; his food was locusts and wild honey.

TIME FOR A CHANGE

John chose to live in the desert (1) to get away from distractions so he could hear God's instructions; (2) to capture the undivided attention of the people; (3) to symbolize a sharp break with the hypocrisy of the religious leaders who preferred their luxurious homes and positions of authority over doing God's work; (4) to fulfill Old Testament prophecies that said John would be a voice calling in the wilderness to prepare the way for the Lord (Isaiah 40:3). The purpose of John's preaching was to prepare people to accept Jesus as God's Son. When John challenged the people to confess sin individually, he signaled the start of a new way to relate to God. Is change needed in your life before you can hear and understand Jesus' message? You have to admit that you need forgiveness before you can accept it. To prepare to receive Christ, repent. Denounce the world's dead-end attractions, sinful temptations, and harmful attitudes.

John's clothes were not the latest style of his day. He dressed much like the prophet Elijah (2 Kings 1:8) in order to distinguish himself from the religious leaders, whose long flowing robes reflected their great pride in their position. John's striking appearance reinforced his striking message.

January 31

John the Baptist prepares the way for Jesus
Luke 3:7-14 (also in Matthew 3:7-10) *(Harmony 16b)*

*H*ere is a sample of John's preaching to the crowds that came for baptism: "You brood of snakes! Who warned you to flee God's coming judgment? Prove by the way you live that you have really turned from your sins and turned to God. Don't just say, 'We're safe—we're the descendants of Abraham.' That proves nothing. God can change these stones here into children of Abraham. Even now the ax of God's judgment is poised, ready to sever your roots. Yes, every tree that does not produce good fruit will be chopped down and thrown into the fire."

The crowd asked, "What should we do?"

John replied, "If you have two coats, give one to the poor. If you have food, share it with those who are hungry."

Even corrupt tax collectors came to be baptized and asked, "Teacher, what should we do?"

"Show your honesty," he replied. "Make sure you collect no more taxes than the Roman government requires you to."

"What should we do?" asked some soldiers.

John replied, "Don't extort money, and don't accuse people of things you know they didn't do. And be content with your pay."

BEYOND WORDS

John's message demanded at least three specific responses: (1) Share what you have with those who need it; (2) whatever your job is, do it well and with fairness; and (3) be content with what you're earning. John had no time to address comforting messages to those who lived careless or selfish lives—he was calling the people to right living. Just as a fruit tree is expected to bear fruit, God's people should produce a crop of good works. God has no use for people who call themselves Christians but do nothing about it. Like many people in John's day who were God's people in name only, we are of no value if we are Christians in name only. If others can't see our faith in the way we treat them, we may not be God's people at all.

Many of John's hearers were shocked when he said that being Abraham's descendants was not enough for God. The religious leaders relied more on their family lines than on their faith for their standing with God. For them, religion was inherited. But a personal relationship with God is not handed down from parents

February 1

John baptizes Jesus
Matthew 3:13-17 (also in Mark 1:9-11; Luke 3:21-22) *(Harmony 17)*

*T*hen Jesus went from Galilee to the Jordan River to be baptized by John. But John didn't want to baptize him. "I am the one who needs to be baptized by you," he said, "so why are you coming to me?"

But Jesus said, "It must be done, because we must do everything that is right." So then John baptized him.

After his baptism, as Jesus came up out of the water, the heavens were opened and he saw the Spirit of God descending like a dove and settling on him. And a voice from heaven said, "This is my beloved Son, and I am fully pleased with him."

LET GO OF EGO

Put yourself in John's situation. Your work is going well, people are taking notice, everything is growing. But you know that the purpose of your work is to prepare the people for Jesus (John 1:35-37). Then Jesus arrives, and his coming tests your integrity. Will you be able to turn your followers over to him? John passed the test by publicly baptizing Jesus. Soon he would say, "He must become greater and greater, and I must become less and less" (John 3:30). Can you, like John, put your ego and profitable work aside in order to point others to Jesus? Are you willing to lose some of your status so that everyone will benefit?

Why did Jesus ask to be baptized? It was not for repentance for sin because Jesus never sinned. He was baptized because (1) he was confessing sin on behalf of the nation, as Nehemiah, Ezra, Moses, and Daniel had done; (2) he was showing support for what John was doing; (3) he was inaugurating his public ministry; and (4) he was identifying with the penitent people of God, not with the critical Pharisees who were only watching.

February 2

Satan tempts Jesus in the wilderness
Matthew 4:1-4 (also in Mark 1:12-13; Luke 4:1-4) *(Harmony 18a)*

*T*hen Jesus was led out into the wilderness by the Holy Spirit to be tempted there by the Devil. For forty days and forty nights he ate nothing and became very hungry. Then the Devil came and said to him, "If you are the Son of God, change these stones into loaves of bread."

But Jesus told him, "No! The Scriptures say, 'People need more than bread for their life; they must feed on every word of God.'"

TEMPTATION
The Devil, also called Satan, tempted Eve in the Garden of Eden; here he tempted Jesus in the wilderness. Satan is a fallen angel. He is *real*, not symbolic, and is constantly fighting against those who follow and obey God. Satan's temptations are strong, and he is always trying to get us to live his way or our way rather than God's way. One day Jesus will reign over all creation, but Satan tried to force his hand and get him to declare his kingship prematurely. The Devil's temptations focused on three crucial areas: (1) physical needs and desires, (2) possessions and power, and (3) pride. If Jesus had given in, his mission on earth—to die for our sins and give us the opportunity to have eternal life—would have been lost. But Jesus did *not* give in! When temptations seem especially strong, or when you think you can rationalize giving in, consider whether Satan may be trying to block God's purposes for your life or for someone else's life.

Jesus was tempted by the Devil, but he never sinned! Although we may feel dirty after being tempted, we should remember that temptation itself is not sin. We sin when we give in and disobey God. Remembering this will help us turn away from the temptation.

February 3

Satan tempts Jesus in the wilderness
Matthew 4:5-7 (also in Luke 4:9-13) *(Harmony 18b)*

*T*hen the Devil took him to Jerusalem, to the highest point of the Temple, and said, "If you are the Son of God, jump off! For the Scriptures say, 'He orders his angels to protect you. And they will hold you with their hands to keep you from striking your foot on a stone.'"

Jesus responded, "The Scriptures also say, 'Do not test the Lord your God.'"

THE WHOLE TRUTH

Satan used Scripture to try to convince Jesus to sin! Sometimes friends or associates will present attractive and convincing reasons why you should do something you know is wrong. They may even find Bible verses that *seem* to support their viewpoint. Study the Bible carefully, especially the broader contexts of specific verses, so that you understand God's principles for living and what he wants for your life. Only if you really understand what the *whole* Bible says will you be able to recognize errors of interpretation when people take verses out of context and twist them to say what they want them to say. Jesus was able to resist all of the Devil's temptations because he not only knew Scripture, he also obeyed it. Ephesians 6:17 says that God's Word is a sword to use in spiritual combat. Knowing Bible verses is an important step in helping us resist the Devil's attacks, but we must also obey the Bible. Satan had memorized Scripture, but he failed to submit to it. Knowing and obeying the Bible helps us follow God's desires rather than the Devil's.

The Temple was the religious center of the Jewish nation and the place where the people expected the Messiah to arrive (Malachi 3:1). The Temple was the tallest building in the area, and its highest point was actually a pinnacle on the corner wall that jutted out of the hillside, overlooking the valley below. From this spot, Jesus could see all of Jerusalem behind him and the country for miles in front of him.

February 4

Satan tempts Jesus in the wilderness
Matthew 4:8-11 (also in Luke 4:5-8) *(Harmony 18c)*

*N*ext the Devil took him to the peak of a very high mountain and showed him the nations of the world and all their glory. "I will give it all to you," he said, "if you will only kneel down and worship me."

"Get out of here, Satan," Jesus told him. "For the Scriptures say, 'You must worship the Lord your God; serve only him.'"

Then the Devil went away, and angels came and cared for Jesus.

Did the Devil have the power to give Jesus the kingdoms of the world? Satan may have been lying about his implied power, or he may have based his offer on his temporary control and free rein over the earth because of humanity's sinfulness.

THE TEST

This time of testing showed that Jesus really was the Son of God, able to overcome the Devil and his temptations. A person has not shown true obedience if he or she has never had an opportunity to disobey. We read in

Deuteronomy 8:2 that God led Israel into the wilderness to humble and test them. God wanted to see whether or not his people would really obey him. We, too, will be tested. Because we know that testing will come, we should be alert and ready for it. Remember, your convictions are strong only if they hold up under pressure!

February 5

John the Baptist declares his mission
John 1:19-23 *(Harmony 19a)*

*T*his was the testimony of John when the Jewish leaders sent priests and Temple assistants from Jerusalem to ask John whether he claimed to be the Messiah. He flatly denied it. "I am not the Messiah," he said.

"Well then, who are you?" they asked. "Are you Elijah?"

"No," he replied.

"Are you the Prophet?"

"No."

"Then who are you? Tell us, so we can give an answer to those who sent us. What do you have to say about yourself?"

John replied in the words of Isaiah: "I am a voice shouting in the wilderness, 'Prepare a straight pathway for the Lord's coming!'"

WHO WAS JOHN THE BAPTIST?

In the Pharisees' minds, there were four options regarding John the Baptist's identity: He was (1) the prophet foretold by Moses (Deuteronomy 18:15), (2) Elijah (Malachi 4:5), (3) the Prophet (the Messiah), or (4) a false prophet. John denied being any of the first three personages. Instead he called himself, in the words of the Old Testament prophet Isaiah, "a voice shouting in the wilderness, 'Prepare a straight pathway for the Lord's coming!'" (Isaiah 40:3). The leaders kept pressing John to say who he was because people were expecting the Messiah to come (Luke 3:15). But John emphasized only *why* he had come—to prepare the way for the Messiah. The Pharisees missed the point. They wanted to know who John was, but John wanted to point them to Jesus. Believers need to be like John, preparing the way for the Savior. What can you do to point people to Christ?

The priests and Temple assistants were respected religious leaders in Jerusalem. Priests served in the Temple. These leaders that came to see John were Pharisees. Many of them outwardly obeyed God's laws to look pious, while inwardly their hearts were filled with pride and greed. They believed that their own oral traditions were just as important as God's inspired Word.

February 6

John the Baptist declares his mission
John 1:24-28 *(Harmony 19b)*

*T*hen those who were sent by the Pharisees asked him, "If you aren't the Messiah or Elijah or the Prophet, what right do you have to baptize?"

John told them, "I baptize with water, but right here in the crowd is someone you do not know, who will soon begin his ministry. I am not even worthy to be his slave." This incident took place at Bethany, a village east of the Jordan River, where John was baptizing.

TO FORGIVE SINS
John was baptizing Jews. The Essenes (a strict, monastic sect of Judaism) practiced baptism for purification, but normally only non-Jews (Gentiles) were baptized when they converted to Judaism. When the Pharisees questioned John's authority to baptize, they were asking who gave John the right to treat God's chosen people like Gentiles. John said, "I merely baptize with water"—he was helping the people perform a symbolic act of repentance. But soon one would come who would truly *forgive* sins, something only the Son of God—the Messiah—could do. Jesus can forgive your sins, no matter how big or small they may be. Have you accepted his forgiveness? Confess to Christ.

John the Baptist said he was not even worthy to be Christ's slave. But according to Luke 7:28, Jesus said that John was the greatest of all prophets. If such a great person felt inadequate even to be Christ's slave, how much more should we lay aside our pride to serve Christ!

February 7

John the Baptist proclaims Jesus as the Messiah
John 1:29-34 *(Harmony 20)*

*T*he next day John saw Jesus coming toward him and said, "Look! There is the Lamb of God who takes away the sin of the world! He is the one I was talking about when I said, 'Soon a man is coming who is far greater than I am, for he existed long before I did.' I didn't know he was the one, but I have been baptizing with water in order to point him out to Israel."

Then John said, "I saw the Holy Spirit descending like a dove from heaven and resting upon him. I didn't know he was the one, but when God sent me to baptize with water, he told me, 'When you see the Holy Spirit descending and resting upon someone, he is the one you are looking for. He is the one who baptizes with the Holy Spirit.' I saw this happen to Jesus, so I testify that he is the Son of God."

THE LAMB OF GOD

Every morning and evening, a lamb was sacrificed in the Temple for the sins of the people (Exodus 29:38-42). Isaiah 53:7 prophesied that the Messiah, God's servant, would be led to the slaughter like a lamb. To pay the penalty for sin, a life had to be given—and God chose to provide the sacrifice himself. The sins of the world were removed when Jesus died as the perfect sacrifice. This is the way our sins are forgiven (1 Corinthians 5:7). The "sin of the world" means everyone's sin, the sin of each individual. Jesus paid the price of *your* sin by his death. You can receive forgiveness by confessing your sin to him and asking for his forgiveness.

John the Baptist's baptism with water was preparatory, because it was for repentance and symbolized the washing away of sins. Jesus, by contrast, would baptize with the Holy Spirit. He would send the Holy Spirit upon all believers, empowering them to live and to teach the message of salvation. This outpouring of the Spirit came after Jesus had risen from the dead and ascended into heaven (see 20:22; Acts 2).

February 8

The first disciples follow Jesus
John 1:35-42 *(Harmony 21a)*

*T*he following day, John was again standing with two of his disciples. As Jesus walked by, John looked at him and then declared, "Look! There is the Lamb of God!" Then John's two disciples turned and followed Jesus.

Jesus looked around and saw them following. "What do you want?" he asked them.

They replied, "Rabbi" (which means Teacher), "where are you staying?"

"Come and see," he said. It was about four o'clock in the afternoon when they went with him to the place, and they stayed there the rest of the day.

Andrew, Simon Peter's brother, was one of these men who had heard what John said and then followed Jesus. The first thing Andrew did was to find his brother, Simon, and tell him, "We have found the Messiah" (which means the Christ).

Then Andrew brought Simon to meet Jesus. Looking intently at Simon, Jesus said, "You are Simon, the son of John—but you will be called Cephas" (which means Peter).

NAMES OF JESUS

These new disciples used several names for Jesus: Lamb of God (1:36), Messiah (1:41), Son of God (1:49), and King of Israel (1:49). As they got to know Jesus, their appreciation for him grew. The more time we spend getting to know Christ, the more we will understand and appreciate who he is. We may be drawn to him for his teaching, but we will come to know him as the Son of God. Although these disciples made this verbal shift in a few days, they would not fully understand Jesus until three years later (Acts 2). What they so easily professed had to be worked out in experience. We may find that words of faith come easily, but deep appreciation for Christ comes with living by faith.

One of the two disciples was Andrew (1:40). The other was probably John, the writer of this book. These were Jesus' first disciples, along with Peter (1:42) and Nathanael (1:45).

February 9

The first disciples follow Jesus
John 1:43-51 (Harmony 21b)

The next day Jesus decided to go to Galilee. He found Philip and said to him, "Come, be my disciple." Philip was from Bethsaida, Andrew and Peter's hometown.

Philip went off to look for Nathanael and told him, "We have found the very person Moses and the prophets wrote about! His name is Jesus, the son of Joseph from Nazareth."

"Nazareth!" exclaimed Nathanael. "Can anything good come from there?"

"Just come and see for yourself," Philip said.

As they approached, Jesus said, "Here comes an honest man—a true son of Israel."

"How do you know about me?" Nathanael asked.

And Jesus replied, "I could see you under the fig tree before Philip found you."

Nathanael replied, "Teacher, you are the Son of God—the King of Israel!"

Jesus asked him, "Do you believe all this just because I told you I had seen you under the fig tree? You will see greater things than this." Then he said, "The truth is, you will all see heaven open and the angels of God going up and down upon the Son of Man."

DON'T MISS JESUS

When Nathanael heard that the Messiah was from Nazareth, he was surprised. Philip responded, "Come and see for yourself." Fortunately for Nathanael, he went to meet Jesus and became a disciple. If he had stuck to his prejudice without investigating further, he would have missed the Messiah! Don't let people's stereotypes about Christ keep them from his power and love. Invite them to come and see the real Jesus.

Nazareth was despised by the Jews because a Roman army garrison was located there. Some have speculated that an aloof attitude or a poor reputation in morals and religion on the part of the people of Nazareth led to Nathanael's harsh comment. Nathanael's hometown was Cana, about four miles from Nazareth.

February 10

Jesus turns water into wine
John 2:1-12 *(Harmony 22)*

The next day Jesus' mother was a guest at a wedding celebration in the village of Cana in Galilee. Jesus and his disciples were also invited to the celebration. The wine supply ran out during the festivities, so Jesus' mother spoke to him about the problem. "They have no more wine," she told him.

"How does that concern you and me?" Jesus asked. "My time has not yet come."

But his mother told the servants, "Do whatever he tells you."

Six stone waterpots were standing there; they were used for Jewish ceremonial purposes and held twenty to thirty gallons each. Jesus told the servants, "Fill the jars with water." When the jars had been filled to the brim, he said, "Dip some out and take it to the master of ceremonies." So they followed his instructions.

When the master of ceremonies tasted the water that was now wine, not knowing where it had come from (though, of course, the servants knew), he called the bridegroom over. "Usually a host serves the best wine first," he said. "Then, when everyone is full and doesn't care, he brings out the less expensive wines. But you have kept the best until now!"

This miraculous sign at Cana in Galilee was Jesus' first display of his glory. And his disciples believed in him.

After the wedding he went to Capernaum for a few days with his mother, his brothers, and his disciples.

GOD'S WAY

Mary was probably not asking Jesus to do a miracle; she was simply hoping that her son would help solve this major problem and find some wine. Tradition says that Joseph, Mary's husband, was dead, so she probably was used to asking for her eldest son's help in certain situations. Jesus' answer to Mary is difficult to understand, but maybe that is the point. Although Mary did not understand what Jesus was going to do, she trusted him to do what was right. Those who believe in Jesus but encounter situations they cannot understand must continue to trust that he will work in the best way. Mary submitted to Jesus' way of doing things. She recognized that he was more than her human son—he was the Son of God. When we bring our problems to Christ, we may think we know how he should take care of them. But he may have a completely different plan. Like Mary, we should submit and allow Christ to deal with the problem as he sees fit.

Beyond mere superhuman events, miracles demonstrate God's power. Almost every miracle Jesus did was a renewal of fallen creation-restoring sight, making the lame walk, even bringing the dead back to life. When the disciples saw Jesus' miracle, they believed. The miracle showed his power over nature and revealed the way he would go about his ministry—helping others, speaking with authority, and being in personal touch with people.

February 11

Jesus clears the Temple
John 2:13-17 (Harmony 23a)

*I*t was time for the annual Passover celebration, and Jesus went to Jerusalem. In the Temple area he saw merchants selling cattle, sheep, and doves for sacrifices; and he saw money changers behind their counters. Jesus made a whip from some ropes and chased them all out of the Temple. He drove out the sheep and oxen, scattered the money changers' coins over the floor, and turned over their tables. Then, going over to the people who sold doves, he told them, "Get these things out of here. Don't turn my Father's house into a marketplace!"

Then his disciples remembered this prophecy from the Scriptures: "Passion for God's house burns within me."

RIGHTEOUS ANGER

The Temple area was always crowded with thousands of out-of-town visitors during Passover. The religious leaders crowded it even further by allowing money changers and merchants to set up booths in the Court of the Gentiles.

They rationalized this practice as a convenience for the worshipers and as a way to make money for Temple upkeep. But the religious leaders did not seem to care that the Court of the Gentiles was so full of merchants that foreigners found it difficult to worship. Yet worship was the main purpose for visiting the Temple. No wonder Jesus was angry at

The Passover celebration took place yearly at the Temple in Jerusalem. Every Jewish male was expected to make a pilgrimage to Jerusalem during this time (Deuteronomy 16:16).

the merchants who exploited those worshipers. There is a difference between uncontrolled rage and righteous indignation—yet both are called anger. We must be very careful how we use the powerful emotion of anger. It is right to be angry about injustice and sin; it is wrong to be angry over trivial personal offenses.

February 12

Jesus clears the Temple
John 2:18-25 *(Harmony 23b)*

*W*hat right do you have to do these things?" the Jewish leaders demanded. "If you have this authority from God, show us a miraculous sign to prove it."

"All right," Jesus replied. "Destroy this temple, and in three days I will raise it up."

"What!" they exclaimed. "It took forty-six years to build this Temple, and you can do it in three days?" But by "this temple," Jesus meant his body. After he was raised from the dead, the disciples remembered that he had said this. And they believed both Jesus and the Scriptures.

Because of the miraculous signs he did in Jerusalem at the Passover celebration, many people were convinced that he was indeed the Messiah. But Jesus didn't trust them, because he knew what people were really like. No one needed to tell him about human nature.

The Son of God knows all about human nature. Jesus was well aware of the truth of Jeremiah 17:9, which states, "The human heart is most deceitful and desperately wicked. Who really knows how bad it is!" Jesus was discerning, and he knew that the faith of some followers was superficial. Some of the same people claiming to believe in Jesus at this time would later yell, "Crucify him!"

STRONG PROOF
The Jews understood Jesus to mean the Temple out of which he had just driven the merchants and money changers. This was the Temple Zerubbabel had built more than five hundred years earlier, but Herod the Great had begun remodeling it, making it much

larger and far more beautiful. It had been forty-six years since this remodeling had started (20 B.C.), and it still was not completely finished. They understood Jesus' words to mean that this imposing building could be torn down and rebuilt in three days, and they were startled. However, Jesus was not talking about the Temple made of stones, but about his body. His listeners didn't realize it, but Jesus was greater than the Temple (Matthew 12:6). His words would take on meaning for his disciples after his resurrection. That Christ so perfectly fulfilled this prediction became the strongest proof for his claims to be God. If you ever have doubts about Jesus' divinity, remember that he fulfilled his promise to rise from the dead. You worship a *living* Savior.

February 13

Nicodemus visits Jesus at night
John 3:1-8 *(Harmony 24a)*

*A*fter dark one evening, a Jewish religious leader named Nicodemus, a Pharisee, came to speak with Jesus. "Teacher," he said, "we all know that God has sent you to teach us. Your miraculous signs are proof enough that God is with you."

Jesus replied, "I assure you, unless you are born again, you can never see the Kingdom of God."

"What do you mean?" exclaimed Nicodemus. "How can an old man go back into his mother's womb and be born again?"

Jesus replied, "The truth is, no one can enter the Kingdom of God without being born of water and the Spirit. Humans can reproduce only human life, but the Holy Spirit gives new life from heaven. So don't be surprised at my statement that you must be born again. Just as you can hear the wind but can't tell where it comes from or where it is going, so you can't explain how people are born of the Spirit."

A NIGHT MEETING

Nicodemus was a Pharisee and a member of the ruling council called the Sanhedrin. The Pharisees were a group of religious leaders whom Jesus and John the Baptist often criticized for being hypocrites. Most Pharisees were intensely jealous of Jesus because he undermined their authority and challenged their views. But Nicodemus was searching, and he believed that Jesus had some answers.

What did Nicodemus know about the Kingdom? From the Bible he knew it would be ruled by God, it would be restored on earth, and it would incorporate God's people. Jesus revealed to this devout Pharisee that the Kingdom would come to the whole world (3:16), not just the Jews, and that Nicodemus wouldn't be a part of it unless he was personally born again (3:5).

A learned teacher himself, he came to Jesus to be taught. Nicodemus came to Jesus personally, although he could have sent one of his assistants. He wanted to examine Jesus for himself in order to separate fact from rumor. Perhaps Nicodemus was afraid of what his peers, the Pharisees, would say about his visit, so he came after dark. Later, when he understood that Jesus was truly the Messiah, he spoke up boldly in his defense (7:50-51). Like Nicodemus, we must examine Jesus for ourselves—others cannot do it for us. If we believe he is who he says, we will want to speak up for him.

February 14

Nicodemus visits Jesus at night
John 3:9-17 *(Harmony 24b)*

*W*hat do you mean?" Nicodemus asked.

Jesus replied, "You are a respected Jewish teacher, and yet you don't understand these things? I assure you, I am telling you what we know and have seen, and yet you won't believe us. But if you don't even believe me when I tell you about things that happen here on earth, how can you possibly believe if I tell you what is going on in heaven? For only I, the Son of Man, have come to earth and will return to heaven again. And as Moses lifted up the bronze snake on a pole in the wilderness, so I, the Son of Man, must be lifted up on a pole, so that everyone who believes in me will have eternal life.

"For God so loved the world that he gave his only Son, so that everyone who believes in him will not perish but have eternal life. God did not send his Son into the world to condemn it, but to save it."

THE GOSPEL

The entire gospel comes to a focus in John 3:16. God's love is not static or self-centered; it reaches out and draws others in. Here God sets the pattern of true love, the basis for all love relationships—when you love someone dearly, you are willing to give freely to the point of self-sacrifice. God paid dearly with the life of his Son, the highest price he could pay. Jesus accepted our punishment, paid the price for our sins, and then offered us the new life that he had bought for us. When we share the gospel with others, our love must be like Jesus'—willingly giving up our own comfort and security so that others might join us in receiving God's

When the Israelites were wandering in the wilderness, God sent a plague of serpents to punish them for their rebellious attitude. Those doomed to die from snakebite could be healed by obeying God's command to look up at the elevated bronze snake and by believing that God would heal them if they did.

love. To "believe" is more than intellectual agreement that Jesus is God. It means to put our trust and confidence in him that he alone can save us. It is to put Christ in charge of our present plans and eternal destiny. Believing is both trusting his words as reliable and relying on him for the power to change. If you have never trusted Christ, let this promise of everlasting life be yours—and believe.

February 15

Nicodemus visits Jesus at night
John 3:18-21 *(Harmony 24c)*

*T*here is no judgment awaiting those who trust him. But those who do not trust him have already been judged for not believing in the only Son of God. Their judgment is based on this fact: The light from heaven came into the world, but they loved the darkness more than the light, for their actions were evil. They hate the light because they want to sin in the darkness. They stay away from the light for fear their sins will be exposed and they will be punished. But those who do what is right come to the light gladly, so everyone can see that they are doing what God wants."

LIVING IN THE LIGHT
Many people don't want their lives exposed to God's light because they are afraid of what will be revealed. They don't want to be changed. Don't be surprised when these same people are threatened by your desire to obey God and do what is right, because they are afraid that the light in you may expose some of the darkness in their lives. Rather than giving in to discouragement, keep praying that they will come to see how much better it is to live in light than in darkness.

People often try to protect themselves from their fears by putting their faith in something they do or have: good works, skill or intelligence, money or possessions. But only God can save us from the one thing that we really need to fear—eternal condemnation.

John the Baptist tells more about Jesus
John 3:22-30 *(Harmony 25a)*

*A*fterward Jesus and his disciples left Jerusalem, but they stayed in Judea for a while and baptized there.

At this time John the Baptist was baptizing at Aenon, near Salim, because there was plenty of water there and people kept coming to him for baptism. This was before John was put into prison. At that time a certain Jew began an argument with John's disciples over ceremonial cleansing. John's disciples came to him and said, "Teacher, the man you met on the other side of the Jordan River, the one you said was the Messiah, is also baptizing people. And everybody is going over there instead of coming here to us."

John replied, "God in heaven appoints each person's work. You yourselves know how plainly I told you that I am not the Messiah. I am here to prepare the way for him—that is all. The bride will go where the bridegroom is. A bridegroom's friend rejoices with him. I am the bridegroom's friend, and I am filled with joy at his success. He must become greater and greater, and I must become less and less."

FOLLOWING GOD'S CALL

Why did John the Baptist continue to baptize after Jesus came onto the scene? Why didn't he become a disciple too? John explained that because God had given him his work, he had to continue it until God called him to do something else. John's main purpose was to point people to Christ. Even with Jesus beginning his own ministry, John could still turn people to Jesus. Although John was the first genuine prophet in four hundred years, Jesus the Messiah would be infinitely greater than he. What John began, Jesus finished. What John prepared, Jesus fulfilled. Yet John willingly did the task to which he had been called. We must do the same, serving where we are called, and doing the tasks set before us to the best of our ability. While others may get the glory and we may feel jealous of others or wish we had their gifts or positions, we must remember that our goal is to glorify Christ and complete his work on earth.

John's willingness to decrease in importance shows unusual humility. Pastors and other Christian leaders can be tempted to focus more on the success of their ministries than on Christ. Beware of those who put more emphasis on their own achievements than on God's Kingdom.

John the Baptist tells more about Jesus
John 3:31-36 *(Harmony 25b)*

*H*e has come from above and is greater than anyone else. I am of the earth, and my understanding is limited to the things of earth, but he has come from heaven. He tells what he has seen and heard, but how few believe what he tells them! Those who believe him discover that God is true. For he is sent by God. He speaks God's words, for God's Spirit is upon him without measure or limit. The Father loves his Son, and he has given him authority over everything. And all who believe in God's Son have eternal life. Those who don't obey the Son will never experience eternal life, but the wrath of God remains upon them."

THE CHOICE

Jesus' testimony was trustworthy because he had come from heaven and was speaking of what he had seen there. His words were the very words of God. Your whole spiritual life depends on your answer to one question: "Who is Jesus Christ?" If you accept Jesus as only a prophet or teacher, you have to reject his teaching, for he claimed to be God's Son, even God himself. The heartbeat of John's Gospel is the dynamic truth that Jesus Christ is God's Son, the Messiah, the Savior, who was from the beginning and will continue to live forever. This same Jesus has invited us to accept him and live with him eternally. When we understand who Jesus is, we are compelled to believe what he said. We are responsible to decide today whom we will obey (Joshua 24:15), and God wants us to choose him and life (Deuteronomy 30:15-20). The wrath of God is his final judgment and rejection of the sinner. To put off the choice is to choose not to follow Christ. Indecision is a fatal decision.

Jesus said that those who believe in him have (not will have) everlasting life. To receive eternal life is to join in God's life, which by nature is eternal. Thus, eternal life begins at the moment of spiritual rebirth.

February 18

Herod puts John in prison
Luke 3:19-20 *(Harmony 26)*

*J*ohn also publicly criticized Herod Antipas, ruler of Galilee, for marrying Herodias, his brother's wife, and for many other wrongs he had done. So Herod put John in prison, adding this sin to his many others.

THROWING AWAY THE KEY
John the Baptist publicly spoke out against Herod's adultery. This was Herod Antipas, tetrarch of Galilee and Perea, and he had married Herodias, who was previously married to his brother, Herod Philip I. Besides being his brother's wife, Herodias was also his niece. Rather than accept John's rebuke, Herod moved to silence John. People hate to be confronted with their sin. We should not be surprised when the world tries to silence Christians today. Yet we should have the courage of John the Baptist and speak the truth in love, regardless of the consequences.

The Herods were a murderous and deceitful family. Rebuking a tyrannical Roman official who could imprison and execute him was extremely dangerous, yet that is what John did. He fearlessly risked his life to speak out against sin.

February 19

Jesus talks to a woman at the well
John 4:1-15 *(Harmony 27a)*

*J*esus learned that the Pharisees had heard, "Jesus is baptizing and making more disciples than John" (though Jesus himself didn't baptize them—his disciples did). So he left Judea to return to Galilee.

He had to go through Samaria on the way. Eventually he came to the Samaritan village of Sychar, near the parcel of ground that Jacob gave to his son Joseph. Jacob's well was there; and Jesus, tired from the long walk, sat wearily beside the well about noontime. Soon a Samaritan woman came to draw water, and Jesus said to her, "Please give me a drink." He was alone at the time because his disciples had gone into the village to buy some food.

The woman was surprised, for Jews refuse to have anything to do with Samaritans. She said to Jesus, "You are a Jew, and I am a Samaritan woman. Why are you asking me for a drink?"

Jesus replied, "If you only knew the gift God has for you and who I am, you would ask me, and I would give you living water."

"But sir, you don't have a rope or a bucket," she said, "and this is a very deep well. Where would you get this living water? And besides, are you greater than our ancestor Jacob who gave us this well? How can you offer better water than he and his sons and his cattle enjoyed?"

Jesus replied, "People soon become thirsty again after drinking this water. But the water I give them takes away thirst altogether. It becomes a perpetual spring within them, giving them eternal life."

"Please, sir," the woman said, "give me some of that water! Then I'll never be thirsty again, and I won't have to come here to haul water."

THIRST QUENCHER

Many spiritual functions parallel physical functions. As our bodies hunger and thirst, so do our souls. But our souls need *spiritual* food and water. The woman confused the two kinds of water, perhaps because no one had ever talked with her about her spiritual hunger and thirst before. We would not think of depriving our bodies of food and water when they hunger or thirst. Why then should we deprive our souls? The living Word, Jesus Christ, and the written Word, the Bible, can satisfy our hungry and thirsty souls. The woman mistakenly believed that if she received the water Jesus offered, she would not have to return to the well each day. She was interested in Jesus' message because she thought it could make her life easier. But if that were always the case, people would accept Christ's message for the wrong reasons. Christ did not come to take away challenges but to change us on the inside, helping us see our problems from God's perspective and empowering us to deal with them. Jesus wants to help you too. Let him change you from the inside out.

Jacob's well was on the property originally owned by Jacob (Genesis 33:18-19). It was not a spring-fed well but a well into which water seeped from rain and dew, collecting at the bottom. Wells were almost always located outside the city along the main road. Twice each day, morning and evening, women came to draw water. This woman came at noon, however, probably to avoid meeting people who knew her reputation.

February 20

Jesus talks to a woman at the well
John 4:16-26 *(Harmony 27b)*

*G*o and get your husband," Jesus told her.

"I don't have a husband," the woman replied.

Jesus said, "You're right! You don't have a husband—for you have had five husbands, and you aren't even married to the man you're living with now."

"Sir," the woman said, "you must be a prophet. So tell me, why is it that you Jews insist that Jerusalem is the only place of worship, while we Samaritans claim it is here at Mount Gerizim, where our ancestors worshiped?"

Jesus replied, "Believe me, the time is coming when it will no longer matter whether you worship the Father here or in Jerusalem. You Samaritans know so little about the one you worship, while we Jews know all about him, for salvation comes through the Jews. But the time is coming and is already here when true worshipers will worship the Father in spirit and in truth. The Father is looking for anyone who will worship him that way. For God is Spirit, so those who worship him must worship in spirit and in truth."

The woman said, "I know the Messiah will come—the one who is called Christ. When he comes, he will explain everything to us."

Then Jesus told her, "I am the Messiah!"

THE HOLY SPIRIT'S HELP
"God is Spirit" means he is not a physical being limited to one place. He is present everywhere and he can be worshiped anywhere, at any time. It is not *where* we worship that counts, but *how* we worship. Is your worship genuine and true? Do you have the Holy Spirit's help? How does the Holy Spirit help us worship? The Holy Spirit prays for us (Romans 8:26), teaches us the words of Christ (14:26), and tells us we are loved (Romans 5:5). Focus your worship on who God is and what he has done for you. Ask for the Holy Spirit's help.

The woman brought up a popular theological issue—the correct place to worship. But her question was a diversion to keep Jesus away from her deepest need. Jesus directed the conversation to a much more important point: The location of worship is not nearly as important as the attitude of the worshipers.

February 21

Jesus tells about the spiritual harvest
John 4:27-38 *(Harmony 28)*

*J*ust then his disciples arrived. They were astonished to find him talking to a woman, but none of them asked him why he was doing it or what they had been discussing. The woman left her water jar beside the well and went back to the village and told everyone, "Come and meet a man who told me everything I ever did! Can this be the Messiah?" So the people came streaming from the village to see him.

Meanwhile, the disciples were urging Jesus to eat. "No," he said, "I have food you don't know about."

"Who brought it to him?" the disciples asked each other.

Then Jesus explained: "My nourishment comes from doing the will of God, who sent me, and from finishing his work. Do you think the work of harvesting will not begin until the summer ends four months from now? Look around you! Vast fields are ripening all around us and are ready now for the harvest. The harvesters are paid good wages, and the fruit they harvest is people brought to eternal life. What joy awaits both the planter and the harvester alike! You know the saying, 'One person plants and someone else harvests.' And it's true. I sent you to harvest where you didn't plant; others had already done the work, and you will gather the harvest."

WAGES OF JOY

The wages Jesus offers are the joy of working for him and seeing the harvest of believers. These wages come to sower and reaper alike because both find joy in seeing new believers come into Christ's Kingdom. The phrase "others have already done the work" (4:38) may refer to the Old Testament prophets and to John the Baptist, who paved the way for the gospel. Sometimes Christians excuse themselves from witnessing by saying that their family or friends aren't ready to believe. Jesus makes it clear, however, that around us a continual harvest waits to be reaped. Don't let Jesus find you making excuses. Look around. You will find people ready to hear God's Word.

The "food" about which Jesus was speaking was his spiritual nourishment. It includes more than Bible study, prayer, and attending church. Spiritual nourishment also comes from doing God's will and helping to bring his work of salvation to completion. We are nourished not only by what we take in but also by what we give out for God.

February 22

Many Samaritans believe in Jesus
John 4:39-42 *(Harmony 29)*

*M*any Samaritans from the village believed in Jesus because the woman had said, "He told me everything I ever did!" When they came out to see him, they begged him to stay at their village. So he stayed for two days, long enough for many of them to hear his message and believe. Then they said to the woman, "Now we believe because we have heard him ourselves, not just because of what you told us. He is indeed the Savior of the world."

BREAKING THE BARRIERS

After the northern kingdom, with its capital at Samaria, fell to the Assyrians, many Jews were deported to Assyria, and foreigners were brought in to settle the land and help keep the peace (2 Kings 17:24). The intermarriage between those foreigners and the remaining Jews resulted in a mixed race, impure in the opinion of Jews who lived in the southern kingdom. Thus, the pure Jews hated this mixed race, called Samaritans, because they felt that their fellow Jews who had intermarried had betrayed their people and nation. The Samaritans had set up an alternate center for worship on Mount Gerizim (referred to in 4:20) to parallel the Temple at Jerusalem, but it had been destroyed 150 years earlier. The Jews did everything they could to avoid traveling through Samaria. But Jesus had no reason to live by such cultural restrictions. The route through Samaria was shorter, so that was the route he took. As a result, many Samaritans became believers. Never let cultural or social prejudices keep you from sharing the gospel.

The Samaritan woman immediately shared her experience with others. Despite her reputation, many took her invitation and came out to meet Jesus. Perhaps there are sins in our past of which we're ashamed. But Christ changes us. As people see these changes, they become curious. We share these opportunities to introduce people to Christ.

February 23

Jesus preaches in Galilee

Matthew 4:12-17 (also in Mark 1:14-15; Luke 4:14-15; John 4:43-45) *(Harmony 30)*

*W*hen Jesus heard that John had been arrested, he left Judea and returned to Galilee. But instead of going to Nazareth, he went to Capernaum, beside the Sea of Galilee, in the region of Zebulun and Naphtali. This fulfilled Isaiah's prophecy: "In the land of Zebulun and of Naphtali, beside the sea, beyond the Jordan River—in Galilee where so many Gentiles live—the people who sat in darkness have seen a great light. And for those who lived in the land where death casts its shadow, a light has shined."

From then on, Jesus began to preach, "Turn from your sins and turn to God, because the Kingdom of Heaven is near."

THE KINGDOM

The "Kingdom of Heaven" has the same meaning as the "Kingdom of God" in Mark and Luke. Matthew used this phrase because the Jews, out of their intense reverence and respect, did not pronounce God's name. The Kingdom of Heaven began when God himself entered human history as a man. Today Jesus Christ reigns in the hearts of believers, but the Kingdom of Heaven will not be fully realized until all evil in the world is judged and removed. Christ came to earth first as a suffering servant; he will come again as King and Judge to rule victoriously over all the earth. The Kingdom of Heaven is still near because it has arrived in our hearts. When you feel overwhelmed by life and destroyed by circumstances, remember that this world isn't all there is. Jesus will return—the Kingdom of Heaven is near.

Jesus moved from Nazareth, his hometown, to Capernaum, about twenty miles farther north. Capernaum became Jesus' home base during his ministry in Galilee. Capernaum was a thriving city with great wealth as well as great decadence. Because it was the headquarters for many Roman troops, word about Jesus could spread all over the Roman Empire. Jesus' move fulfilled the prophecy of Isaiah 9:1-2, which stated that the Messiah would be a light to the land of Zebulun and Naphtali, the region of Galilee where Capernaum was located. Zebulun and Naphtali were two of the original twelve tribes of Israel.

February 24

Jesus heals a government official's son
John 4:46-54 *(Harmony 31)*

*I*n the course of his journey through Galilee, he arrived at the town of Cana, where he had turned the water into wine. There was a government official in the city of Capernaum whose son was very sick. When he heard that Jesus had come from Judea and was traveling in Galilee, he went over to Cana. He found Jesus and begged him to come to Capernaum with him to heal his son, who was about to die.

Jesus asked, "Must I do miraculous signs and wonders before you people will believe in me?"

The official pleaded, "Lord, please come now before my little boy dies."

Then Jesus told him, "Go back home. Your son will live!" And the man believed Jesus' word and started home.

While he was on his way, some of his servants met him with the news that his son was alive and well. He asked them when the boy had begun to feel better, and they replied, "Yesterday afternoon at one o'clock his fever suddenly disappeared!" Then the father realized it was the same time that Jesus had told him, "Your son will live." And the officer and his entire household believed in Jesus. This was Jesus' second miraculous sign in Galilee after coming from Judea.

This government official was probably in Herod's service. He had walked twenty miles to see Jesus and addressed him as "Lord," putting himself under Jesus even though he had legal authority over Jesus. This official not only believed Jesus could heal; he also obeyed Jesus by returning home, thus demonstrating his faith. It isn't enough for us to say we believe that Jesus can take care of our problems. We need to act as if he can. When you pray about a need or problem, live as though you believe Jesus can do what he says. Notice how the official's faith grew. First, he believed enough to ask Jesus to help his son. Second, he believed Jesus' assurance that his son would live, and he acted on it. Third, he and his whole house believed in Jesus. Faith is a gift that grows as we use it.

Jesus' miracles were not mere illusions, the product of wishful thinking. Although the official's son was twenty miles away, he was healed when Jesus spoke the word. Distance was no problem because Christ has mastery over space. We can never put so much space between ourselves and Christ that he can no longer help us.

February 25

Jesus is rejected at Nazareth
Luke 4:16-30 *(Harmony 32)*

*W*hen he came to the village of Nazareth, his boyhood home, he went as usual to the synagogue on the Sabbath and stood up to read the Scriptures. The scroll containing the messages of Isaiah the prophet was handed to him, and he unrolled the scroll to the place where it says: "The Spirit of the Lord is upon me, for he has appointed me to preach Good News to the poor. He has sent me to proclaim that captives will be released, that the blind will see, that the downtrodden will be freed from their oppressors, and that the time of the Lord's favor has come."

He rolled up the scroll, handed it back to the attendant, and sat down. Everyone in the synagogue stared at him intently. Then he said, "This Scripture has come true today before your very eyes!"

All who were there spoke well of him and were amazed by the gracious words that fell from his lips. "How can this be?" they asked. "Isn't this Joseph's son?"

Then he said, "Probably you will quote me that proverb, 'Physician, heal yourself'—meaning, 'Why don't you do miracles here in your hometown like those you did in Capernaum?' But the truth is, no prophet is accepted in his own hometown.

"Certainly there were many widows in Israel who needed help in Elijah's time, when there was no rain for three and a half years and hunger stalked the land. Yet Elijah was not sent to any of them. He was sent instead to a widow of Zarephath—a foreigner in the land of Sidon. Or think of the prophet Elisha, who healed Naaman, a Syrian, rather than the many lepers in Israel who needed help."

When they heard this, the people in the synagogue were furious. Jumping up, they mobbed him and took him to the edge of the hill on which the city was built. They intended to push him over the cliff, but he slipped away through the crowd and left them.

GOOD NEWS

Jesus was quoting from Isaiah 61:1-2. Isaiah pictured the deliverance of Israel from exile in Babylon as a Year of Jubilee when all debts are cancelled, all slaves are freed, and all property is returned to original owners (Leviticus 25). But the release from Babylonian exile had not brought the fulfillment the people had expected; they were still a conquered and oppressed people. So Isaiah must have been referring to a future messianic age. Jesus boldly announced, "This Scripture has come true today before your very eyes!" Jesus was proclaiming himself as the one who would bring this good news to pass, but in a way that the people would not yet be able to grasp. Even Jesus himself was not accepted as a prophet in his hometown. Many people have a similar attitude —an expert is anyone who carries a briefcase and comes from more than two hundred miles away. Don't be surprised when your Christian life and faith are not easily understood or accepted by those who know you well.

Jesus' remarks filled the people of Nazareth with rage because he was saying that God sometimes chooses to reach Gentiles rather than Jews. Jesus implied that his hearers were as unbelieving as the citizens of the northern kingdom of Israel in the days of Elijah and Elisha, a time notorious for its great wickedness.

February 26

Four fishermen follow Jesus
Mark 1:16-20 (also in Matthew 4:18-22) (Harmony 33)

*O*ne day as Jesus was walking along the shores of the Sea of Galilee, he saw Simon and his brother, Andrew, fishing with a net, for they were commercial fishermen. Jesus called out to them, "Come, be my disciples, and I will show you how to fish for people!" And they left their nets at once and went with him.

A little farther up the shore Jesus saw Zebedee's sons, James and John, in a boat mending their nets. He called them, too, and immediately they left their father, Zebedee, in the boat with the hired men and went with him.

TRUE FOLLOWERS

We often assume that Jesus' disciples were great men of faith from the first time they met Jesus. But they had to grow in their faith just as all believers do (14:48-50, 66-72; John 14:1-9; 20:26-29). This is apparently not the only time Jesus called Peter (Simon), James, and John to follow him (see Luke 5:1-11 and John 1:35-42 for two other times). Although it took time for Jesus' call and his message to get through, the disciples still *followed*. In the same way, we may question and falter, but we must never stop following Jesus.

Fishing was a major industry around the Sea of Galilee. Fishing with nets was the most common method. Capernaum, the largest of the more than thirty fishing towns around the lake at that time, became Jesus' new home (Matthew 4:12-13).

February 27

Jesus teaches with great authority
Luke 4:31-37 (also in Mark 1:21-28) *(Harmony 34)*

*T*hen Jesus went to Capernaum, a town in Galilee, and taught there in the synagogue every Sabbath day. There, too, the people were amazed at the things he said, because he spoke with authority.

Once when he was in the synagogue, a man possessed by a demon began shouting at Jesus, "Go away! Why are you bothering us, Jesus of Nazareth? Have you come to destroy us? I know who you are—the Holy One sent from God."

Jesus cut him short. "Be silent!" he told the demon. "Come out of the man!" The demon threw the man to the floor as the crowd watched; then it left him without hurting him further.

Amazed, the people exclaimed, "What authority and power this man's words possess! Even evil spirits obey him and flee at his command!" The story of what he had done spread like wildfire throughout the whole region.

JESUS VS. SATAN

A man possessed by a demon was in the synagogue where Jesus was teaching. This man made his way into the place of worship and verbally abused Jesus. The people were amazed at Jesus' authority to drive out demons—evil (unclean) spirits ruled by Satan

Why was Jesus allowed to teach in the synagogues? Jesus was taking advantage of the policy of allowing visitors to teach. Itinerant rabbis were always welcome to speak to those gathered each Sabbath in the synagogues. The apostle Paul also profited from this practice (see Acts 13:5; 14:1).

and sent to harass people and tempt them to sin. Demons are fallen angels who have joined Satan in rebellion against God. Demons can cause a person to become mute, deaf, blind, or insane. Jesus faced many demons during his time on earth, and he always exerted authority over them. Not only did the evil spirit leave this man; Luke records that the man was not even injured. Evil permeates our world, and it is no wonder that people are often fearful. But Jesus' power is far greater than Satan's. The first step toward conquering fear of evil is to recognize Jesus' authority and power. He has overcome all evil, including Satan himself.

February 28

Jesus heals Peter's mother-in-law and many others
Luke 4:38-41 (also in Matthew 8:14-17; Mark 1:29-34) *(Harmony 35)*

*A*fter leaving the synagogue that day, Jesus went to Simon's home, where he found Simon's mother-in-law very sick with a high fever. "Please heal her," everyone begged. Standing at her bedside, he spoke to the fever, rebuking it, and immediately her temperature returned to normal. She got up at once and prepared a meal for them.

As the sun went down that evening, people throughout the village brought sick family members to Jesus. No matter what their diseases were, the touch of his hand healed every one. Some were possessed by demons; and the demons came out at his command, shouting, "You are the Son of God." But because they knew he was the Messiah, he stopped them and told them to be silent.

Why didn't Jesus want the demons to reveal who he was? (1) By commanding the demons to remain silent, Jesus proved his authority and power over them. (2) Jesus wanted the people to believe he was the Messiah because of what he said and did, not because of the demons' words. (3) Jesus wanted to reveal his identity as the Messiah according to his timetable, not according to Satan's timetable. Satan wanted the people to follow Jesus around for what they could get out of him, not because he was the Son of God who could truly set them free from sin's guilt and power.

READY TO SERVE
Jesus healed Simon's (Peter's) mother-in-law so completely that not only did the fever leave, but her strength was restored, and she immediately got up and prepared a meal for them. Peter's mother-in-law gives us a beautiful example to follow. Her response to Jesus' touch was to wait on Jesus and his disciples—immediately. Has God ever helped you through a dangerous or difficult situation? If so, you should ask, *How can I express my gratitude to him?* Because God has promised us all the rewards of his Kingdom, we should look for ways to serve him and his followers now. God gives us health so that we may serve others.

March 1

Jesus preaches throughout Galilee
Mark 1:35-39 (also in Matthew 4:23-25; Luke 4:42-44)
(Harmony 36)

*T*he next morning Jesus awoke long before daybreak and went out alone into the wilderness to pray. Later Simon and the others went out to find him. They said, "Everyone is asking for you."

But he replied, "We must go on to other towns as well, and I will preach to them, too, because that is why I came." So he traveled throughout the region of Galilee, preaching in the synagogues and expelling demons from many people.

TIME TO PRAY
Jesus took time to pray. Finding time to pray is not easy, but prayer is the vital link between us and God. Like Jesus, we must break away from others to talk with God, even if we have to get up early in the morning to do it! If Jesus needed solitude for prayer and refreshment, how much more is this true for us? Don't become so busy that life turns into a flurry of activity, leaving no room for quiet fellowship alone with God. No matter how much you have to do, you should always have time for prayer.

The Romans divided the land of Israel into three separate regions: Galilee, Samaria, and Judea. Galilee was the northernmost region, an area about sixty miles long and thirty miles wide. Jesus did much of his ministry in this area, an ideal place for him to teach because there were more than 250 towns concentrated there, with many synagogues.

March 2

Jesus provides a miraculous catch of fish
Luke 5:1-11 *(Harmony 37)*

*O*ne day as Jesus was preaching on the shore of the Sea of Galilee, great crowds pressed in on him to listen to the word of God. He noticed two empty boats at the water's edge, for the fishermen had left them and were washing their nets. Stepping into one of the boats,

Jesus asked Simon, its owner, to push it out into the water. So he sat in the boat and taught the crowds from there.

When he had finished speaking, he said to Simon, "Now go out where it is deeper and let down your nets, and you will catch many fish."

"Master," Simon replied, "we worked hard all last night and didn't catch a thing. But if you say so, we'll try again." And this time their nets were so full they began to tear! A shout for help brought their partners in the other boat, and soon both boats were filled with fish and on the verge of sinking.

When Simon Peter realized what had happened, he fell to his knees before Jesus and said, "Oh, Lord, please leave me—I'm too much of a sinner to be around you." For he was awestruck by the size of their catch, as were the others with him. His partners, James and John, the sons of Zebedee, were also amazed.

Jesus replied to Simon, "Don't be afraid! From now on you'll be fishing for people!" And as soon as they landed, they left everything and followed Jesus.

DAY TO DAY WITH JESUS

This was the disciples' second call. After the first call (Matthew 4:18-22; Mark 1:16-20), Peter, Andrew, James, and John had gone back to fishing. They continued to watch Jesus, however, as he established his authority in the synagogue, healed the sick, and drove out demons. Here he also established his authority in their lives—he met them on their level and helped them in their work. Simon Peter was awestruck at this miracle, and his first response was to feel his own insignificance in comparison to this man's greatness. Peter knew that Jesus had healed the sick and driven out demons, but he was amazed that Jesus cared about his day-to-day routine and understood his needs. God is interested not only in saving us but also in helping us in our daily activities. From this point on, they left their nets and remained with Jesus. For us, following Jesus means more than just acknowledging him as Savior. We must leave our past behind and commit our future to him.

Lake Gennesaret was also known as the Sea of Galilee or the Sea of Tiberias. Fishermen on the Sea of Galilee used nets, often bell-shaped, with lead weights around the edges. A net would be thrown flat onto the water, and the lead weights would cause it to sink around the fish. Then the fishermen would pull on a cord, drawing the net around the fish. Nets had to be kept in good condition, so they were washed to remove weeds and then mended.

March 3

Jesus heals a man with leprosy
Mark 1:40-45 (also in Matthew 8:1-4; Luke 5:12-16) *(Harmony 38)*

A man with leprosy came and knelt in front of Jesus, begging to be healed. "If you want to, you can make me well again," he said. Moved with pity, Jesus touched him. "I want to," he said. "Be healed!" Instantly the leprosy disappeared—the man was healed. Then Jesus sent him on his way and told him sternly, "Go right over to the priest and let him examine you. Don't talk to anyone along the way. Take along the offering required in the law of Moses for those who have been healed of leprosy, so everyone will have proof of your healing."

But as the man went on his way, he spread the news, telling everyone what had happened to him. As a result, such crowds soon surrounded Jesus that he couldn't enter a town anywhere publicly. He had to stay out in the secluded places, and people from everywhere came to him there.

THE HEALING TOUCH

Leprosy was a feared disease because it had no known cure, and some forms of it were highly contagious. Leprosy had an emotional impact and terror associated with it as AIDS does today. (Sometimes called Hansen's disease, leprosy still exists in a less contagious form that can be treated.) The priests monitored the disease, banishing lepers who were in a contagious stage to prevent the spread of infection and readmitting lepers whose disease was in remission. Because leprosy destroys the nerve endings, lepers often would unknowingly damage their fingers, toes, and noses. This man with leprosy had an advanced case, so he undoubtedly had lost much bodily tissue. Lepers were considered untouchable because people feared contracting their disease. Yet Jesus reached out and touched the leper to heal him.

Although leprosy was incurable, many different types of skin diseases were classified together as "leprosy." According to the Old Testament laws about leprosy (Leviticus 13–14), when a leper was cured, he or she had to go to a priest to be examined. Then the leper was to give an offering of thanks at the Temple. Jesus adhered to these laws by sending the man to the priest. This demonstrated Jesus' complete regard for God's Law. Sending a healed leper to a priest was also a way to verify Jesus' great miracle to the community.

The real value of a person is inside, not outside. Although a person's body may be diseased or deformed, the person inside is no less valuable to God. No person is too disgusting for God's touch. In a sense, we are all people with leprosy because we have all been deformed by the ugliness of sin. But by sending his Son, Jesus, God has touched us, giving us the opportunity to be healed. When you feel repulsed by someone, remember how God feels about that person—and about you.

March 4

Jesus heals a paralyzed man
Mark 2:1-12 (also in Matthew 9:1-8; Luke 5:17-26) *(Harmony 39)*

*S*everal days later Jesus returned to Capernaum, and the news of his arrival spread quickly through the town. Soon the house where he was staying was so packed with visitors that there wasn't room for one more person, not even outside the door. And he preached the word to them. Four men arrived carrying a paralyzed man on a mat. They couldn't get to Jesus through the crowd, so they dug through the clay roof above his head. Then they lowered the sick man on his mat, right down in front of Jesus. Seeing their faith, Jesus said to the paralyzed man, "My son, your sins are forgiven."

But some of the teachers of religious law who were sitting there said to themselves, "What? This is blasphemy! Who but God can forgive sins!"

Jesus knew what they were discussing among themselves, so he said to them, "Why do you think this is blasphemy? Is it easier to say to the paralyzed man, 'Your sins are forgiven' or 'Get up, pick up your mat, and walk'? I will prove that I, the Son of Man, have the authority on earth to forgive sins." Then Jesus turned to the paralyzed man and said, "Stand up, take your mat, and go on home, because you are healed!"

The man jumped up, took the mat, and pushed his way through the stunned onlookers. Then they all praised God. "We've never seen anything like this before!" they exclaimed.

MOVED TO ACTION

It wasn't the paralyzed man's faith that impressed Jesus, but the faith of his friends. The paralyzed man's need moved his friends to action, and they brought him to Jesus. Jesus responded to their faith and healed the man. For better or worse, our faith affects others. When you recognize someone's need, do you act? Many people have physical and spiritual needs you can meet, either by yourself or with others who are also concerned. Human need moved these four men; let it also move you to compassionate action.

Houses in Bible times were built of stone. They had flat roofs made of mud mixed with straw. Outside stairways led to the roofs. These friends may have carried the paralyzed man up the outside stairs to the roof. They then could easily have taken apart the mud and straw mixture to make a hole through which to lower their friend to Jesus.

We cannot make another person a Christian, but we can do much through our words, actions, and love to give him or her a chance to respond. Look for opportunities to bring your friends to the living Christ.

Jesus eats with sinners at Matthew's house

Matthew 9:9-13 (also in Mark 2:13-17; Luke 5:27-32) *(Harmony 40)*

*A*s Jesus was going down the road, he saw Matthew sitting at his tax-collection booth. "Come, be my disciple," Jesus said to him. So Matthew got up and followed him.

That night Matthew invited Jesus and his disciples to be his dinner guests, along with his fellow tax collectors and many other notorious sinners. The Pharisees were indignant. "Why does your teacher eat with such scum?" they asked his disciples.

When he heard this, Jesus replied, "Healthy people don't need a doctor—sick people do." Then he added, "Now go and learn the meaning of this Scripture: 'I want you to be merciful; I don't want your sacrifices.' For I have come to call sinners, not those who think they are already good enough."

LEAVE IT BEHIND!

Matthew was a Jew who was appointed by the Romans to be the area's tax collector. He collected taxes from the citizens as well as from merchants passing through town. Tax collectors were expected to take a commission on the taxes they collected, but most of them overcharged and kept the profits. Thus, tax collectors were hated by the Jews because of their reputation for cheating and because of their support of Rome. When Jesus called Matthew to be one of his disciples, Matthew got up and followed, leaving a lucrative career. When God calls you to follow or obey him, do you do it with as much abandon as Matthew? Sometimes the decision to follow Christ requires difficult or painful choices. Like Matthew, we must decide to leave behind those things that would keep us from following Christ.

The Pharisees constantly tried to trap Jesus, and they thought his association with these "lowlifes" was the perfect opportunity. They were more concerned with their own appearance of holiness than with helping people, with criticism than with encouragement, with outward respectability than with practical help.

March 6

Religious leaders ask Jesus about fasting

Luke 5:33-39 (also in Matthew 9:14-17; Mark 2:18-22) *(Harmony 41)*

*T*he religious leaders complained that Jesus' disciples were feasting instead of fasting. "John the Baptist's disciples always fast and pray," they declared, "and so do the disciples of the Pharisees. Why are yours always feasting?"

Jesus asked, "Do wedding guests fast while celebrating with the groom? Someday he will be taken away from them, and then they will fast."

Then Jesus gave them this illustration: "No one tears a piece of cloth from a new garment and uses it to patch an old garment. For then the new garment would be torn, and the patch wouldn't even match the old garment. And no one puts new wine into old wineskins. The new wine would burst the old skins, spilling the wine and ruining the skins. New wine must be put into new wineskins. But no one who drinks the old wine seems to want the fresh and the new. 'The old is better,' they say."

SOFT HEARTS

Wineskins were goatskins sewed together at the edges to form watertight bags. Because new wine expands as it ages, it had to be put in new, pliable wineskins. A used skin, having become more rigid, would burst and spill the wine. Like old wineskins, the Pharisees were too rigid to accept Jesus, who could not be contained by their traditions or rules. Christianity required new approaches, new traditions, new structures. Our church programs and ministries should not be so structured that they have no room for a fresh touch of the Spirit, a new method, or a new idea. We, too, must be careful that our hearts do not become so hard that they prevent us from accepting the new way of thinking that Christ brings. We need to keep our hearts pliable so we can accept Jesus' life-changing message.

John's disciples fasted (went without food) as a sign of mourning for sin and to prepare for the Messiah's coming. Jesus' disciples did not need to fast because he is the Messiah and was with them! Jesus did not condemn fasting—he himself fasted (Luke 4:1-2). He emphasized that fasting must be done for the right reasons.

March 7

Jesus heals a lame man by the pool
John 5:1-9 *(Harmony 42a)*

*A*fterward Jesus returned to Jerusalem for one of the Jewish holy days. Inside the city, near the Sheep Gate, was the pool of Bethesda, with five covered porches. Crowds of sick people—blind, lame, or paralyzed—lay on the porches. One of the men lying there had been sick for thirty-eight years. When Jesus saw him and knew how long he had been ill, he asked him, "Would you like to get well?"

"I can't, sir," the sick man said, "for I have no one to help me into the pool when the water is stirred up. While I am trying to get there, someone else always gets in ahead of me."

Jesus told him, "Stand up, pick up your sleeping mat, and walk!"

Instantly, the man was healed! He rolled up the mat and began walking! But this miracle happened on the Sabbath day.

GOD MEETS NEEDS
Jesus appropriately asked, "Would you like to get well?" After thirty-eight years, this man's problem had become a way of life. No one had ever helped him. He had no hope of ever being healed and no desire to help himself. The man's situation looked hopeless. But no matter how trapped you feel in your infirmities, God can minister to your deepest needs. Don't let a problem or hardship cause you to lose hope. God may have special work for you to do in spite of your condition, or even because of it. Many have ministered effectively to hurting people because they have triumphed over their own hurts.

Some ancient authorities do not include the reference to an angel disturbing the waters. Whether or not this occurred, Jesus healed this man who had been waiting for years to be healed.

March 8

Jesus heals a lame man by the pool
John 5:10-15 *(Harmony 42b)*

*S*o the Jewish leaders objected. They said to the man who was cured, "You can't work on the Sabbath! It's illegal to carry that sleeping mat!"

He replied, "The man who healed me said to me, 'Pick up your sleeping mat and walk.'"

"Who said such a thing as that?" they demanded.

The man didn't know, for Jesus had disappeared into the crowd. But afterward Jesus found him in the Temple and told him, "Now you are well; so stop sinning, or something even worse may happen to you." Then the man went to find the Jewish leaders and told them it was Jesus who had healed him.

According to the Pharisees, carrying one's bed (a mat) on the Sabbath was work and was therefore unlawful. It did not break an Old Testament law, but merely the Pharisees' interpretation of God's command to "remember to observe the Sabbath as a holy day" (Exodus 20:8). This was just one of hundreds of rules they had added to the Old Testament law.

THE GREATEST MIRACLE

This man had been lame, or paralyzed, and suddenly he could walk. This was a great miracle. But he needed an even greater miracle—to have his sins forgiven. The man was delighted to be physically healed, but he had to turn from his sins and seek God's forgiveness to be spiritually healed. God's forgiveness is the greatest gift you will ever receive. Don't neglect his gracious offer.

March 9

Jesus claims to be God's Son
John 5:16-23 *(Harmony 43a)*

S o the Jewish leaders began harassing Jesus for breaking the Sabbath rules. But Jesus replied, "My Father never stops working, so why should I?" So the Jewish leaders tried all the more to kill him. In addition to disobeying the Sabbath rules, he had spoken of God as his Father, thereby making himself equal with God.

Jesus replied, "I assure you, the Son can do nothing by himself. He does only what he sees the Father doing. Whatever the Father does, the Son also does. For the Father loves the Son and tells him everything he is doing, and the Son will do far greater things than healing this man. You will be astonished at what he does. He will even raise from the dead anyone he wants to, just as the Father does. And the Father leaves all judgment to his Son, so that everyone will honor the Son, just as they honor the Father. But if you refuse to honor the Son, then you are certainly not honoring the Father who sent him.

If God stopped every kind of work on the Sabbath, nature would fall into chaos, and sin would overrun the world. Genesis 2:2 says that God rested on the seventh day, but this doesn't mean that he stopped doing good. Jesus was teaching that when the opportunity to do good presents itself, we should act, even on the Sabbath.

Jesus was identifying himself with God, his Father. There could be no doubt as to his claim to be God. Jesus does not leave us the option to believe in God while ignoring God's Son. Because of his unity with God, Jesus lived as God wanted him to live. Because of our identification with Jesus, we must honor him and live as he wants us to live. The questions "What would Jesus do?" and "What would Jesus have me do?" may help you make the right choices.

March 10

Jesus claims to be God's Son
John 5:24-30 *(Harmony 43b)*

I assure you, those who listen to my message and believe in God who sent me have eternal life. They will never be condemned for their sins, but they have already passed from death into life.

"And I assure you that the time is coming, in fact it is here, when the dead will hear my voice—the voice of the Son of God. And those who listen will live. The Father has life in himself, and he has granted his Son to have life in himself. And he has given him authority to judge all mankind because he is the Son of Man. Don't be so surprised! Indeed, the time is coming when all the dead in their graves will hear the voice of God's Son, and they will rise again. Those who have done good will rise to eternal life, and those who have continued in evil will rise to judgment. But I do nothing without consulting the Father. I judge as I am told. And my judgment is absolutely just, because it is according to the will of God who sent me; it is not merely my own."

TO LIVE FOREVER
In saying that the dead will hear his voice, Jesus was talking about the spiritually dead who hear, understand, and accept him. Those who accept Jesus, the Word, will have eternal life. Jesus was also talking about the physically dead. He raised several dead people while he was on earth, and at his second coming, "Christians who have died will rise from their graves" (1 Thessalonians 4:16). "Eternal life"—living forever with God—begins when you accept Jesus Christ as Savior. At that moment new life begins in you (2 Corinthians 5:17). It is a completed transaction. You still will face physical death, but when Christ returns, your body will be resurrected to live forever with him (1 Corinthians 15). Those who have rebelled against Christ, who have ignored God and lived only for themselves, will find that death does not end it all. There is a

God is the source and Creator of life. Because Jesus is eternally existent with God, the Creator, he, too, is "the life" (14:6) through whom we may live eternally (see 1 John 5:11).

judgment to face. They will be resurrected too, but to stand before God's throne and be sentenced to an eternity apart from him. You can help people be saved from eternal death by telling them the good news about Christ's eternal life.

March 11

Jesus supports his claim
John 5:31-40 *(Harmony 44a)*

*I*f I were to testify on my own behalf, my testimony would not be valid. But someone else is also testifying about me, and I can assure you that everything he says about me is true. In fact, you sent messengers to listen to John the Baptist, and he preached the truth. But the best testimony about me is not from a man, though I have reminded you about John's testimony so you might be saved. John shone brightly for a while, and you benefited and rejoiced. But I have a greater witness than John—my teachings and my miracles. They have been assigned to me by the Father, and they testify that the Father has sent me. And the Father himself has also testified about me. You have never heard his voice or seen him face to face, and you do not have his message in your hearts, because you do not believe me—the one he sent to you.

Jesus claimed to be equal with God (John 5:18), to give everlasting life (5:24), to be the source of life (5:26), and to judge sin (5:27). These statements make it clear that Jesus was claiming to be divine— an almost unbelievable claim, but one that was supported by another witness, John the Baptist.

"You search the Scriptures because you believe they give you eternal life. But the Scriptures point to me! Yet you refuse to come to me so that I can give you this eternal life."

MISSING THE SAVIOR
The religious leaders knew what the Bible said but failed to apply its words to their lives. They knew the teachings of the Scriptures but failed to see the Messiah to whom the Scriptures pointed. They knew the rules but missed the Savior. Entrenched in their own religious system, they refused to let the Son of God change their lives. Don't become so involved in "religion" that you miss Christ.

March 12

Jesus supports his claim
John 5:41-47 *(Harmony 44b)*

*Y*our approval or disapproval means nothing to me, because I know you don't have God's love within you. For I have come to you representing my Father, and you refuse to welcome me, even though you readily accept others who represent only themselves. No wonder you can't believe! For you gladly honor each other, but you don't care about the honor that comes from God alone.

"Yet it is not I who will accuse you of this before the Father. Moses will accuse you! Yes, Moses, on whom you set your hopes. But if you had believed Moses, you would have believed me because he wrote about me. And since you don't believe what he wrote, how will you believe what I say?"

PRAISE SEEKERS
Whose praise do you seek? The religious leaders enjoyed great prestige in Israel, but their stamp of approval meant nothing to Jesus. He was concerned about God's approval. This is a good principle for us. If even the highest officials in the world approve of our actions and God does not, we should be concerned. But if God approves, even though others don't, we should be content.

The Pharisees prided themselves on being the true followers of their ancestor Moses. They were trying to follow every one of his laws to the letter. Jesus' warning that Moses would accuse them stung them to fury. Moses wrote about Jesus (Genesis 3:15; Numbers 24:17; Deuteronomy 18:15), yet the religious leaders refused to believe Jesus when he came.

March 13

The disciples pick wheat on the Sabbath
Matthew 12:1-8 (also in Mark 2:23-28; Luke 6:1-5) *(Harmony 45)*

*A*t about that time Jesus was walking through some grainfields on the Sabbath. His disciples were hungry, so they began breaking off heads of wheat and eating the grain. Some Pharisees saw them do it and protested, "Your disciples shouldn't be doing that! It's against the law to work by harvesting grain on the Sabbath."

But Jesus said to them, "Haven't you ever read in the Scriptures what King David did when he and his companions were hungry? He went into the house of God, and they ate the special bread reserved for the priests alone. That was breaking the law, too. And haven't you ever read in the law of Moses that the priests on duty in the Temple may work on the Sabbath? I tell you, there is one here who is even greater than the Temple! But you would not have condemned those who aren't guilty if you knew the meaning of this Scripture: 'I want you to be merciful; I don't want your sacrifices.' For I, the Son of Man, am master even of the Sabbath."

REMEMBERING THE SABBATH
The Pharisees had established thirty-nine categories of actions forbidden on the Sabbath, based on interpretations of God's law and on Jewish custom. Harvesting was one of those forbidden actions. By picking wheat and rubbing it in their hands, the disciples were technically harvesting, according to the religious leaders. Jesus and the disciples were picking grain because they were hungry, not because they wanted to harvest the grain for a profit. They were not working on the Sabbath. The Pharisees, however, could not (and did not want to) see beyond their law's technicalities.

Many of the Pharisees were so caught up in their man-made laws and traditions that they lost sight of what was good and right. The Ten Commandments prohibit work on the Sabbath (Exodus 20:8-11). That was the *letter* of the law. But because the *purpose* of the Sabbath is to rest and to worship God, the priests were allowed to work by performing sacrifices and conducting worship services. This "work" was serving and worshiping God. Jesus always emphasized the intent of the law, the meaning behind the letter. God is far more important than the created instruments of worship. If we become more concerned with the means of worship than with the one we worship, we will miss God even as we think we are worshiping him.

This story of David and the consecrated bread is recorded in 1 Samuel 21:1-6. The special bread was replaced every week, and the old loaves were eaten by the priests. The loaves given to David were the old loaves that had just been replaced with fresh ones. Although the priests were the only ones allowed to eat this bread, God did not punish David because his need for food was more important than the priestly regulations. Jesus was saying, "If you condemn me, you must also condemn David."

March 14

Jesus heals a man's hand on the Sabbath
Mark 3:1-6 (also in Matthew 12:9-14; Luke 6:6-11) *(Harmony 46)*

*J*esus went into the synagogue again and noticed a man with a deformed hand. Since it was the Sabbath, Jesus' enemies watched him closely. Would he heal the man's hand on the Sabbath? If he did, they planned to condemn him. Jesus said to the man, "Come and stand in front of everyone." Then he turned to his critics and asked, "Is it legal to do good deeds on the Sabbath, or is it a day for doing harm? Is this a day to save life or to destroy it?" But they wouldn't answer him. He looked around at them angrily, because he was deeply disturbed by their hard hearts. Then he said to the man, "Reach out your hand." The man reached out his hand, and it became normal again! At once the Pharisees went away and met with the supporters of Herod to discuss plans for killing Jesus.

WHEN THERE IS A NEED . . .
As the Pharisees watched the man with the deformed hand, they wondered if Jesus would heal him, thereby breaking the Sabbath. Their Sabbath rules said that people could be helped on the Sabbath only if their lives were in danger. Jesus healed on the Sabbath several times, and none of those healings was in response to an emergency. If Jesus had waited until another day, he would have been submitting to the Pharisees' authority, showing that their petty rules were equal to God's law. If he healed the man on the Sabbath, the Pharisees could claim that because Jesus broke their rules, his power was not from God. But Jesus made it clear how ridiculous and petty their rules were. God is more concerned about people than rules. The best time to reach out to someone is when he or she needs help. The Pharisees placed their laws above human need. They were so concerned about Jesus' breaking one of their rules that they did not care about the man's deformed hand. What is your attitude toward others? If your convictions don't allow you to help certain people, those convictions are not in tune with God's Word. Don't allow dogma to blind you to human need.

The Pharisees plotted Jesus' death because they were outraged. Jesus had overruled their authority (Luke 6:11) and had exposed their evil attitudes in front of the entire crowd in the synagogue. Jesus had shown that the Pharisees were more loyal to their religious system than to God.

March 15

Large crowds follow Jesus
Mark 3:7-12 (also in Matthew 12:15-21) *(Harmony 47a)*

*J*esus and his disciples went out to the lake, followed by a huge crowd from all over Galilee, Judea, Jerusalem, Idumea, from east of the Jordan River, and even from as far away as Tyre and Sidon. The news about his miracles had spread far and wide, and vast numbers of people came to see him for themselves.

Jesus instructed his disciples to bring around a boat and to have it ready in case he was crowded off the beach. There had been many healings that day. As a result, many sick people were crowding around him, trying to touch him. And whenever those possessed by evil spirits caught sight of him, they would fall down in front of him shrieking, "You are the Son of God!" But Jesus strictly warned them not to say who he was.

THE TRUE MESSIAH
Jesus warned the demons not to reveal his identity because he did not want them to reinforce a popular misconception. The huge crowds were looking for a political and military leader who would free them from Rome's control, and they thought that the Messiah predicted by the Old Testament prophets would be this kind of man. Jesus wanted to teach the people about the kind of Messiah he was—one who was far different from their expectations. Christ's Kingdom is spiritual. It begins not with the overthrow of governments but with the overthrow of sin in people's hearts. The demons knew that Jesus was the Son of God, but they refused to turn from their evil purposes. Knowing about Jesus, or even believing that he is God's Son, does not guarantee salvation. You must also want to follow and obey him (see also James 2:17). Have you allowed Christ to reign in your heart?

While Jesus was drawing fire from the religious leaders, he was gaining great popularity among the people. Some were curious, some sought healing, some wanted evidence to use against him, and others wanted to know if Jesus truly was the Messiah. Most of these leaders could only dimly guess at the real meaning of what was happening among them.

March 16

Large crowds follow Jesus
Matthew 12:15-21 (also in Mark 3:7-12) *(Harmony 47b)*

*B*ut Jesus knew what they were planning. He left that area, and many people followed him. He healed all the sick among them, but he warned them not to say who he was. This fulfilled the prophecy of Isaiah concerning him: "Look at my Servant, whom I have chosen. He is my Beloved, and I am very pleased with him. I will put my Spirit upon him, and he will proclaim justice to the nations. He will not fight or shout; he will not raise his voice in public. He will not crush those who are weak, or quench the smallest hope, until he brings full justice with his final victory. And his name will be the hope of all the world."

THE SERVANT KING

The people expected the Messiah to be a king. This quotation from Isaiah's prophecy (Isaiah 42:1-4) showed that the Messiah was indeed a king, but it illustrated what *kind* of king—a quiet, gentle ruler who brings justice to the nations. His final victory puts the cross before a crown, brings justice without courtly pomp, and yields victory without an army. As a servant, he brings hope. He brings life by offering his own. Like the crowd in Jesus' day, we may want Christ to rule as a king and bring great and visible victories in our lives. But often Christ's work is quiet, and it happens according to *his* perfect timing, not ours. Take time to reflect on Christ's quiet work in your life. Thank him for what he has done and continue to stay close to him.

Jesus did not want those he healed to tell others about his miracles because he didn't want the people coming to him for the wrong reasons. That would hinder his teaching ministry and arouse false hopes about an earthly kingdom. But the news of Jesus' miracles spread, and many came to see for themselves.

March 17

Jesus selects the twelve disciples
Mark 3:13-19 (also in Luke 6:12-16) *(Harmony 48)*

*A*fterward Jesus went up on a mountain and called the ones he wanted to go with him. And they came to him. Then he selected twelve of them to be his regular companions, calling them apostles. He sent them out to preach, and he gave them authority to cast out demons. These are the names of the twelve he chose: Simon (he renamed him Peter), James and John (the sons of Zebedee, but Jesus nicknamed them "Sons of Thunder"), Andrew, Philip, Bartholomew, Matthew, Thomas, James (son of Alphaeus), Thaddaeus, Simon (the Zealot), Judas Iscariot (who later betrayed him).

WILLING DISCIPLES

From the hundreds of people who followed him from place to place, Jesus chose twelve to "be his regular companions" and be sent out to preach and to cast out demons. He did not choose these twelve to be his companions because of their faith; their faith often faltered. He didn't choose them because of their talent and ability; no one stood out with

Why did Jesus choose twelve men? The number twelve corresponds to the twelve tribes of Israel (Matthew 19:28), showing the continuity between the old religious system and the new one based on Jesus' message. Many people followed Jesus, but these twelve received the most intense training. We see the impact of these men throughout the rest of the New Testament.

unusual ability. The disciples represented a wide range of backgrounds and life experiences, but apparently they had no more leadership potential than those who were not chosen. The one characteristic they all shared was their willingness to obey Jesus. After Jesus' ascension, they were filled with the Holy Spirit and empowered to carry out special roles in the growth of the early church. We should not disqualify ourselves from service to Christ because we do not have the expected credentials. Being a good disciple is simply a matter of following Jesus with a willing heart.

March 18

Jesus gives the Beatitudes
Matthew 5:1 (also in Luke 6:17-19) *(Harmony 49a)*

ne day as the crowds were gathering, Jesus went up the mountainside with his disciples and sat down to teach them.

WHAT A DISCIPLE CAN EXPECT

Enormous crowds were following Jesus—he was the talk of the town, and everyone wanted to see him. The disciples, who were the closest associates of this popular man, were certainly tempted to feel important, proud, and possessive. Being with Jesus gave them not only prestige but also opportunity for receiving money and power.

The crowds were gathering once again. But before speaking to them, Jesus pulled his disciples aside and warned them about the temptations they would face as his associates. Don't expect fame and fortune, Jesus was saying, but mourning, hunger, and persecution. Nevertheless, Jesus assured his disciples, they would be rewarded—but perhaps not in this life. There may be times when following Jesus will bring us great popularity. If we don't live by Jesus' words in this sermon, we will find ourselves using God's message only to promote our personal interests.

Matthew 5–7 is called the Sermon on the Mount because Jesus gave it on a hillside near Capernaum. This "sermon" probably covered several days of preaching. The Sermon on the Mount challenged the proud and legalistic religious leaders of the day. It called them back to the messages of the Old Testament prophets who, like Jesus, taught that heartfelt obedience is more important than legalistic observance.

March 19

Jesus gives the Beatitudes
Matthew 5:2-3 (also in Luke 6:20) *(Harmony 49b)*

*T*his is what he taught them:
God blesses those who realize their need for him, for the Kingdom of Heaven is given to them."

REWARDS OF HUMILITY
With Jesus' announcement that the Kingdom was near (4:17), people were naturally asking, "How do I qualify to be in God's Kingdom?" Jesus said that God's Kingdom is organized differently from worldly kingdoms. In the Kingdom of Heaven, wealth and power and authority are unimportant. Kingdom people seek different blessings and benefits, and they have different attitudes. They desire humility rather than chasing after the things of the world that lead to pride. Are your attitudes a carbon copy of the world's selfishness, pride, and lust for power, or do they reflect the humility and self-sacrifice of Jesus, your King?

The blessings of the Beatitudes aren't a promise of laughter, pleasure, or earthly prosperity. To Jesus, "blessed" means the experience of hope and joy, independent of outward circumstances. To find hope and joy, the deepest form of happiness, follow Jesus no matter what the cost.

March 20

Jesus gives the Beatitudes
Matthew 5:4 *(Harmony 49c)*

*G*od blesses those who mourn, for they will be comforted."

FORTUNATE MOURNERS
Jesus' words seem to contradict each other. How can people who mourn be blessed? But God's way of living usually contradicts the world's. If you want to live for God, you must be ready to say and do what seems strange to the world. You must be willing to give when others take, to love when others hate, to help when others abuse. By giving up your own rights in order to serve others, you will one day receive everything God has in store for you.

The Greek word for mourn is the strongest word in that language to designate it—thus it refers to mourning for the dead. People who mourn loved ones know there is no other hope but in the Savior. They experience the reality of the comfort brought by the certainty of eternal life.

March 21

Jesus gives the Beatitudes
Matthew 5:5 *(Harmony 49d)*

*G*od blesses those who are gentle and lowly, for the whole earth will belong to them."

MEEK, NOT WEAK

Gentle people are not wimps. Rather, they have tenderhearted spirits that allow them to truly enjoy life. Because they are humble, willing to learn, willing to forgive and be forgiven, willing to take life in stride, it is true that "the whole earth will belong to them." Too often it seems that the movers, pushers, and shakers are the ones who own everything. But how much can they appreciate, really? Instead, it is the people who have learned balance in life and genuine humility who can enjoy all that God has given them. How much of "the whole earth" have you accepted by God's grace? Can you set aside pride and desires in order to be one of God's gentle and lowly ones?

Being gentle and lowly (humble) means having a true perspective on ourselves. It does not mean that we should put ourselves down. We see that we are sinners, saved only by God's grace; but we are saved and therefore have great worth in God's Kingdom. We should place ourselves in his hands to be used as he wants in order to spread his Word and share his love with others.

March 22

Jesus gives the Beatitudes
Matthew 5:6 (also in Luke 6:21) *(Harmony 49e)*

*G*od blesses those who are hungry and thirsty for justice, for they will receive it in full."

THE JUST AND GOOD

The reference in Luke reads, "God blesses you who are hungry now, for you will be satisfied." Some believe that the hunger about which Jesus was speaking is a hunger for righteousness, a desire for "justice," as here in Matthew's verse. Others say this is physical hunger. In any case, in a nation where riches were seen as a sign of God's favor, Jesus startled his hearers by pronouncing blessings on

Only God is truly just and good; we should long to be like him.

those who hunger. In doing so, however, he was in line with an ancient tradition. The Old Testament is filled with texts proclaiming God's concern for the poor and needy. See, for example, 1 Samuel 2:5; Psalm 146:7; Isaiah 58:6-7; and Jesus' own mother's prayer in Luke 1:53. This promise gives hope to all who are hungry and poor. When you experience loss and are struggling financially, remember God's covenant and look for God's blessings in the midst of poverty.

March 23

Jesus gives the Beatitudes
Matthew 5:7 *(Harmony 49f)*

"God blesses those who are merciful, for they will be shown mercy."

THE KIND AND MERCIFUL

Kindness and mercy go hand in hand. Mercy is often used to describe God—the mercy we receive from him allows us to be saved. It is God's mercy alone that brought Jesus to the cross for undeserving sinners. Precisely because of this incredible mercy, believers ought to demonstrate that quality toward others. If we withhold mercy from others after having received it from God, we show that we don't understand or appreciate God's mercy toward us. Showing mercy means we don't make hasty criticisms, we don't set down demands and expectations of others, we show great patience, and we treat others with the same kindness, generosity, compassion, and understanding that God shows to us every day.

James wrote that "if you have been merciful, then God's mercy toward you will win out over his judgment against you" (James 2:13). In other words, showing mercy places us under God's mercy as well. Merciful actions are evidence of a vital relationship with Christ.

March 24

Jesus gives the Beatitudes
Matthew 5:8 *(Harmony 49g)*

"God blesses those whose hearts are pure, for they will see God."

PURE HAPPINESS
A follower of Christ becomes pure and holy through believing and obeying the Word of God (Hebrews 4:12). He or she has already accepted forgiveness through Christ's sacrificial death (Hebrews 7:26-27). But daily application of God's Word purifies our minds and hearts. Scripture points out sin, motivates us to confess, renews our relationship with Christ, and guides us back to the right path. Continue to read, study and apply God's Word, allowing it to purify your life.

The word for "pure" means "unmixed," without alloy, as with a pure metal. Pure people are transparent with unmixed motives. Their integrity shines through without question. Their only goal is to do God's will.

March 25

Jesus gives the Beatitudes
Matthew 5:9 *(Harmony 49h)*

"God blesses those who work for peace, for they will be called the children of God."

WORKING FOR PEACE
Many barriers can divide us from other Christians: age, appearance, intelligence, political persuasion, economic status, race, theological perspective. One of the best ways to stifle Christ's love is to be friendly with only those people we like. Fortunately, Christ has knocked down the barriers and unified all believers in one family through his death on the cross. The Holy Spirit helps us look beyond the barriers to the unity we are called to enjoy. People who want peace allow the Holy Spirit to work in their lives and strive to live at peace with everyone (Romans 12:18). Because conflict with the world and its authorities is sometimes inevitable for a Christian (John 15:18; Acts 5:29), there will be situations where you cannot obey both God and man. Then you must obey God.

Because of Christ's death, we have peace with God and peace with one another. We are no longer foreigners or aliens to God; and we are all being built into a holy temple with Christ as our chief cornerstone.

Jesus gives the Beatitudes
Matthew 5:10 *(Harmony 49i)*

*G*od blesses those who are persecuted because they live for God, for the Kingdom of Heaven is theirs."

TOUGH HAPPINESS

Jesus said that people persecuted for their faith are blessed! Persecution can be good because (1) it takes our eyes off earthly rewards, (2) it strips away superficial belief, (3) it strengthens the faith of those who endure, and (4) it serves as an example to others who follow. The fact that we are being persecuted proves that we have been faithful; faithless people would be unnoticed. Later, two of the disciples, Peter and John, would be imprisoned for their faith (see Acts 5:17-41). Yet because they knew how Jesus had suffered, they praised God that he had allowed them to be persecuted like their Lord. If you are mocked or persecuted for your faith, it isn't because you're doing something wrong but because God has counted you "worthy to suffer dishonor for the name of Jesus" (Acts 5:41). You can then be happy in the middle of persecution, for you have understood what it means to have the Kingdom of Heaven within you.

Notice the progression in the Beatitudes. People who live differently from society, exposing its evil values by their humility, kindness, gentleness, and peacemaking, will find themselves at odds and persecuted for their beliefs and lifestyle. Jesus would later warn his disciples, "The people of the world will hate you because you belong to me, for they don't know God who sent me" (John 15:21).

Jesus gives the Beatitudes
Matthew 5:11 (also in Luke 6:22) (Harmony 49j)

*G*od blesses you when you are mocked and persecuted and lied about because you are my followers."

REJOICING IN PERSECUTION

All believers face trials when they live for Christ in a hostile world. We must accept trials as part of the refining process that burns away impurities and prepares us to meet Christ. Trials teach us patience and help us grow to be the kind of people God wants. Those who stand for Christ will be persecuted because the world is ruled by Christ's greatest enemy. But just as the small group of early believers stood against persecution, so we must be willing to stand for our faith with patience, endurance, and courage.

The early Christians were misunderstood, harassed, tortured, and even put to death. Persecution from Rome came for several reasons: (1) Christians refused to worship the emperor as a god and thus were viewed as atheists and traitors. (2) Christians refused to worship at heathen temples, so business for these moneymaking enterprises dropped wherever Christianity took hold. (3) Christians didn't support the Roman ideals of self, power, and conquest; and Romans scorned the Christian ideal of self-sacrificing service. (4) Christians exposed and rejected the immorality of heathen culture.

Jesus gives the Beatitudes
Matthew 5:12 (also in Luke 6:23) (Harmony 49k)

*B*e happy about it! Be very glad! For a great reward awaits you in heaven. And remember, the ancient prophets were persecuted, too."

FUTURE REWARDS

Persecution would become a harsh reality for many early Christians. At the time the apostle John wrote Revelation, the Roman government had stepped up its persecution of Christians, causing John to wonder if the church could survive and stand against the opposition. But Jesus appeared in glory and splendor, reassuring John that he and his fellow believers had access to God's strength to

We can be comforted to know that God's greatest prophets were persecuted. Read about Jeremiah (Jeremiah 38:1-6); Isaiah (tradition says he was killed by King Manasseh; see 2 Kings 21:16); Amos (Amos 7:10-13); Zechariah (2 Chronicles 24:20-22); and Elijah (1 Kings 19:2).

low believers had access to God's strength to face these trials (see Revelation 1:17-18) and that tremendous rewards awaited them. If you are facing difficult problems, remember that the power available to John and the early church is also available to you. In the end, all believers will finally be with God in heaven. All who have been faithful through the ages will sing before God's throne (Revelation 7:14-17). Their tribulations and sorrows will be over: There will be no more tears for sin, for all sins will have been forgiven; no more tears for suffering, for all suffering will be over; no more tears for death, for all believers will have been resurrected to die no more.

March 29

Jesus gives the Beatitudes
Luke 6:24-26 *(Harmony 49l)*

*W*hat sorrows await you who are rich, for you have your only happiness now. What sorrows await you who are satisfied and prosperous now, for a time of awful hunger is before you. What sorrows await you who laugh carelessly, for your laughing will turn to mourning and sorrow. What sorrows await you who are praised by the crowds, for their ancestors also praised false prophets."

THE POOR RICH
Despite overwhelming evidence to the contrary, most people still believe that money brings happiness. Rich people craving greater riches can be caught in an endless cycle that only ends in ruin and destruction. How can you keep away from the love of money? (1) Realize that one day riches will all be gone. (2) Be content with what you have. (3) Monitor what you are willing to do to get more money. (4) Love people more than money. (5) Love God's work more than money. (6) Freely share what you have with others.

There were many false prophets in Old Testament times. They were praised by kings and crowds because their predictions— prosperity and victory in war—were exactly what the people wanted to hear. But popularity is no guarantee of truth, and human flattery does not bring God's approval. Sadness lies ahead for those who chase after the crowd's praise rather than God's truth.

March 30

Jesus teaches about salt and light
Matthew 5:13 *(Harmony 50a)*

*Y*ou are the salt of the earth. But what good is salt if it has lost its flavor? Can you make it useful again? It will be thrown out and trampled underfoot as worthless."

GOOD TASTE

If a seasoning has no flavor, it has no value. If we Christians make no effort to affect the world around us, we are of little value to God. If we are too much like the world, we are worthless. Christians should not blend in with everyone else. Instead, we should affect others positively, just as seasoning brings out the best flavor in food. God wants to be active in your life, bringing out the best in you as well. Let him become part of you, penetrating every aspect of your life, preserving you from the evil all around, and healing you of your sins and shortcomings.

In Leviticus 2:13 we read that the offerings were seasoned with salt as a reminder of the people's covenant (contract) with God. Salt is a good symbol of God's activity in a person's life because it penetrates, preserves, and aids in healing.

March 31

Jesus teaches about salt and light
Matthew 5:14-16 *(Harmony 50b)*

*Y*ou are the light of the world—like a city on a mountain, glowing in the night for all to see. Don't hide your light under a basket! Instead, put it on a stand and let it shine for all. In the same way, let your good deeds shine out for all to see, so that everyone will praise your heavenly Father."

GOOD LIGHT

Can you hide a city that is sitting on top of a hill? Its light at night can be seen for miles. If we live for Christ, we will glow like lights, showing others what Christ is like. We hide our light by (1) being quiet when we should speak, (2) going along with the crowd,

Light represents what is good, pure, true, holy, and reliable. Darkness represents what is sinful and evil. Light is also related to truth in that light exposes whatever exists, whether it is good or bad. In the dark, good and evil look alike; in the light, they can be clearly distinguished. Just as darkness cannot exist in the presence of light, sin cannot exist in the presence of a holy God.

(3) denying the light, (4) letting sin dim our light, (5) not explaining our light to others, or (6) ignoring the needs of others. If we want to have a relationship with God, we must put aside our sinful ways of living. To claim that we belong to him but then go out and live for ourselves is hypocrisy. Be a beacon of truth—don't shut your light off from the rest of the world.

April 1

Jesus teaches about the Law
Matthew 5:17-20 *(Harmony 51)*

*D*on't misunderstand why I have come. I did not come to abolish the law of Moses or the writings of the prophets. No, I came to fulfill them. I assure you, until heaven and earth disappear, even the smallest detail of God's law will remain until its purpose is achieved. So if you break the smallest commandment and teach others to do the same, you will be the least in the Kingdom of Heaven. But anyone who obeys God's laws and teaches them will be great in the Kingdom of Heaven.

"But I warn you—unless you obey God better than the teachers of religious law and the Pharisees do, you can't enter the Kingdom of Heaven at all!"

GREATER RIGHTEOUSNESS
The Pharisees were exacting and scrupulous in their attempts to follow their laws. So how can Jesus reasonably call us to a greater righteousness than theirs? The Pharisees' weakness was that they were content to obey the laws outwardly without allowing God to change their hearts (or attitudes). Jesus was saying, therefore, that the *quality* of our goodness should be greater than that of the Pharisees. They looked pious, but they were far from the Kingdom of God. God judges our heart as well as our works, for it is in the heart that our real allegiance lies. Jesus was saying that his listeners needed a different kind of righteousness altogether (love and obedience), not just a more intense version of the Pharisees' righteousness (legal compliance). Our righteousness must (1) come from what God does in us, not what we can do by ourselves; (2) be God-centered, not self-centered; (3) be based on reverence for God, not approval from people; and (4) go beyond keeping the law to living by the principles behind the law.

If Jesus did not come to destroy the law, does that mean all the Old Testament laws still apply to us today? In the Old Testament, there were three categories of law: ceremonial, civil, and moral. The ceremonial law related specifically to Israel's worship. Its primary purpose was to point forward to Jesus Christ. The civil law applied to daily living in Israel. The moral law (such as the Ten Commandments) is the direct command of God, and it still requires strict obedience from God's people.

April 2

Jesus teaches about anger
Matthew 5:21-22 *(Harmony 52a)*

*Y*ou have heard that the law of Moses says, 'Do not murder. If you commit murder, you are subject to judgment.' But I say, if you are angry with someone, you are subject to judgment! If you say to your friend, 'You idiot,' you are in danger of being brought before the court. And if you curse someone, you are in danger of the fires of hell."

THOUGHT CONTROL
Killing is a terrible sin, but *anger* is a great sin too because it also violates God's command to love. Anger in this case refers to a seething, brooding bitterness against someone. It is a dangerous emotion that always threatens to leap out of control, leading to violence, emotional hurt, increased mental stress, and spiritual damage. Anger keeps us from developing a spirit pleasing to God. Have you ever been proud that you didn't strike out and say what was really on your mind? Self-control is good, but Christ wants us to practice thought control as well. Jesus said that we will be held accountable even for our attitudes.

Jesus was not doing away with the law or adding his own beliefs. Rather, he was giving a fuller understanding of why God made the specific law in the first place.

April 3

Jesus teaches about anger
Matthew 5:23-26 *(Harmony 52b)*

*S*o if you are standing before the altar in the Temple, offering a sacrifice to God, and you suddenly remember that someone has something against you, leave your sacrifice there beside the altar. Go and be reconciled to that person. Then come and offer your sacrifice to God. Come to terms quickly with your enemy before it is too late and you are dragged into court, handed over to an officer, and thrown in jail. I assure you that you won't be free again until you have paid the last penny."

GET THINGS RIGHT
Broken relationships can hinder our relationship with God. If we have a problem or grievance with a friend, we should resolve the

In Jesus' day, someone who couldn't pay a debt was thrown into prison until someone paid his debt. It is practical advice to resolve our differences with our enemies before their anger causes more trouble (Proverbs 25:8-10).

problem as soon as possible. We are hypocrites if we claim to love God while we hate others. A person's attitude toward others reflects his or her relationship with God. You may not get into a disagreement that takes you to court, but even small conflicts mend more easily if you try to make peace right away. In a broader sense, these verses advise us to get things right with our brothers and sisters before we have to stand before God.

April 4

Jesus teaches about lust
Matthew 5:27-30 *(Harmony 53)*

*Y*ou have heard that the law of Moses says, 'Do not commit adultery.' But I say, anyone who even looks at a woman with lust in his eye has already committed adultery with her in his heart. So if your eye— even if it is your good eye—causes you to lust, gouge it out and throw it away. It is better for you to lose one part of your body than for your whole body to be thrown into hell. And if your hand—even if it is your stronger hand—causes you to sin, cut it off and throw it away. It is better for you to lose one part of your body than for your whole body to be thrown into hell."

DESIRES
The Old Testament law said that it was wrong for you to have sex with someone other than your spouse (Exodus 20:14). But Jesus said that the *desire* to have sex with someone other than your spouse is mental adultery and thus sin. Jesus emphasized that if the *act* is wrong, then so is the *intention*. To be faithful to your spouse with your body but not your mind is to break the trust so vital to a strong marriage. Jesus is not condemning natural interest in the opposite sex or even healthy sexual desire, but rather the deliberate and repeated filling of one's mind with fantasies that would be evil if acted out. Sinful desires can be just as damaging as sinful actions. Left unchecked, wrong desires will result in wrong actions and turn people away from God. Guard your thoughts—don't give sin a foothold through lust.

When Jesus said to get rid of your hand or your eye, he was speaking figuratively. He didn't mean literally to gouge out your eye, because even a blind person can lust. We sometimes tolerate sins in our lives that, left unchecked, could eventually destroy us. It is better to experience the pain of removal (getting rid of a bad habit or something we treasure, for instance) than to allow the sin to bring judgment and condemnation.

April 5

Jesus teaches about divorce
Matthew 5:31-32 *(Harmony 54)*

*Y*ou have heard that the law of Moses says, 'A man can divorce his wife by merely giving her a letter of divorce.' But I say that a man who divorces his wife, unless she has been unfaithful, causes her to commit adultery. And anyone who marries a divorced woman commits adultery."

A LIFETIME COMMITMENT
Divorce is as hurtful and destructive today as it was in Jesus' day. God intends marriage to be a lifetime commitment (Genesis 2:24). When entering into marriage, people should never consider divorce an option for solving problems or a way out of a relationship that seems dead. In these verses, Jesus is also attacking those who purposefully abuse the marriage contract, using divorce to satisfy their lustful desire to marry someone else. Are your actions today helping your marriage grow stronger, or are you tearing it apart?

Jesus said that divorce is not permissible except for unfaithfulness. This does not mean that divorce should automatically occur when a spouse commits adultery. "Fornication" implies a sexually immoral lifestyle, not a confessed and repented act of adultery. Those who discover that their partner has been unfaithful should first make every effort to forgive, reconcile, and restore their relationship.

April 6

Jesus teaches about vows
Matthew 5:33-37 *(Harmony 55)*

*A*gain, you have heard that the law of Moses says, 'Do not break your vows; you must carry out the vows you have made to the Lord.' But I say, don't make any vows! If you say, 'By heaven!' it is a sacred vow because heaven is God's throne. And if you say, 'By the earth!' it is a sacred vow because the earth is his footstool. And don't swear, 'By Jerusalem!' for Jerusalem is the city of the great King. Don't even swear, 'By my

The Bible condemns making vows or taking oaths casually, giving your word while knowing that you won't keep it, or swearing falsely in God's name (Exodus 20:7; Leviticus 19:12; Numbers 30:1-2; Deuteronomy 19:16-20). Oaths are needed in certain situations only because we live in a sinful society that breeds distrust.

head!' for you can't turn one hair white or black. Just say a simple, 'Yes, I will,' or 'No, I won't.' Your word is enough. To strengthen your promise with a vow shows that something is wrong."

PROMISES, PROMISES

Jesus was emphasizing the importance of telling the truth. People were breaking promises and using sacred language casually and carelessly. Keeping oaths and promises is important; it builds trust and makes committed human relationships possible. Are you known as a person of your word? Truthfulness seems so rare that we feel we must end our statements with "I promise." If we tell the truth all the time, we will have less pressure to back up our words with an oath or promise.

April 7

Jesus teaches about retaliation
Matthew 5:38-42 *(Harmony 56)*

*Y*ou have heard that the law of Moses says, 'If an eye is injured, injure the eye of the person who did it. If a tooth gets knocked out, knock out the tooth of the person who did it.' But I say, don't resist an evil person! If you are slapped on the right cheek, turn the other, too. If you are ordered to court and your shirt is taken from you, give your coat, too. If a soldier demands that you carry his gear for a mile, carry it two miles. Give to those who ask, and don't turn away from those who want to borrow."

GETTING EVEN

When we are wronged, often our first reaction is to get even. Jesus said, however, that we should do *good* to those who wrong us! Our desire should not be to keep score but to love and forgive. This is not natural—it is supernatural. Only God can give us the strength to love as he does. Instead of planning vengeance, pray for those who hurt you.

God's purpose behind this law was to limit vengeance and help the court administer punishment that was neither too strict nor too lenient.

April 8

Jesus teaches about loving enemies
Luke 6:27-36 (also in Matthew 5:43-48) *(Harmony 57)*

*B*ut if you are willing to listen, I say, love your enemies. Do good to those who hate you. Pray for the happiness of those who curse you. Pray for those who hurt you. If someone slaps you on one cheek, turn the other cheek. If someone demands your coat, offer your shirt also. Give what you have to anyone who asks you for it; and when things are taken away from you, don't try to get them back. Do for others as you would like them to do for you.

"Do you think you deserve credit merely for loving those who love you? Even the sinners do that! And if you do good only to those who do good to you, is that so wonderful? Even sinners do that much! And if you lend money only to those who can repay you, what good is that? Even sinners will lend to their own kind for a full return.

"Love your enemies! Do good to them! Lend to them! And don't be concerned that they might not repay. Then your reward from heaven will be very great, and you will truly be acting as children of the Most High, for he is kind to the unthankful and to those who are wicked. You must be compassionate, just as your Father is compassionate."

LOVING YOUR ENEMIES
By telling us not to retaliate, Jesus keeps us from taking the law into our own hands. By loving and praying for our enemies, we can overcome evil with good. If you love your enemies and treat them well, you will truly show that Jesus is Lord of your life. This is possible only for those who give themselves fully to God, because only he can deliver people from natural selfishness. Loving our enemies means acting in their best interests. We can pray for them and think of ways to help them. Jesus loved the whole world, even though the world was in rebellion against God. Jesus asks us to follow his example by loving our enemies. Grant your enemies the same respect and rights as you desire for yourself.

Jesus wasn't talking about having affection for enemies; he was talking about an act of will. You can't "fall into" this kind of love—it takes conscious effort. We must trust the Holy Spirit to help us show love to those for whom we may not feel love.

April 9

Jesus teaches about giving to the needy
Matthew 6:1-4 (Harmony 58)

*T*ake care! Don't do your good deeds publicly, to be admired, because then you will lose the reward from your Father in heaven. When you give a gift to someone in need, don't shout about it as the hypocrites do—blowing trumpets in the synagogues and streets to call attention to their acts of charity! I assure you, they have received all the reward they will ever get. But when you give to someone, don't tell your left hand what your right hand is doing. Give your gifts in secret, and your Father, who knows all secrets, will reward you."

GOOD SECRETS
When Jesus says not to tell the left hand what the right hand is doing, he is teaching that our motives for giving to God and to others must be pure. It's easier to do what is right when we gain recognition and praise. To be sure that our motives are not selfish, we should do our good works quietly or in secret, with no thought of reward. Our actions should not be self-centered but God-centered; done not to make us look good, but to make God look good. The reward God promises is not material, and it is never given to those who seek it. Doing something only for ourselves is not a loving sacrifice. With your next good deed, ask, *Would I still do this if no one would ever know I did it?*

The term hypocrites, *as used here, describes people who do good acts for appearances only—not out of compassion or other good motives. Their actions may be good, but their motives are hollow.*

April 10

Jesus teaches about prayer
Matthew 6:5-8 (Harmony 59a)

*A*nd now about prayer. When you pray, don't be like the hypocrites who love to pray publicly on street corners and in the synagogues where everyone can see them. I assure you, that is all the reward they will ever get. But when you pray, go away by yourself, shut the door behind you, and pray to your Father secretly. Then your Father, who knows all secrets, will reward you.

"When you pray, don't babble on and on as people of other religions do. They think their prayers are answered only by repeating their words again and again. Don't be like them, because your Father knows exactly what you need even before you ask him!"

OVER AND OVER
Repeating the same words over and over like an incantation is no way to ensure that God will hear your prayer. It's not wrong to come to God many times with the same requests—Jesus encourages *persistent* prayer. But he condemns the mindless repetition of words that are not offered with a sincere heart. We can never pray too much if our prayers are honest and sincere. Before you start to pray, make sure you mean what you say.

Some people, especially the religious leaders, wanted to be seen as "holy," and public prayer was one way to get attention. Jesus saw through their self-righteous acts, however, and taught that the essence of prayer is not public style but private communication with God.

April 11

Jesus teaches about prayer
Matthew 6:9-15 *(Harmony 59b)*

*P*ray like this: Our Father in heaven, may your name be honored. May your Kingdom come soon. May your will be done here on earth, just as it is in heaven. Give us our food for today, and forgive us our sins, just as we have forgiven those who have sinned against us. And don't let us yield to temptation, but deliver us from the evil one.

"If you forgive those who sin against you, your heavenly Father will forgive you. But if you refuse to forgive others, your Father will not forgive your sins."

FORGIVENESS
Jesus gives a startling warning about forgiveness: If we refuse to forgive others, God will also refuse to forgive us. Why? Because when we don't forgive others, we are denying our common ground as sinners in need of God's forgiveness. God's forgiveness of sin is not the direct result of our forgiving others, but it is based on our realizing what forgiveness means (see Ephesians 4:32). It is easy to ask God for forgiveness but difficult to grant it to others. Whenever we ask God to forgive us for sin, we should ask ourselves, *Have I forgiven the people who have wronged me?"*

This is often called the Lord's Prayer because Jesus gave it to the disciples. It can be a pattern for our prayers.

April 12

Jesus teaches about fasting
Matthew 6:16-18 *(Harmony 60)*

*A*nd when you fast, don't make it obvious, as the hypocrites do, who try to look pale and disheveled so people will admire them for their fasting. I assure you, that is the only reward they will ever get. But when you fast, comb your hair and wash your face. Then no one will suspect you are fasting, except your Father, who knows what you do in secret. And your Father, who knows all secrets, will reward you."

SPIRITUAL DISCIPLINE
Fasting—going without food in order to spend time in prayer—is noble *and* difficult. It gives us time to pray, teaches self-discipline, reminds us that we can live with a lot less, and helps us appreciate God's gifts. Jesus was not condemning fasting, but hypocrisy—fasting in order to gain public approval. Fasting was mandatory for the Jewish people once a year, on the Day of Atonement (Leviticus 23:32) The Pharisees voluntarily fasted twice a week to impress the people with their "holiness." Jesus commended acts of self-sacrifice done quietly and sincerely. He wanted people to adopt spiritual disciplines for the right reasons, not from a selfish desire for praise.

By separating yourself from the daily routine of food preparation and eating, you can devote extra time to prayer. Hunger pangs remind you of your weakness and your dependence upon God. Fasting still can be helpful today as you seek God's will in special situations.

April 13

Jesus teaches about money
Matthew 6:19-24 *(Harmony 61)*

*D*on't store up treasures here on earth, where they can be eaten by moths and get rusty, and where thieves break in and steal. Store your treasures in heaven, where they will never become moth-eaten or rusty and where they will be safe from thieves. Wherever your treasure is, there your heart and thoughts will also be.

"Your eye is a lamp for your body. A pure eye lets sunshine into your soul. But an evil eye shuts out the light and plunges you into darkness. If the light you think you have is really darkness, how deep that darkness will be!

"No one can serve two masters. For you will hate one and love the other, or be devoted to one and despise the other. You cannot serve both God and money."

ONE MASTER

Jesus says we can have only one master. We live in a materialistic society where many people serve money. They spend all their lives collecting and storing it, only to die and leave it behind. Their desire for money and what it can buy far outweighs their commitment to God and spiritual matters. You will spend much of your time and energy thinking about whatever you have stored up. Don't fall into the materialism trap, because "the love of money is at the root of all kinds of evil" (1 Timothy 6:10). Can you honestly say that God, and not money, is your master? One test is to ask which one occupies more of your thoughts, time, and efforts.

Spiritual vision is the capacity to see clearly what God wants us to do and to see the world from his point of view. But this spiritual insight can be easily clouded. Self-serving desires, interests, and goals block that vision. Serving God is the best way to restore it. A "pure" eye is one that is fixed on God.

April 14

Jesus teaches about worry
Matthew 6:25-30 *(Harmony 62a)*

So I tell you, don't worry about everyday life—whether you have enough food, drink, and clothes. Doesn't life consist of more than food and clothing? Look at the birds. They don't need to plant or harvest or put food in barns because your heavenly Father feeds them. And you are far more valuable to him than they are. Can all your worries add a single moment to your life? Of course not.

"And why worry about your clothes? Look at the lilies and how they grow. They don't work or make their clothing, yet Solomon in all his glory was not dressed as beautifully as they are. And if God cares so wonderfully for flowers that are here today and gone tomorrow, won't he more surely care for you? You have so little faith!"

Jesus referred to King Solomon "in all his glory." When Solomon asked for wisdom, God promised him riches and honor as well (1 Kings 3:13). Solomon's riches became legendary. Yet the great glory of his expensive robes and jewels cannot compare with the beauty of God's creation in the form of the tiniest flowers.

WHY WORRY?

Because of the ill effects of worry, Jesus tells us not to worry about those needs that God promises to supply. Worry may (1) damage your health, (2) cause the object of your worry to consume your thoughts, (3) disrupt your productivity, (4) negatively affect the way you treat others, and (5) reduce your ability to trust in God. How many ill effects of worry are you experiencing? Here is the difference between worry and genuine concern—worry immobilizes, but concern moves you to action. Take your worry and turn it into prayer. Do you want to worry less? Then pray more! Whenever you start to worry, stop and pray.

April 15

Jesus teaches about worry
Matthew 6:31-34 *(Harmony 62b)*

S o don't worry about having enough food or drink or clothing. Why be like the pagans who are so deeply concerned about these things? Your heavenly Father already knows all your needs, and he will give you all you need from day to day if you live for him and make the Kingdom of God your primary concern.

"So don't worry about tomorrow, for tomorrow will bring its own worries. Today's trouble is enough for today."

WHO'S ON FIRST?
To make the Kingdom of God your primary concern means that your thoughts are so centered on God and his will for your life that you desire to serve and obey him in everything. What is really important to you? People, objects, goals, and other desires all compete for priority. Any of these can quickly bump God out of first place if you don't actively choose to give him first place in *every* area of your life.

Planning for tomorrow is time well spent; worrying about tomorrow is time wasted. Sometimes it's difficult to tell the difference. Careful planning is thinking ahead about goals, steps, and schedules, and trusting in God's guidance.

Jesus teaches about criticizing others
Luke 6:37-42 (also in Matthew 7:1-6) *(Harmony 63)*

*S*top judging others, and you will not be judged. Stop criticizing others, or it will all come back on you. If you forgive others, you will be forgiven. If you give, you will receive. Your gift will return to you in full measure, pressed down, shaken together to make room for more, and running over. Whatever measure you use in giving—large or small—it will be used to measure what is given back to you."

Then Jesus gave the following illustration: "What good is it for one blind person to lead another? The first one will fall into a ditch and pull the other down also. A student is not greater than the teacher. But the student who works hard will become like the teacher.

"And why worry about a speck in your friend's eye when you have a log in your own? How can you think of saying, 'Friend, let me help you get rid of that speck in your eye,' when you can't see past the log in your own eye? Hypocrite! First get rid of the log from your own eye; then perhaps you will see well enough to deal with the speck in your friend's eye."

VISION TEST
Jesus doesn't mean we should ignore wrongdoing, but we should not be so worried about others' sins that we overlook our own. Jesus tells us to examine our own motives and conduct instead of judging others. The traits that bother us in others are often the habits we dislike in ourselves. Our untamed bad habits and behavior patterns are the very ones that we most want to change in others.

An object in the eye quickly blurs a person's vision, causing him or her to see things imagined, blurred, or double. When one's vision is clear, that person will be better able to help someone else remove a speck in his or her eye (if one actually exists).

Do you find it easy to magnify others' faults while excusing your own? If you are ready to criticize someone, check to see if you deserve the same criticism. Judge yourself first, and then lovingly forgive and help your neighbor. Remember your own "logs" when you feel like criticizing, and you may find that you have less to say.

April 17

Jesus teaches about asking, seeking, knocking
Matthew 7:7-11 *(Harmony 64a)*

*K*eep on asking, and you will be given what you ask for. Keep on looking, and you will find. Keep on knocking, and the door will be opened. For everyone who asks, receives. Everyone who seeks, finds. And the door is opened to everyone who knocks. You parents—if your children ask for a loaf of bread, do you give them a stone instead? Or if they ask for a fish, do you give them a snake? Of course not! If you sinful people know how to give good gifts to your children, how much more will your heavenly Father give good gifts to those who ask him."

ASKING FOR SNAKES
When children ask their parents for food, they usually are granted their request.

Parents most certainly would not give their children a stone or poisonous snake instead! As we learn to know God better as a loving Father, we will come to realize that he desires to grant us only good gifts.

Jesus told us to persist in pursuing God. People often give up after a few halfhearted efforts and conclude that God cannot be found. But knowing God takes faith, focus, and follow-through, and Jesus assures us that we will be rewarded.

April 18

Jesus teaches about asking, seeking, knocking
Matthew 7:12 *(Harmony 64b)*

*D*o for others what you would like them to do for you. This is a summary of all that is taught in the law and the prophets."

GOLDEN ACTIONS
This is commonly known as the Golden Rule. In many religions it is stated negatively: "Don't do to others what you don't want done to you." By stating it positively, Jesus made it more significant. It is not very difficult to refrain from harming others; it is much more difficult to take the initiative in doing something good for them. The Golden Rule

Jesus called this the "summary of all that is taught in the law and the prophets." If we do to others what we want done to us, we will naturally keep all the laws. This looks at God's law positively. Rather than worrying about all we should not do, we should concentrate on all we can do to show our love for God and others.

as Jesus formulated it is the foundation of active goodness and mercy—the kind of love God shows to us every day. Think of a good and merciful action you can do today.

April 19

Jesus teaches about the way to heaven
Matthew 7:13-14 *(Harmony 65)*

*Y*ou can enter God's Kingdom only through the narrow gate. The highway to hell is broad, and its gate is wide for the many who choose the easy way. But the gateway to life is small, and the road is narrow, and only a few ever find it."

ONE WAY
The gate that leads to eternal life is called "narrow." This does not mean that it is difficult to become a Christian but that there is only *one* way to live eternally with God, and only a few decide to take that way. Believing in Jesus is the only way to heaven because he

In John 10:7, Jesus called himself "the gate for the sheep." Jesus is the only way into God's Kingdom. Only by accepting his sacrifice on your behalf can you find eternal life.

alone died for our sins and opened the way. Going Jesus' way may not be popular, but it is true and right. Thank God there *is* one way!

April 20

Jesus teaches about fruit in people's lives
Matthew 7:15-20 (also in Luke 6:43-45) *(Harmony 66)*

*B*eware of false prophets who come disguised as harmless sheep, but are really wolves that will tear you apart. You can detect them by the way they act, just as you can identify a tree by its fruit. You don't pick grapes from thornbushes, or figs from thistles. A healthy tree produces good fruit, and an unhealthy tree produces bad fruit. A good tree can't produce bad fruit, and a bad tree can't produce good fruit. So every tree that does not produce good fruit is chopped down and thrown into the fire. Yes, the way to identify a tree or a person is by the kind of fruit that is produced."

FRUIT CHECK

We should evaluate teachers' words by examining their lives. Just as trees are consistent in the kind of fruit they produce, good teachers consistently exhibit good behavior and high moral character as they attempt to live out the truths of Scripture. This does not mean we should throw out church teachers, pastors, and others who are less than perfect. Every one of us is subject to sin, and we must show the same mercy to others that we need for ourselves. When Jesus talks about bad trees, he means teachers who deliberately teach false doctrine. We must examine teachers' motives, the direction they are taking, and the results they are seeking.

False prophets were common in Old Testament times. They prophesied only what the king and the people wanted to hear, claiming it was God's message. False teachers are just as common today. Jesus said to beware of those whose words sound religious but who are motivated by money, fame, or power.

April 21

Jesus teaches about those who build houses on rock and sand
Matthew 7:21-29 (also in Luke 6:46-49) *(Harmony 67)*

Not all people who sound religious are really godly. They may refer to me as 'Lord,' but they still won't enter the Kingdom of Heaven. The decisive issue is whether they obey my Father in heaven. On judgment day many will tell me, 'Lord, Lord, we prophesied in your name and cast out demons in your name and performed many miracles in your name.' But I will reply, 'I never knew you. Go away; the things you did were unauthorized.'

"Anyone who listens to my teaching and obeys me is wise, like a person who builds a house on solid rock. Though the rain comes in torrents and the floodwaters rise and the winds beat against that house, it won't collapse, because it is built on rock. But anyone who hears my teaching and ignores it is foolish, like a person who builds a house on sand. When the rains and floods come and the winds beat against that house, it will fall with a mighty crash."

After Jesus finished speaking, the crowds were amazed at his teaching, for he taught as one who had real authority—quite unlike the teachers of religious law.

Living on the edge of a desert, Jesus' listeners were well aware of sand—its shifts and sudden movements in the wind. Tents, not houses, were used on sand. The people were also very aware of the deceptive nature of water, having experienced violent storms on the Sea of Galilee.

A SOLID FOUNDATION

Like a house of cards, the fool's life crumbles under pressure. Most people do not deliberately seek to build on a false or inferior foundation; instead, they just don't think about their life's purpose. Many people are headed for destruction, not out of stubbornness but out of thoughtlessness. Part of our responsibility as believers is to help others stop and think about where their lives are headed and to point out the consequences of ignoring Christ's message. Obeying God is like building a house on a strong, solid foundation that stands firm when storms come. When life is calm, our foundations don't seem to matter. But when crises come, our foundations are tested. Be sure your life is built on the solid foundation of knowing and trusting Jesus Christ.

April 22

A Roman soldier demonstrates faith
Luke 7:1-10 (also in Matthew 8:5-13) *(Harmony 68)*

*W*hen Jesus had finished saying all this, he went back to Capernaum. Now the highly valued slave of a Roman officer was sick and near death. When the officer heard about Jesus, he sent some respected Jewish leaders to ask him to come and heal his slave. So they earnestly begged Jesus to come with them and help the man. "If anyone deserves your help, it is he," they said, "for he loves the Jews and even built a synagogue for us."

So Jesus went with them. But just before they arrived at the house, the officer sent some friends to say, "Lord, don't trouble yourself by coming to my home, for I am not worthy of such an honor. I am not even worthy to come and meet you. Just say the word from where you are, and my servant will be healed. I know because I am under the authority of my superior officers, and I have authority over my soldiers. I only need to say, 'Go,' and they go, or 'Come,' and they come. And if I say to my slaves, 'Do this or that,' they do it."

When Jesus heard this, he was amazed. Turning to the crowd, he said, "I tell you, I haven't seen faith like this in all the land of Israel!" And when the officer's friends returned to his house, they found the slave completely healed.

Since he was well aware of the Jewish hatred for Roman soldiers, the Roman army officer may not have wanted to interrupt a Jewish gathering. As a centurion, he daily delegated work and sent groups on missions, so this was how he chose to get his message to Jesus.

BETWEEN YOU AND JESUS

This officer was a *centurion,* in charge of one hundred men in the Roman army. This man turned to Jesus, not as a last resort or magic charm, but because he believed Jesus was sent from God. Yet he didn't come himself to Jesus, and he didn't expect Jesus to come to him. Just as this officer did not need to be present to have his orders carried out, so Jesus did not need to be present to heal. The captain's faith was especially amazing because he was a Gentile who had not been brought up to know a loving God. The Roman officer could have let many obstacles stand between him and Jesus—pride, doubt, money, language, distance, time, self-sufficiency, power, race. But he didn't. Neither should we.

April 23

Jesus raises a widow's son from the dead
Luke 7:11-17 *(Harmony 69)*

*S*oon afterward Jesus went with his disciples to the village of Nain, with a great crowd following him. A funeral procession was coming out as he approached the village gate. The boy who had died was the only son of a widow, and many mourners from the village were with her. When the Lord saw her, his heart overflowed with compassion. "Don't cry!" he said. Then he walked over to the coffin and touched it, and the bearers stopped. "Young man," he said, "get up." Then the dead boy sat up and began to talk to those around him! And Jesus gave him back to his mother.

Great fear swept the crowd, and they praised God, saying, "A mighty prophet has risen among us," and "We have seen the hand of God at work today." The report of what Jesus had done that day spread all over Judea and even out across its borders.

ACCEPT THE GIFT

This story illustrates salvation. The whole world was dead in sin (Ephesians 2:1), just as the widow's son was dead. Being dead, we could do nothing to help ourselves—we couldn't even ask for help. But God had compassion on us, and he sent Jesus to raise us to life with him (Ephesians 2:4-7). The dead boy did not earn his second chance at life, and we cannot earn our new life in Christ. But we can accept God's gift of life, praise God for it, and use our lives to do his will.

Honoring the dead was important in Jewish tradition. A funeral procession—the relatives of the dead person following the body, which was wrapped and carried on a kind of stretcher—would make its way through town, and bystanders would be expected to join the procession. In addition, hired mourners would cry aloud and draw attention to the procession.

April 24

Jesus eases John's doubt
Luke 7:18-28 (also in Matthew 11:1-15) *(Harmony 70a)*

*T*he disciples of John the Baptist told John about everything Jesus was doing. So John called for two of his disciples, and he sent them to the Lord to ask him, "Are you the Messiah we've been expecting, or should we keep looking for someone else?"

John's two disciples found Jesus and said to him, "John the Baptist sent us to ask, 'Are you the Messiah we've been expecting, or should we keep looking for someone else?'"

At that very time, he cured many people of their various diseases, and he cast out evil spirits and restored sight to the blind. Then he told John's disciples, "Go back to John and tell him what you have seen and heard—the blind see, the lame walk, the lepers are cured, the deaf hear, the dead are raised to life, and the Good News is being preached to the poor. And tell him, 'God blesses those who are not offended by me.'"

After they left, Jesus talked to the crowd about John. "Who is this man in the wilderness that you went out to see? Did you find him weak as a reed, moved by every breath of wind? Or were you expecting to see a man dressed in expensive clothes? No, people who wear beautiful clothes and live in luxury are found in palaces, not in the wilderness. Were you looking for a prophet? Yes, and he is more than a prophet. John is the man to whom the Scriptures refer when they say,

> *'Look, I am sending my messenger before you,*
> *and he will prepare your way before you.'*

I tell you, of all who have ever lived, none is greater than John. Yet even the most insignificant person in the Kingdom of God is greater than he is!"

DEALING WITH DOUBTS

John was confused because the reports he received about Jesus were unexpected and incomplete. John's doubts were natural, and Jesus didn't rebuke him for them. Instead, Jesus responded in a way that John would understand: Jesus explained that he had accomplished what the Messiah was supposed to accomplish. God can handle our doubts, and he welcomes our questions. Do you have questions about Jesus—about who he is or what he expects of you? Admit them to yourself and to God, and begin looking for answers. Only as you face your doubts honestly can you begin to resolve them.

Of all people, no one fulfilled his God-given purpose better than John. Yet in God's Kingdom, all who come after John have a greater spiritual heritage because they have clearer knowledge of the purpose of Jesus' death and resurrection.

Jesus eases John's doubt
Luke 7:29-35 (also in Matthew 11:16-19) *(Harmony 70b)*

*W*hen they heard this, all the people, including the unjust tax collectors, agreed that God's plan was right, for they had been baptized by John. But the Pharisees and experts in religious law had rejected God's plan for them, for they had refused John's baptism.

"How shall I describe this generation?" Jesus asked. "With what will I compare them? They are like a group of children playing a game in the public square. They complain to their friends, 'We played wedding songs, and you weren't happy, so we played funeral songs, but you weren't sad.' For John the Baptist didn't drink wine and he often fasted, and you say, 'He's demon possessed.' And I, the Son of Man, feast and drink, and you say, 'He's a glutton and a drunkard, and a friend of the worst sort of sinners!' But wisdom is shown to be right by the lives of those who follow it."

HYPOCRISY
The religious leaders hated anyone who spoke the truth and exposed their own hypocrisy, and they did not bother to be consistent in their faultfinding. They criticized John the Baptist because he fasted and drank no wine; they criticized Jesus because he ate heartily and drank wine with tax collectors and "lowlifes." Their real objection to both men, of course, had nothing to do with dietary habits. What the Pharisees and experts in the law couldn't stand was being exposed for their hypocrisy. Most of us can find compelling reasons to do or believe whatever suits our purposes. If we do not examine our ideas in the light of God's truth, however, we may be just as obviously self-serving as the Pharisees.

The tax collectors (who embodied evil in most people's minds) and common people heard John's message and repented. In contrast, the Pharisees and experts in religious law rejected his words. Wanting to live their own way, they justified their own point of view and refused to listen to other ideas.

April 26

Jesus promises rest for the soul
Matthew 11:20-24 *(Harmony 71a)*

*T*hen Jesus began to denounce the cities where he had done most of his miracles, because they hadn't turned from their sins and turned to God. "What horrors await you, Korazin and Bethsaida! For if the miracles I did in you had been done in wicked Tyre and Sidon, their people would have sat in deep repentance long ago, clothed in sackcloth and throwing ashes on their heads to show their remorse. I assure you, Tyre and Sidon will be better off on the judgment day than you! And you people of Capernaum, will you be exalted to heaven? No, you will be brought down to the place of the dead. For if the miracles I did for you had been done in Sodom, it would still be here today. I assure you, Sodom will be better off on the judgment day than you."

NO EXCUSES

Tyre, Sidon, and Sodom were ancient cities with a long-standing reputation for wickedness (Genesis 18–19; Ezekiel 27–28). Each was destroyed by God for its evil. The people of Bethsaida, Korazin, and Capernaum saw Jesus firsthand, and yet they stubbornly refused to repent of their sins and believe in him. Jesus said that if some of the wickedest cities in the world had seen him, they would have repented. Because Bethsaida, Korazin, and Capernaum saw Jesus and didn't believe, they would suffer even greater punishment than that of the wicked cities who didn't see Jesus. Similarly, nations and cities with churches on every corner and Bibles in every home will have no excuse on judgment day if they do not repent and believe. What evidence do you have for the truth of the gospel? How have you responded to the truth?

God had promised to spare Sodom if only ten godly people could be found in the city (Genesis 18:32), and not even ten could be found. The cities of Tyre and Sidon on the sea were beautiful, but the beauty was a source of pride, guaranteeing their judgment.

April 27

Jesus promises rest for the soul
Matthew 11:25-30 *(Harmony 71b)*

*T*hen Jesus prayed this prayer: "O Father, Lord of heaven and earth, thank you for hiding the truth from those who think themselves so wise and clever, and for revealing it to the childlike. Yes, Father, it pleased you to do it this way!

"My Father has given me authority over everything. No one really knows the Son except the Father, and no one really knows the Father except the Son and those to whom the Son chooses to reveal him."

Then Jesus said, "Come to me, all of you who are weary and carry heavy burdens, and I will give you rest. Take my yoke upon you. Let me teach you, because I am humble and gentle, and you will find rest for your souls. For my yoke fits perfectly, and the burden I give you is light."

THE YOKE
A yoke is a heavy wooden harness that fits over the shoulders of oxen. It is attached to a piece of equipment the oxen are to pull. A person may be carrying heavy burdens of (1) sin, (2) excessive demands of religious leaders (23:4; Acts 15:10), (3) oppression and persecution, or (4) weariness in the search for God. Jesus frees people from all these burdens. Jesus promises us his love, healing, and rest for our souls. A relationship with God changes meaningless, wearisome toil into spiritual productivity and purpose. Come to Jesus with your burdens. Turn them over to him—he will give you rest.

Jesus mentions two kinds of people in his prayer: The "wise"—arrogant in their own knowledge—and the "little children"—humbly open to receive the truth of God's Word. Are you wise in your own eyes, or do you seek the truth in childlike faith, realizing that only God holds all the answers?

April 28

A sinful woman anoints Jesus' feet
Luke 7:36-50 *(Harmony 72)*

*O*ne of the Pharisees asked Jesus to come to his home for a meal, so Jesus accepted the invitation and sat down to eat. A certain immoral woman heard he was there and brought a beautiful jar filled with expensive perfume. Then she knelt behind him at his feet, weeping. Her tears fell on his feet, and she wiped them off with her hair. Then she kept kissing his feet and putting perfume on them.

When the Pharisee who was the host saw what was happening and who the woman was, he said to himself, "This proves that Jesus is no prophet. If God had really sent him, he would know what kind of woman is touching him. She's a sinner!"

Then Jesus spoke up and answered his thoughts. "Simon," he said to the Pharisee, "I have something to say to you."

"All right, Teacher," Simon replied, "go ahead."

Then Jesus told him this story: "A man loaned money to two people—five hundred pieces of silver to one and fifty pieces to the other. But neither of them could repay him, so he kindly forgave them both, canceling their debts. Who do you suppose loved him more after that?"

Simon answered, "I suppose the one for whom he canceled the larger debt."

"That's right," Jesus said. Then he turned to the woman and said to Simon, "Look at this woman kneeling here. When I entered your home, you didn't offer me water to wash the dust from my feet, but she has washed them with her tears and wiped them with her hair. You didn't give me a kiss of greeting, but she has kissed my feet again and again from the time I first came in. You neglected the courtesy of olive oil to anoint my head, but she has anointed my feet with rare perfume. I tell you, her sins—and they are many—have been forgiven, so she has shown me much love. But a person who is forgiven little shows only little love." Then Jesus said to the woman, "Your sins are forgiven."

The men at the table said among themselves, "Who does this man think he is, going around forgiving sins?"

And Jesus said to the woman, "Your faith has saved you; go in peace."

COMPLETE FORGIVENESS

Simon had committed several social errors in neglecting to wash Jesus' feet (a courtesy extended to guests because sandaled feet got very dirty), anoint his head with oil, and offer him the kiss of greeting. Did Simon perhaps feel that he was too good to treat Jesus as an equal? The immoral woman, by contrast, lavished tears, expensive perfume, and kisses on her Savior. In this story it is this grateful woman, and not the stingy religious leader, whose sins were forgiven. Although it is God's grace through faith that saves us and not acts of love or generosity, this woman demonstrated true faith, and Jesus honored her faith. Overflowing love is the natural response to forgiveness and the appropriate consequence of faith. But only those who realize the depth of their sin can appreciate the complete forgiveness God offers them. Do you appreciate the wideness of God's mercy? Are you grateful for his forgiveness?

In Jesus' day, it was customary to recline while eating. Dinner guests would lie on couches with their heads near the table, propping themselves up on one elbow and stretching their feet out behind them. The woman could easily anoint Jesus' feet without approaching the table.

April 29

Women accompany Jesus and his disciples
Luke 8:1-3 *(Harmony 73)*

*N*ot long afterward Jesus began a tour of the nearby cities and villages to announce the Good News concerning the Kingdom of God. He took his twelve disciples with him, along with some women he had healed and from whom he had cast out evil spirits. Among them were Mary Magdalene, from whom he had cast out seven demons; Joanna, the wife of Chuza, Herod's business manager; Susanna; and many others who were contributing from their own resources to support Jesus and his disciples.

EQUAL IN VALUE
Jesus lifted women up from the agony of degradation and servitude to the joy of fellowship and service. In Jewish culture, women were not supposed to learn from rabbis. By allowing these women to travel with him, Jesus was showing that all people are valuable under God. These women supported Jesus' ministry with their own money.

God equips men and women for various tasks, but all lead to the same goal— honoring God. Each has a role which carries exclusive privileges that should eliminate any attitudes about an inferior or superior sex.

They owed a great debt to him because he had driven demons out of some and had healed others. Here we catch a glimpse of a few of the people behind the scenes in Jesus' ministry. The ministry of those in the foreground is often supported by those whose work is less visible but just as essential. Offer your resources to God, whether or not you will be on center stage.

April 30

Religious leaders accuse Jesus of being Satan
Matthew 12:22-32 (also in Mark 3:20-30) *(Harmony 74a)*

*T*hen a demon-possessed man, who was both blind and unable to talk, was brought to Jesus. He healed the man so that he could both speak and see. The crowd was amazed. "Could it be that Jesus is the Son of David, the Messiah?" they wondered out loud.

But when the Pharisees heard about the miracle, they said, "No wonder he can cast out demons. He gets his power from Satan, the prince of demons."

Jesus knew their thoughts and replied, "Any kingdom at war with itself is doomed. A city or home divided against itself is doomed. And if Satan is casting out Satan, he is fighting against himself. His own kingdom will not survive. And if I am empowered by the prince of demons, what about your own followers? They cast out demons, too, so they will judge you for what you have said. But if I am casting out demons by the Spirit of God, then the Kingdom of God has arrived among you. Let me illustrate this. You can't enter a strong man's house and rob him without first tying him up. Only then can his house be robbed! Anyone who isn't helping me opposes me, and anyone who isn't working with me is actually working against me.

"Every sin or blasphemy can be forgiven—except blasphemy against the Holy Spirit, which can never be forgiven. Anyone who blasphemes against me, the Son of Man, can be forgiven, but blasphemy against the Holy Spirit will never be forgiven, either in this world or in the world to come.

THE UNFORGIVABLE SIN

The Pharisees had blasphemed against the Spirit by attributing the power by which Christ did miracles to Satan (12:24) instead of the Holy Spirit. The unforgivable sin is the deliberate refusal to acknowledge God's power in Christ. It indicates a deliberate and irreversible hardness of heart. Sometimes believers worry that they have accidentally committed this unforgivable sin. But only those who have turned their backs on God and rejected faith in Christ have any need to

The Pharisees had already accused Jesus of being in league with Satan (9:34). They were trying to discredit him by using an emotional argument. Refusing to believe that Jesus came from God, they said he was from Satan. Jesus easily exposed the foolishness of their argument.

worry. Jesus said they can't be forgiven—not because their sin is worse than any other, but because they will never ask for forgiveness. Those who reject the prompting of the Holy Spirit remove themselves from the only force that can lead them to repentance and restoration to God.

May 1

Religious leaders accuse Jesus of being Satan
Matthew 12:33-37 *(Harmony 74b)*

A tree is identified by its fruit. Make a tree good, and its fruit will be good. Make a tree bad, and its fruit will be bad. You brood of snakes! How could evil men like you speak what is good and right? For whatever is in your heart determines what you say. A good person produces good words from a good heart, and an evil person produces evil words from an evil heart. And I tell you this, that you must give an account on judgment day of every idle word you speak. The words you say now reflect your fate then; either you will be justified by them or you will be condemned."

MOUTHWASH

Jesus reminds us that what we say reveals what is in our heart. What kinds of words come from your mouth? That is an indication of what your heart is really like. You can't solve your heart problem, however, just by cleaning up your speech. You must allow the Holy Spirit to fill you with new attitudes and motives; then your speech will be cleansed at its source.

Jesus Christ has been given the authority to judge all the earth (Romans 14:9-11; Philippians 2:9-11). Although his judgment is already at work in our lives, there will be a future, final judgment when Christ returns (Matthew 25:31-46) and everyone's life is reviewed and evaluated.

May 2

Religious leaders ask Jesus for a miracle
Matthew 12:38-42 *(Harmony 75a)*

O ne day some teachers of religious law and Pharisees came to Jesus and said, "Teacher, we want you to show us a miraculous sign to prove that you are from God."
But Jesus replied, "Only an evil, faithless generation would ask for a miraculous sign; but the only sign I will give them is the sign of the prophet Jonah. For as Jonah was in the belly of the great fish for three days and three nights, so I, the Son of Man, will be in the heart of the earth for three

days and three nights. The people of Nineveh will rise up against this generation on judgment day and condemn it, because they repented at the preaching of Jonah. And now someone greater than Jonah is here—and you refuse to repent. The queen of Sheba will also rise up against this generation on judgment day and condemn it, because she came from a distant land to hear the wisdom of Solomon. And now someone greater than Solomon is here—and you refuse to listen to him."

MORE EVIDENCE?

The Pharisees were asking for another miraculous sign, but they were not sincerely seeking to know Jesus. Jesus knew they had already seen enough miraculous proof to convince them that he was the Messiah if they would just open their hearts. But they had already decided not to believe in him, and more miracles would not change that.

Many people have said, "If I could just see a real miracle, then I could really believe in God." But Jesus' response to the Pharisees applies to us. We have plenty of evidence—Jesus' birth, death, resurrection, and ascension, and centuries of his work in believers around the world. Instead of looking for additional evidence or miracles, accept what God has already given and move forward. He may use your life as evidence to reach another person.

Jonah was a prophet sent to the Assyrian city of Nineveh (see the book of Jonah). Because Assyria was such a cruel and warlike nation, Jonah tried to run from his assignment and ended up spending three days in the stomach of a huge fish. When Jonah got out, he grudgingly went to Nineveh, preached God's message, and saw the city repent. By contrast, when Jesus came to his people, they refused to repent.

May 3

Religious leaders ask Jesus for a miracle
Matthew 12:43-45 *(Harmony 75b)*

*W*hen an evil spirit leaves a person, it goes into the desert, seeking rest but finding none. Then it says, 'I will return to the person I came from.' So it returns and finds its former home empty, swept, and clean. Then the spirit finds seven other spirits more evil than itself, and they all enter the person and live there. And so that person is worse off than before. That will be the experience of this evil generation."

Jesus told this parable to warn the Jewish religious leaders, who were opposing him. The nation had benefited from the exorcisms and miracles of Jesus. But because they rejected the Savior, the nation would now be defenseless against evil and worse off than before—just like the man in the parable.

EMPTY IT OUT, FILL IT UP

Jesus was describing the attitude of the nation of Israel, and the religious leaders in particular. Just cleaning up one's life without filling it with God leaves plenty of room for Satan to enter. The book of Ezra records how the people rid themselves of idolatry but failed to replace it with love for God and obedience to him. Ridding our lives of sin is only the first step. We must also take the second step: filling our lives with God's Word and the Holy Spirit. Unfilled and complacent people are easy targets for Satan.

May 4

Jesus describes his true family

Mark 3:31-35 (also in Matthew 12:46-50; Luke 8:19-21) *(Harmony 76)*

*J*esus' mother and brothers arrived at the house where he was teaching. They stood outside and sent word for him to come out and talk with them. There was a crowd around Jesus, and someone said, "Your mother and your brothers and sisters are outside, asking for you."

Jesus replied, "Who is my mother? Who are my brothers?" Then he looked at those around him and said, "These are my mother and brothers. Anyone who does God's will is my brother and sister and mother."

GOD'S FAMILY

God's family is accepting and doesn't exclude anyone. Although Jesus cared for his mother and brothers, he also cared for all those who loved him. Jesus did not show partiality; he allowed everyone the privilege of obeying God and becoming part of his family. In our increasingly computerized, impersonal world, warm relationships among members of God's family take on major importance. The church can give the loving, personalized care found nowhere else.

Jesus' family did not yet fully understand his ministry. Jesus explained that in our spiritual family, the relationships are ultimately more important and longer lasting than those formed in our physical families.

May 5

Jesus tells the parable of the four soils
Mark 4:1-9 (also in Matthew 13:1-9; Luke 8:4-8) *(Harmony 77)*

*O*nce again Jesus began teaching by the lakeshore. There was such a large crowd along the shore that he got into a boat and sat down and spoke from there. He began to teach the people by telling many stories such as this one:

"Listen! A farmer went out to plant some seed. As he scattered it across his field, some seed fell on a footpath, and the birds came and ate it. Other seed fell on shallow soil with underlying rock. The plant sprang up quickly, but it soon wilted beneath the hot sun and died because the roots had no nourishment in the shallow soil. Other seed fell among thorns that shot up and choked out the tender blades so that it produced no grain. Still other seed fell on fertile soil and produced a crop that was thirty, sixty, and even a hundred times as much as had been planted." Then he said, "Anyone who is willing to hear should listen and understand!"

KEEP ON SOWING
This parable should encourage spiritual "sowers"—those who teach, preach, and lead others. The farmer sowed good seed, but not all the seed sprouted, and even the plants that grew had varying yields. Don't be discouraged if you do not always see results as you faithfully teach the Word. Belief does not follow a formula (for example, a 4:1 ratio of seeds planted to seeds sprouted). Rather, it is a miracle of God's Holy Spirit as he uses your words to lead others to him.

Jesus taught the people by telling parables, short stories using familiar scenes to explain spiritual truth. This method of teaching compels the listener to think. It conceals the truth from those who are too stubborn or prejudiced to hear what is being taught. Most parables have one main point, so we must be careful not to go beyond what Jesus intended to teach.

May 6

Jesus explains the parable of the four soils
Mark 4:10-25 (also in Matthew 13:10-23; Luke 8:9-18) *(Harmony 78)*

*L*ater, when Jesus was alone with the twelve disciples and with the others who were gathered around, they asked him, "What do your stories mean?"

He replied, "You are permitted to understand the secret about the Kingdom of God. But I am using these stories to conceal everything about it from outsiders, so that the Scriptures might be fulfilled: 'They see what I do, but they don't perceive its meaning. They hear my words, but they don't understand. So they will not turn from their sins and be forgiven.'

"But if you can't understand this story, how will you understand all the others I am going to tell? The farmer I talked about is the one who brings God's message to others. The seed that fell on the hard path represents those who hear the message, but then Satan comes at once and takes it away from them. The rocky soil represents those who hear the message and receive it with joy. But like young plants in such soil, their roots don't go very deep. At first they get along fine, but they wilt as soon as they have problems or are persecuted because they believe the word. The thorny ground represents those who hear and accept the Good News, but all too quickly the message is crowded out by the cares of this life, the lure of wealth, and the desire for nice things, so no crop is produced. But the good soil represents those who hear and accept God's message and produce a huge harvest—thirty, sixty, or even a hundred times as much as had been planted."

Then Jesus asked them, "Would anyone light a lamp and then put it under a basket or under a bed to shut out the light? Of course not! A lamp is placed on a stand, where its light will shine.

"Everything that is now hidden or secret will eventually be brought to light. Anyone who is willing to hear should listen and understand! And be sure to pay attention to what you hear. The more you do this, the more you will understand—and even more, besides. To those who are open to my teaching, more understanding will be given. But to those who are not listening, even what they have will be taken away from them."

SOILED AGAIN

The four soils represent four different ways people respond to God's message. Usually we think that Jesus was talking about four different kinds of people. But he may also have been talking about (1) different times or phases in a person's life or (2) how we willingly receive God's message in some areas of our lives and resist it in others. For example, you may be open to God about your future but closed concerning how you spend your money. You may respond like good soil to God's demand for worship but like rocky soil to his demand to give to people in need. We must strive to be like good soil in every area of our lives at all times.

We hear with our ears, but there is a deeper kind of listening with the mind and heart that is necessary in order to gain spiritual understanding from Jesus' words. Some people in the crowd were looking for evidence to use against Jesus; others truly wanted to learn and grow. Jesus' words were for the honest seekers.

May 7

Jesus tells the parable of the growing seed
Mark 4:26-29 *(Harmony 79)*

*J*esus also said, "Here is another illustration of what the Kingdom of God is like: A farmer planted seeds in a field, and then he went on with his other activities. As the days went by, the seeds sprouted and grew without the farmer's help, because the earth produces crops on its own. First a leaf blade pushes through, then the heads of wheat are formed, and finally the grain ripens. And as soon as the grain is ready, the farmer comes and harvests it with a sickle."

KINGDOM GROWTH
This parable about the Kingdom of God, recorded only by Mark, reveals that spiritual growth is a continual, gradual process that is finally consummated in a harvest of spiritual maturity. We can understand the process of

Seed was sown by hand. As the farmer walked across the field he threw handfuls of seed onto the ground from a large bag slung across his shoulders.

spiritual growth by comparing it to the slow but certain growth of a plant. God's Kingdom grows. We don't know how. We do our part, and God does his, so that in due time a harvest is ready. Are you doing your part in helping the Kingdom of God grow to maturity?

May 8

Jesus tells the parable of the weeds
Matthew 13:24-30 *(Harmony 80)*

*H*ere is another story Jesus told: "The Kingdom of Heaven is like a farmer who planted good seed in his field. But that night as everyone slept, his enemy came and planted weeds among the wheat. When the crop began to grow and produce grain, the weeds also grew. The farmer's servants came and told him, 'Sir, the field where you planted that good seed is full of weeds!'

" 'An enemy has done it!' the farmer exclaimed.

" 'Shall we pull out the weeds?' they asked.

"He replied, 'No, you'll hurt the wheat if you do. Let both grow together until the harvest. Then I will tell the harvesters to sort out the weeds and burn them and to put the wheat in the barn.' "

THE COMING HARVEST
The young weeds and the young blades of wheat look the same and can't be distinguished until they are grown and ready for harvest. Weeds (unbelievers) and wheat (believers) must live side by side in this world. God allows unbelievers to remain for a while, just as a farmer allows weeds to remain in his field so the surrounding wheat isn't uprooted

The Kingdom of Heaven is not a geographic location, but a spiritual realm where God rules and where we share in his eternal life. We join that Kingdom when we trust in Christ as Savior.

with them. At the harvest, however, the weeds will be uprooted and thrown away. God's harvest (judgment) of all people is coming. We are to make ourselves ready by making sure that our faith is sincere.

May 9

Jesus tells the parable of the mustard seed
Mark 4:30-34 (also in Matthew 13:31-32) *(Harmony 81)*

*J*esus asked, "How can I describe the Kingdom of God? What story should I use to illustrate it? It is like a tiny mustard seed. Though this is one of the smallest of seeds, it grows to become one of the largest of plants, with long branches where birds can come and find shelter."

He used many such stories and illustrations to teach the people as much as they were able to understand. In fact, in his public teaching he taught only with parables, but afterward when he was alone with his disciples, he explained the meaning to them.

WORLDWIDE FELLOWSHIP
Jesus adapted his methods to his audience's ability and desire to understand. He didn't speak in parables to confuse people but to challenge sincere seekers to discover the meaning of his words. Jesus used this parable to explain that although Christianity had very

The mustard seed was the smallest seed a farmer used. Jesus used this parable to show that the Kingdom has small beginnings but will grow and produce great results.

small beginnings, it would grow into a worldwide community of believers. When you feel alone in your stand for Christ, realize that God is building a worldwide Kingdom. He has faithful followers in every part of the world, and your faith, no matter how small, can join with that of others to accomplish great things.

May 10

Jesus tells the parable of the yeast
Matthew 13:33-35 *(Harmony 82)*

*J*esus also used this illustration: "The Kingdom of Heaven is like yeast used by a woman making bread. Even though she used a large amount of flour, the yeast permeated every part of the dough."

Jesus always used stories and illustrations like these when speaking to the crowds. In fact, he never spoke to them without using such parables. This fulfilled the prophecy that said, "I will speak to you in parables. I will explain mysteries hidden since the creation of the world."

JUST ONE SEED

In other Bible passages, yeast is used as a symbol of evil or uncleanness. Here it is a positive symbol of growth. Although yeast looks like a minor ingredient, it permeates the whole loaf. Although the Kingdom began small and was nearly invisible, it would soon grow and have a great impact on the world. You may wonder what kind of impact you as just one person can make on your world. But as the Kingdom grows from one small seed, so it grows from individual believers who serve God. Ask God what you can do to help his Kingdom grow.

All the parables in Matthew 13 teach us about God and his Kingdom. They explain what the Kingdom is really like as opposed to our expectations of it.

May 11

Jesus explains the parable of the weeds
Matthew 13:36-43 *(Harmony 83)*

*T*hen, leaving the crowds outside, Jesus went into the house. His disciples said, "Please explain the story of the weeds in the field."

"All right," he said. "I, the Son of Man, am the farmer who plants the good seed. The field is the world, and the good seed represents the people of the Kingdom. The weeds are the people who belong to the evil one. The enemy who planted the weeds among the wheat is the Devil. The harvest is the end of the world, and the harvesters are the angels.

"Just as the weeds are separated out and burned, so it will be at the end of the world. I, the Son of Man, will send my angels, and they will remove from my Kingdom everything that causes sin and all who do evil, and they will throw them into the furnace and burn them. There will be weeping and gnashing of teeth. Then the godly will shine like the sun in their Father's Kingdom. Anyone who is willing to hear should listen and understand!"

FINAL JUDGMENT

At the end of the world, angels will separate the evil from the good. There are true and false believers in churches today, but we should be cautious in our judgments because only Christ is qualified to make the final separation. If you start judging, you may damage some of the good "plants." It's more important to judge our own response to God than to analyze others' responses.

Those who receive God's favor stand in bright contrast to those who receive his judgment. The weeping indicates sorrow or remorse, and gnashing of teeth shows extreme anxiety or pain.

May 12

Jesus tells the parable of hidden treasure
Matthew 13:44 *(Harmony 84)*

*T*he Kingdom of Heaven is like a treasure that a man discovered hidden in a field. In his excitement, he hid it again and sold everything he owned to get enough money to buy the field—and to get the treasure, too!"

TOTAL RULE

The Kingdom of Heaven is more valuable than anything else we can have, and a person must be willing to give up everything to obtain it. The man who discovered the treasure in the field stumbled upon it by accident but knew its value when he found it. When we decide to become part of God's Kingdom, we are accepted by God. Yet to truly experience citizenship in that Kingdom, we may need to give up some actions or attitudes. Have you set aside "the world" in order to have God's Kingdom? Do you live so that people know your true citizenship?

Believers live in this world, but they're not "of" it; their home is really in heaven. We often feel like strangers in a world that would prefer to ignore God. But we have citizenship in the Kingdom of Heaven.

May 13

Jesus tells the parable of the pearl merchant
Matthew 13:45-46 *(Harmony 85)*

*A*gain, the Kingdom of Heaven is like a pearl merchant on the lookout for choice pearls. When he discovered a pearl of great value, he sold everything he owned and bought it!"

THE KINGDOM'S VALUE

The merchant was earnestly searching for the pearl of great value, and when he found it he sold everything he had to purchase it. Why is the Kingdom so valuable? Someday, after God judges and destroys all sin, the Kingdom of Heaven will rule every corner of this earth.

Heaven is where God dwells, and it operates according to God's principles and values. It is eternal and unshakable. Our hope is in the certainty of heaven.

We will be with Christ in a way not possible in this life. John saw this day in a vision, and he cried out, "Look, the home of God is now among his people! He will live with them, and they will be his people. God himself will be with them" (Revelation 21:3). Our true loyalty is not to the things of this earth, which will be destroyed. It is to God's truth, his way of life, his perfect creation. Can you willingly put aside everything else in order to have God and his Kingdom?

May 14

Jesus tells the parable of the fishing net
Matthew 13:47-52 *(Harmony 86)*

*A*gain, the Kingdom of Heaven is like a fishing net that is thrown into the water and gathers fish of every kind. When the net is full, they drag it up onto the shore, sit down, sort the good fish into crates, and throw the bad ones away. That is the way it will be at the end of the world. The angels will come and separate the wicked people from the godly, throwing the wicked into the fire. There will be weeping and gnashing of teeth. Do you understand?"

"Yes," they said, "we do."

Then he added, "Every teacher of religious law who has become a disciple in the Kingdom of Heaven is like a person who brings out of the storehouse the new teachings as well as the old."

FINAL SORTING

The parable of the fishing net has the same meaning as the parable of the wheat and weeds. We are to obey God and tell others about his grace and goodness, but we cannot dictate who is part of the Kingdom of Heaven and who is not. This sorting will be done at the last judgment by those infinitely more qualified than we. On the day of judgment we will appear before Christ and be held accountable for our lives. With God living in us through Christ, we have no reason to fear this day because we have been saved from punishment. Instead, we can look forward to the judgment because it will mean the end of sin and the beginning of a face-to-face relationship with Jesus Christ. Be careful of judging another's relationship with God. Only God is the true and reliable Judge.

Revelation 14:14-17 describes Christ separating the faithful from the unfaithful like a farmer harvesting his crops. This will be a time of joy for Christians.

May 15

Jesus calms the storm
Mark 4:35-41 (also in Matthew 8:23-27; Luke 8:22-25) *(Harmony 87)*

*A*s evening came, Jesus said to his disciples, "Let's cross to the other side of the lake." He was already in the boat, so they started out, leaving the crowds behind (although other boats followed). But soon a fierce storm arose. High waves began to break into the boat until it was nearly full of water.

Jesus was sleeping at the back of the boat with his head on a cushion. Frantically they woke him up, shouting, "Teacher, don't you even care that we are going to drown?"

When he woke up, he rebuked the wind and said to the water, "Quiet down!" Suddenly the wind stopped, and there was a great calm. And he asked them, "Why are you so afraid? Do you still not have faith in me?"

And they were filled with awe and said among themselves, "Who is this man, that even the wind and waves obey him?"

CALMING THE STORMS

Although the disciples had witnessed many miracles, they panicked in this storm. As experienced sailors, they knew its danger; what they did not know was that Christ could control the forces of nature. There is often a

The Sea of Galilee is an unusual body of water. It is relatively small (thirteen miles long, seven miles wide), but it is 150 feet deep, and the shoreline is 680 feet below sea level. Sudden storms can appear over the surrounding mountains with little warning, stirring the water into violent twenty-foot waves.

stormy area of our human nature where we feel God can't or won't work. When we truly understand who God is, however, we will realize that he controls both the storms of nature and the storms of the troubled heart. Jesus' power that calmed this storm can also help us deal with the problems we face. Jesus is willing to help if we only ask him. We should never discount his power, even in terrible trials.

May 16

Jesus sends the demons into a herd of pigs
Mark 5:1-10 (also in Matthew 8:28-29; Luke 8:26-31) *(Harmony 88a)*

*S*o they arrived at the other side of the lake, in the land of the Gerasenes. Just as Jesus was climbing from the boat, a man possessed by an evil spirit ran out from a cemetery to meet him. This man lived among the tombs and could not be restrained, even with a chain. Whenever he was put into chains and shackles—as he often was—he snapped the chains from his wrists and smashed the shackles. No one was strong enough to control him. All day long and throughout the night, he would wander among the tombs and in the hills, screaming and hitting himself with stones.

When Jesus was still some distance away, the man saw him. He ran to meet Jesus and fell down before him. He gave a terrible scream, shrieking, "Why are you bothering me, Jesus, Son of the Most High God? For God's sake, don't torture me!" For Jesus had already said to the spirit, "Come out of the man, you evil spirit."

Then Jesus asked, "What is your name?"

And the spirit replied, "Legion, because there are many of us here inside this man." Then the spirits begged him again and again not to send them to some distant place.

CHRIST'S AUTHORITY

These demons recognized Jesus and his authority immediately. They knew who Jesus was and what his great power could do to them. Demons, Satan's messengers, are powerful and destructive. Still active today, they attempt to distort and destroy people's relationship with God. Demons and demon-possession are real. It is vital that believers recognize the power of Satan and his demons, but we shouldn't let curiosity lead

The demons begged Jesus not to send them to "some distant land" (to spare them from the abyss, which is also mentioned in Revelation 9:1 and 20:1-3 as the place of confinement for Satan and his messengers). The demons, of course, knew all about this place of confinement, and they didn't want to go there.

us to get involved with demonic forces (Deuteronomy 18:10-12). Demons have no authority over those who trust in Jesus. If we resist the Devil, he will leave us alone (James 4:7).

May 17

Jesus sends the demons into a herd of pigs
Mark 5:11-20 (also in Matthew 8:30-34; Luke 8:32-39)
(Harmony 88b)

*T*here happened to be a large herd of pigs feeding on the hillside nearby. "Send us into those pigs," the evil spirits begged. Jesus gave them permission. So the evil spirits came out of the man and entered the pigs, and the entire herd of two thousand pigs plunged down the steep hillside into the lake, where they drowned.

The herdsmen fled to the nearby city and the surrounding countryside, spreading the news as they ran. Everyone rushed out to see for themselves. A crowd soon gathered around Jesus, but they were frightened when they saw the man who had been demon possessed, for he was sitting there fully clothed and perfectly sane. Those who had seen what happened to the man and to the pigs told everyone about it, and the crowd began pleading with Jesus to go away and leave them alone.

When Jesus got back into the boat, the man who had been demon possessed begged to go, too. But Jesus said, "No, go home to your friends, and tell them what wonderful things the Lord has done for you and how merciful he has been." So the man started off to visit the Ten Towns of that region and began to tell everyone about the great things Jesus had done for him; and everyone was amazed at what he told them.

WHAT'S MORE IMPORTANT?
The demons destroyed the hogs, which hurt the finances of those tending the hogs, but can hogs and money compare with a human life? A man had been freed from the Devil's power, but the people thought only about their livestock. People have always tended to value financial gain above needy people. Throughout history, most wars have been fought to protect economic interests. Much injustice and oppression, both at home and abroad, is the direct result of some individual's or company's urge to get rich. People are continually being sacrificed to the god of money. Don't think more highly of "swine" than of people. Think carefully about how your decisions will affect other

Why didn't Jesus send these demons to the abyss? His time for that has not yet come. But it will come. The book of Revelation portrays the future victory of Jesus over Satan, his demons, and all evil.

human beings, and be willing to choose a simpler lifestyle if it will keep other people from being harmed.

May 18

Jesus heals a bleeding woman and restores a girl to life
Mark 5:21-34 (also in Matthew 9:18-22; Luke 8:40-48)
(Harmony 89a)

*W*hen Jesus went back across to the other side of the lake, a large crowd gathered around him on the shore. A leader of the local synagogue, whose name was Jairus, came and fell down before him, pleading with him to heal his little daughter. "She is about to die," he said in desperation. "Please come and place your hands on her; heal her so she can live."

Jesus went with him, and the crowd thronged behind. And there was a woman in the crowd who had had a hemorrhage for twelve years. She had suffered a great deal from many doctors through the years and had spent everything she had to pay them, but she had gotten no better. In fact, she was worse. She had heard about Jesus, so she came up behind him through the crowd and touched the fringe of his robe. For she thought to herself, "If I can just touch his clothing, I will be healed." Immediately the bleeding stopped, and she could feel that she had been healed!

Jesus realized at once that healing power had gone out from him, so he turned around in the crowd and asked, "Who touched my clothes?"

His disciples said to him, "All this crowd is pressing around you. How can you ask, 'Who touched me?'"

But he kept on looking around to see who had done it. Then the frightened woman, trembling at the realization of what had happened to her, came and fell at his feet and told him what she had done. And he said to her, "Daughter, your faith has made you well. Go in peace. You have been healed."

AVAILABLE POWER
Many people surrounded Jesus as he made his way toward Jairus's house. It was virtually impossible to get through the multitude, but one woman fought her way desperately through the crowd in order to touch Jesus. As soon as she did so, she was healed. What a difference there is between the crowds that are curious about Jesus and the few who

It isn't that Jesus didn't know who had touched him; it's that he wanted the woman to step forward and identify herself. Jesus wanted to teach her that his cloak did not contain magical properties—her faith in him had healed her.

reach out and touch him! Today, many people are vaguely familiar with Jesus, but nothing in their lives is changed or improved by this passing acquaintance. It is only faith that releases God's healing power. Are you just curious about God, or do you reach out to him in faith, knowing that his mercy will bring healing to your body, soul, and spirit?

May 19

Jesus heals a bleeding woman and restores a girl to life
Mark 5:35-43 (also in Matthew 9:23-26; Luke 8:49-56) *(Harmony 89b)*

*W*hile he was still speaking to her, messengers arrived from Jairus's home with the message, "Your daughter is dead. There's no use troubling the Teacher now."

But Jesus ignored their comments and said to Jairus, "Don't be afraid. Just trust me." Then Jesus stopped the crowd and wouldn't let anyone go with him except Peter and James and John. When they came to the home of the synagogue leader, Jesus saw the commotion and the weeping and wailing. He went inside and spoke to the people. "Why all this weeping and commotion?" he asked. "The child isn't dead; she is only asleep."

The crowd laughed at him, but he told them all to go outside. Then he took the girl's father and mother and his three disciples into the room where the girl was lying. Holding her hand, he said to her, "Get up, little girl!" And the girl, who was twelve years old, immediately stood up and walked around! Her parents were absolutely overwhelmed. Jesus commanded them not to tell anyone what had happened, and he told them to give her something to eat.

POWER OVER DEATH
The leader of the synagogue didn't come to Jesus until his daughter was near death—it was too late for anyone else to help. But Jesus simply went to the girl and raised her! In our life Christ can make a difference when it is too late for anyone else to help. He can bring healing to broken relationships, release from bad habits, and forgiveness and healing to emotional scars. If your situation looks hopeless, remember that Christ can do the impossible.

Jesus told the girl's parents not to spread the news of the miracle. He wanted the facts to speak for themselves, and the time was not yet right for a major confrontation with the religious leaders. Jesus still had much to accomplish, and he didn't want people following him just to see his miracles.

May 20

Jesus heals the blind and mute
Matthew 9:27-34 *(Harmony 90)*

*A*fter Jesus left the girl's home, two blind men followed along behind him, shouting, "Son of David, have mercy on us!"

They went right into the house where he was staying, and Jesus asked them, "Do you believe I can make you see?"

"Yes, Lord," they told him, "we do."

Then he touched their eyes and said, "Because of your faith, it will happen." And suddenly they could see! Jesus sternly warned them, "Don't tell anyone about this." But instead, they spread his fame all over the region.

When they left, some people brought to him a man who couldn't speak because he was possessed by a demon. So Jesus cast out the demon, and instantly the man could talk. The crowds marveled. "Nothing like this has ever happened in Israel!" they exclaimed.

But the Pharisees said, "He can cast out demons because he is empowered by the prince of demons."

HEALING POWER

These blind men were persistent. They went right into the house where Jesus was staying. They knew Jesus could heal them. "Son of David" was a popular way of addressing Jesus as the Messiah because it was known that the Messiah would be a descendant of David (Isaiah 9:7). This is the first time the title is used in Matthew. Jesus' ability to give sight to the blind was prophesied in Isaiah 29:18; 35:5; 42:7. These men let nothing stop them from finding the Messiah. That's real faith in action. If you believe Jesus is the answer to your every need, don't let anything or anyone stop you from reaching him.

While the Pharisees questioned, debated, and dissected Jesus, people were being healed and lives changed right in front of them. Their skepticism was based not on insufficient evidence but on jealousy of Jesus' popularity.

May 21

The people of Nazareth refuse to believe
Mark 6:1-6 (also in Matthew 13:53-58) *(Harmony 91)*

*J*esus left that part of the country and returned with his disciples to Nazareth, his hometown. The next Sabbath he began teaching in the synagogue, and many who heard him were astonished. They asked,

"Where did he get all his wisdom and the power to perform such miracles? He's just the carpenter, the son of Mary and brother of James, Joseph, Judas, and Simon. And his sisters live right here among us." They were deeply offended and refused to believe in him.

Then Jesus told them, "A prophet is honored everywhere except in his own hometown and among his relatives and his own family." And because of their unbelief, he couldn't do any mighty miracles among them except to place his hands on a few sick people and heal them. And he was amazed at their unbelief.

Then Jesus went out from village to village, teaching.

SEEING THE REAL JESUS

Jesus was teaching effectively and wisely, but the people of his hometown saw him as just a carpenter. They were offended that others could be impressed by Jesus and follow him. They rejected his authority because he was one of their peers. They thought they knew him, but their preconceived notions about who he was made it impossible for them to accept his message. Don't let prejudice blind you to truth. As you learn more about Jesus, try to see him for who he really is.

Jesus could have done greater miracles in Nazareth, but he chose not to because of the people's pride and unbelief. The miracles he did had little effect on the people because they did not accept his message or believe that he was from God.

May 22

Jesus urges the disciples to pray for workers
Matthew 9:35-38 *(Harmony 92)*

*J*esus traveled through all the cities and villages of that area, teaching in the synagogues and announcing the Good News about the Kingdom. And wherever he went, he healed people of every sort of disease and illness. He felt great pity for the crowds that came, because their problems were so great and they didn't know where to go for help. They were like sheep without a shepherd. He said to his disciples, "The harvest is so great, but the workers are so few. So pray to the Lord who is in charge of the harvest; ask him to send out more workers for his fields."

HELP WANTED

Jesus looked at the crowds following him and referred to them as fields ripe for harvest. Many people are ready to give their lives to Christ if someone would show them how. Jesus commands us to pray that people will

The gospel of the Kingdom was that the promised and long-awaited Messiah had finally come. His healing miracles were a sign that his teaching was true.

respond to this need for workers. Often when we pray for something, God answers our prayers by using *us*. Be prepared for God to use you to show another person the way to him. Jesus needs workers who know how to deal with people's problems. We can comfort others and show them the way to live because we have been helped with our problems by God and his laborers.

May 23

Jesus sends out the twelve disciples
Matthew 10:1-15 (also in Mark 6:7-13; Luke 9:1-6) *(Harmony 93)*

*J*esus called his twelve disciples to him and gave them authority to cast out evil spirits and to heal every kind of disease and illness. Here are the names of the twelve apostles: first Simon (also called Peter), then Andrew (Peter's brother), James (son of Zebedee), John (James's brother), Philip, Bartholomew, Thomas, Matthew (the tax collector), James (son of Alphaeus), Thaddaeus, Simon (the Zealot), Judas Iscariot (who later betrayed him).

Jesus sent the twelve disciples out with these instructions: "Don't go to the Gentiles or the Samaritans, but only to the people of Israel—God's lost sheep. Go and announce to them that the Kingdom of Heaven is near. Heal the sick, raise the dead, cure those with leprosy, and cast out demons. Give as freely as you have received!

"Don't take any money with you. Don't carry a traveler's bag with an extra coat and sandals or even a walking stick. Don't hesitate to accept hospitality, because those who work deserve to be fed. Whenever you enter a city or village, search for a worthy man and stay in his home until you leave for the next town. When you are invited into someone's home, give it your blessing. If it turns out to be a worthy home, let your blessing stand; if it is not, take back the blessing. If a village doesn't welcome you or listen to you, shake off the dust of that place from your feet as you leave. I assure you, the wicked cities of Sodom and Gomorrah will be better off on the judgment day than that place will be."

USED BY GOD

The list of Jesus' twelve disciples doesn't give us many details—probably because there weren't many impressive details to tell. Jesus called people from all walks of life—fishermen, political activists, tax collectors. He called common people and uncommon leaders, rich and poor, educated and uneducated. Today many people think only certain people are fit to follow Christ, but this was not the attitude of the Master himself. Jesus called his twelve disciples. He didn't draft them, force them, or ask them to volunteer; he chose them to serve him in a special way.

Jesus asked his disciples to go only to the Jews because he came first to the Jews (Romans 1:16). God chose them to tell the rest of the world about him. Jewish disciples and apostles preached the gospel of the risen Christ all around the Roman Empire, and soon Gentiles were pouring into the church. The Bible clearly teaches that God's message of salvation is for all people.

Christ calls us today. He doesn't twist our arms and make us do something we don't want to do. We can choose to join him or go our own way. God can use anyone, no matter how insignificant he or she appears. God uses ordinary people to do his extraordinary work. Be one who is used by God.

May 24

Jesus prepares the disciples for persecution
Matthew 10:16-23 *(Harmony 94a)*

*L*ook, I am sending you out as sheep among wolves. Be as wary as snakes and harmless as doves. But beware! For you will be handed over to the courts and beaten in the synagogues. And you must stand trial before governors and kings because you are my followers. This will be your opportunity to tell them about me—yes, to witness to the world. When you are arrested, don't worry about what to say in your defense, because you will be given the right words at the right time. For it won't be you doing the talking—it will be the Spirit of your Father speaking through you.

"Brother will betray brother to death, fathers will betray their own children, and children will rise against their parents and cause them to be killed. And everyone will hate you because of your allegiance to me. But those who endure to the end will be saved. When you are persecuted in one town, flee to the next. I assure you that I, the Son of Man, will return before you have reached all the towns of Israel."

Jesus told the disciples that when arrested for preaching the gospel, they should not worry about what to say in their defense—God's Spirit would speak through them. This promise was fulfilled in Acts 4:8-14 and elsewhere. Some mistakenly think this means that we don't have to prepare to present the gospel because God will take care of everything. Scripture makes it clear however, that we *are* to be prepared (2 Timothy 4:2; 1 Peter 3:15). Jesus is teaching us not to be unprepared but to be unworried about what we will say.

Enduring to the end is not a way to be saved but rather the evidence that a person is really committed to Jesus. Persistence is not a means to earn salvation; it is the by-product of a truly devoted life.

May 25

Jesus prepares the disciples for persecution
Matthew 10:24-33 *(Harmony 94b)*

A student is not greater than the teacher. A servant is not greater than the master. The student shares the teacher's fate. The servant shares the master's fate. And since I, the master of the household, have been called the prince of demons, how much more will it happen to you, the members of the household! But don't be afraid of those who threaten you. For the time is coming when everything will be revealed; all that is secret will be made public. What I tell you now in the darkness, shout abroad when daybreak comes. What I whisper in your ears, shout from the housetops for all to hear!

"Don't be afraid of those who want to kill you. They can only kill your body; they cannot touch your soul. Fear only God, who can destroy both soul and body in hell. Not even a sparrow, worth only half a penny, can fall to the ground without your Father knowing it. And the very hairs on your head are all numbered. So don't be afraid; you are more valuable to him than a whole flock of sparrows.

"If anyone acknowledges me publicly here on earth, I will openly acknowledge that person before my Father in heaven. But if anyone denies me here on earth, I will deny that person before my Father in heaven.

COVERED BY GOD
Jesus said that God is aware of everything that happens, even to sparrows, and you are far more valuable to him than they are. You are so valuable that God sent his only Son to die for you (John 3:16). Because God places such value on you, you need never fear personal threats or difficult trials. These can't shake God's

love or dislodge his Spirit from within you.

But this doesn't mean that God will take away all your troubles (see 10:16). The real test of value is how well something holds up under the wear, tear, and abuse of everyday life. Those who stand up for Christ in spite of their troubles truly have lasting value and will receive great rewards (see 5:11-12). Despite your struggles and trials, remember that you are valuable to God and that he is making you more like Christ (Romans 8:29).

The Pharisees did, in fact, call Jesus "Satan" (see Matthew 9:34). Good is sometimes labeled evil. If Jesus, who is perfect, was called evil, his followers should expect that similar accusations will be directed at them. But those who endure will be vindicated (10:22).

May 26

Jesus prepares the disciples for persecution
Matthew 10:34-39 *(Harmony 94c)*

*D*on't imagine that I came to bring peace to the earth! No, I came to bring a sword. I have come to set a man against his father, and a daughter against her mother, and a daughter-in-law against her mother-in-law. Your enemies will be right in your own household! If you love your father or mother more than you love me, you are not worthy of being mine; or if you love your son or daughter more than me, you are not worthy of being mine. If you refuse to take up your cross and follow me, you are not worthy of being mine. If you cling to your life, you will lose it; but if you give it up for me, you will find it."

FREE TO FOLLOW
Matthew 10:39 is a positive and negative statement of the same truth: Clinging to this life may cause us to forfeit the best from Christ in this world *and* in the next. The more we love this life's rewards (leisure, power, popularity, financial security), the more we will discover how empty they really are. The

To take our cross and follow Jesus means to be willing to publicly identify with him, to experience almost certain opposition, and to be committed to face even suffering and death for his sake.

best way to enjoy life, therefore, is to loosen our greedy grasp on earthly rewards so that we can be free to follow Christ. In doing so, we will inherit eternal life and begin at once to experience the benefits of following Christ. To what are you holding tightly for security and meaning in life? Let go!

May 27

Jesus prepares the disciples for persecution
Matthew 10:40-42 *(Harmony 94d)*

*A*nyone who welcomes you is welcoming me, and anyone who welcomes me is welcoming the Father who sent me. If you welcome a prophet as one who speaks for God, you will receive the same reward a prophet gets. And if you welcome good and godly people because of their godliness, you will be given a reward like theirs. And if you give even a cup of cold water to one of the least of my followers, you will surely be rewarded."

LOVE'S MEASUREMENT
How much we love God can be measured by how well we treat others. Jesus' example of giving a cup of cold water to one of his servants is a good model of unselfish service. People in full-time ministry often can't return the favor. God notices every good deed we do or don't do as if he were the one receiving it. Is there something unselfish you can do for someone else today? Although no one else may see you, God will notice.

Jesus gave the disciples a principle to guide their actions as they ministered to others: "Give as freely as you have received!" (10:8). Because God has showered us with his blessings, we should give generously to others of our time, love, and possessions.

May 28

Herod kills John the Baptist
Mark 6:14-16 (also in Matthew 14:1-2; Luke 9:7-9) *(Harmony 95a)*

*H*erod Antipas, the king, soon heard about Jesus, because people everywhere were talking about him. Some were saying, "This must be John the Baptist come back to life again. That is why he can do such miracles." Others thought Jesus was the ancient prophet Elijah. Still others thought he was a prophet like the other great prophets of the past. When Herod heard about Jesus, he said, "John, the man I beheaded, has come back from the dead."

CHRIST'S TRUE IDENTITY
It was so difficult for the people to accept Jesus as the Son of God that they tried to come up with other solutions—most of which sound quite unbelievable to us. Many thought that he must be someone who had come back to life, perhaps

John the Baptist or another prophet. Some suggested that he was Elijah, the great prophet who did not die but was taken to heaven in a chariot of fire (2 Kings 2:1-11). Very few found the correct answer, as Peter did (Luke 9:20).

Many people still find it difficult to accept Jesus as the fully human yet fully divine Son of God. People are still trying to find alternate explanations—a great prophet, a radical political leader, a self-deceived rabble-rouser. None of these explanations can account for Jesus' miracles or, especially, his glorious resurrection—so these realities, too, have to be explained away. In the end, the attempts to explain away Jesus are far more difficult to believe than the truth. People still have to make up their minds about Jesus. Some think that if they can name what he is—prophet, teacher, good man—they can weaken the power of his claim on their lives. But what they *think* does not change who Jesus *is*. Jesus is the God-man; he is God. Does he rule in your life?

Herod was a tetrarch—one of four rulers over the four districts of Palestine. His territory included the regions of Galilee and Perea. He was the son of Herod the Great, who ordered the killing of the babies in Bethlehem (Matthew 2:16). Also known as Herod Antipas, he heard Jesus' case before Jesus' crucifixion (Luke 23:6-12).

May 29

Herod kills John the Baptist
Mark 6:17-29 (also in Matthew 14:3-12) *(Harmony 95b)*

*F*or Herod had sent soldiers to arrest and imprison John as a favor to Herodias. She had been his brother Philip's wife, but Herod had married her. John kept telling Herod, "It is illegal for you to marry your brother's wife." Herodias was enraged and wanted John killed in revenge, but without Herod's approval she was powerless. And Herod respected John, knowing that he was a good and holy man, so he kept him under his protection. Herod was disturbed whenever he talked with John, but even so, he liked to listen to him.

Herodias's chance finally came. It was Herod's birthday, and he gave a party for his palace aides, army officers, and the leading citizens of Galilee. Then his daughter, also named Herodias, came in and performed a dance that greatly pleased them all. "Ask me for anything you like," the king said to the girl, "and I will give it to you." Then he promised, "I will give you whatever you ask, up to half of my kingdom!"

She went out and asked her mother, "What should I ask for?"

Her mother told her, "Ask for John the Baptist's head!"

So the girl hurried back to the king and told him, "I want the head of John the Baptist, right now, on a tray!"

Then the king was very sorry, but he was embarrassed to break his oath in front of his guests. So he sent an executioner to the prison to cut off John's head and bring it to him. The soldier beheaded John in the prison, brought his head on a tray, and gave it to the girl, who took it to her mother. When John's disciples heard what had happened, they came for his body and buried it in a tomb.

DETERMINE TO DO RIGHT

As a ruler under Roman authority, Herod had no kingdom to give. The offer of half his kingdom was Herod's way to say that he would give Herodias's daughter almost anything she wanted. When Herodias asked for John's head, Herod would have been greatly embarrassed in front of his guests if he had denied her request. Words are powerful. Because they can lead to great sin, we should use them with great care. How easy it is to give in to the crowd and to let ourselves be pressured into doing wrong. Don't get in a situation where it will be too embarrassing to do what is right. Determine to do what is right, no matter how embarrassing or painful it may be.

Philip, Herod's half brother, was another of Palestine's four rulers. His territories were Iturea and Trachonitis, northeast of the Sea of Galilee (Luke 3:1). Philip's wife, Herodias, left Philip to live with Herod Antipas. John the Baptist condemned Herod and Herodias for living immorally.

May 30

Jesus feeds five thousand

Mark 6:30-34 (also in Matthew 14:13-14; Luke 9:10-11; John 6:1-4) *(Harmony 96a)*

*T*he apostles returned to Jesus from their ministry tour and told him all they had done and what they had taught. Then Jesus said, "Let's get away from the crowds for a while and rest." There were so many people coming and going that Jesus and his apostles didn't even have time to eat. They left by boat for a quieter spot. But many people saw them leaving, and people from many towns ran ahead along the shore and met them as they landed. A vast crowd was there as he stepped from the boat, and he had compassion on them because they were like sheep without a shepherd. So he taught them many things.

JESUS LOVED PEOPLE

Jesus had tried to slip quietly away from the crowds, but they found out where he was going and followed him. Instead of showing impatience at this interruption, Jesus welcomed the people and ministered to their needs. This crowd was as pitiful as a flock of sheep without a shepherd. Sheep are easily scattered; without a shepherd they are in grave danger. Jesus was the shepherd who could teach them what they needed to know and keep them from straying from God. How do you see people who interrupt your schedule—as nuisances, or as the reason for your life and ministry?

When the disciples had returned from their mission, Jesus took them away to rest. Doing God's work is very important, but Jesus recognized that to do it effectively we need periodic rest and renewal.

May 31

Jesus feeds five thousand

Mark 6:35-44 (also in Matthew 14:15-21; Luke 9:12-17; John 6:5-13) *(Harmony 96b)*

*L*ate in the afternoon his disciples came to him and said, "This is a desolate place, and it is getting late. Send the crowds away so they can go to the nearby farms and villages and buy themselves some food."

But Jesus said, "You feed them."

"With what?" they asked. "It would take a small fortune to buy food for all this crowd!"

"How much food do you have?" he asked. "Go and find out."

They came back and reported, "We have five loaves of bread and two fish." Then Jesus told the crowd to sit down in groups on the green grass. So they sat in groups of fifty or a hundred.

Jesus took the five loaves and two fish, looked up toward heaven, and asked God's blessing on the food. Breaking the loaves into pieces, he kept giving the bread and fish to the disciples to give to the people. They all ate as much as they wanted, and they picked up twelve baskets of leftover bread and fish. Five thousand men had eaten from those five loaves!

The text states that there were five thousand men present, besides women and children. Therefore the total number of people Jesus fed could have been ten to fifteen thousand. The number of men is listed separately because in the Jewish culture of the day, men and women usually ate separately when in public. The children ate with the women.

GIVE WHAT YOU HAVE

Jesus multiplied five loaves and two fish to feed more than five thousand people. What he was originally given seemed insufficient, but in his hands it became more than enough. We often feel that our contribution to Jesus is meager, but he can use and multiply whatever we give him, whether it is talent, time, or treasure. It is when we give them to Jesus that our resources are multiplied. God gives in abundance. He takes whatever we can offer him in time, ability, or resources and multiplies its effectiveness beyond our wildest expectations. If you take the first step in making yourself available to God, he will show you how greatly you can be used to advance the work of his Kingdom.

June 1

Jesus walks on water
Matthew 14:22-24 (also in Mark 6:45-46; John 6:16-18)
(Harmony 97a)

*I*mmediately after this, Jesus made his disciples get back into the boat and cross to the other side of the lake while he sent the people home. Afterward he went up into the hills by himself to pray. Night fell while he was there alone. Meanwhile, the disciples were in trouble far away from land, for a strong wind had risen, and they were fighting heavy waves.

TIME ALONE
Seeking solitude was an important priority for Jesus (see also 14:13). He made room in his busy schedule to be alone with the Father. Spending time with God in prayer nurtures a vital relationship and equips us to meet life's challenges and struggles. Finding time to pray is not easy, but prayer is the vital link between us and God. Like Jesus, we must break away from others to talk with God, even if we have to get up very early in the morning to do it! Develop the discipline of spending time alone with God—it will help you grow spiritually and become more and more like Christ.

The miraculous feeding of the five thousand occurred on the shores of the Sea of Galilee. Jesus sent his disciples across the lake while he went up into the rolling hills to spend time in prayer.

June 2

Jesus walks on water
Matthew 14:25-33 (also in Mark 6:47-52; John 6:19-21)
(Harmony 97b)

*A*bout three o'clock in the morning Jesus came to them, walking on the water. When the disciples saw him, they screamed in terror, thinking he was a ghost. But Jesus spoke to them at once. "It's all right," he said. "I am here! Don't be afraid."

Then Peter called to him, "Lord, if it's really you, tell me to come to you by walking on water."

"All right, come," Jesus said.

So Peter went over the side of the boat and walked on the water toward Jesus. But when he looked around at the high waves, he was terrified and began to sink. "Save me, Lord!" he shouted.

Instantly Jesus reached out his hand and grabbed him. "You don't have much faith," Jesus said. "Why did you doubt me?" And when they climbed back into the boat, the wind stopped.

Then the disciples worshiped him. "You really are the Son of God!" they exclaimed.

TRANSFER THE TRUTH

The disciples didn't want to believe, perhaps because (1) they couldn't accept the fact that this human named Jesus was really the Son of God; (2) they dared not believe that the Messiah would choose them as his followers—it was too good to be true; (3) they still did not understand the real purpose for Jesus' coming to earth. Their disbelief took the form of misunderstanding.

The disciples were afraid, but Jesus' presence calmed their fears. We all experience fear. Do we try to deal with it ourselves, or do we let Jesus deal with it? In times of fear and uncertainty, it is calming to know that Christ is always with us.

Even after watching Jesus miraculously feed five thousand people, they still could not take the final step of faith and believe that he was God's Son. If they had, they would not have been amazed that Jesus could walk on water. The disciples did not transfer the truth they already knew about Jesus to their own lives. We read that Jesus walked on the water, and yet we often marvel that he is able to work in our lives. We must not only believe that these miracles really occurred; we must also transfer the truth to our own life situations.

June 3

Jesus heals all who touch him
Mark 6:53-56 (also in Matthew 14:34-36) *(Harmony 98)*

*W*hen they arrived at Gennesaret on the other side of the lake, they anchored the boat and climbed out. The people standing there recognized him at once, and they ran throughout the whole area and began carrying sick people to him on mats. Wherever he went—in villages and cities and out on the farms—they laid the sick in the market plazas and streets. The sick begged him to let them at least touch the fringe of his robe, and all who touched it were healed.

Gennesaret was a small fertile plain located on the west side of the Sea of Galilee. Capernaum, Jesus' home, sat at the northern edge of this plain.

THE GREAT HEALER

The people recognized Jesus as a great healer, but how many understood who he truly was? They came to Jesus for physical healing, but did they come for spiritual healing? They came to prolong their lives on earth, but did they come to secure their eternal lives? People may seek Jesus to learn valuable lessons from his life or in hopes of finding relief from pain. But we miss Jesus' whole message if we seek him only to heal our bodies but not our souls—if we look to him for help only in this life and not consider his eternal plan for us. Only when we understand the real Jesus Christ can we appreciate how he can truly change our lives.

June 4

Jesus is the true Bread from heaven

John 6:22-29 *(Harmony 99a)*

*T*he next morning, back across the lake, crowds began gathering on the shore, waiting to see Jesus. For they knew that he and his disciples had come over together and that the disciples had gone off in their boat, leaving him behind. Several boats from Tiberias landed near the place where the Lord had blessed the bread and the people had eaten. When the crowd saw that Jesus wasn't there, nor his disciples, they got into the boats and went across to Capernaum to look for him. When they arrived and found him, they asked, "Teacher, how did you get here?"

Jesus replied, "The truth is, you want to be with me because I fed you, not because you saw the miraculous sign. But you shouldn't be so concerned about perishable things like food. Spend your energy seeking the eternal life that I, the Son of Man, can give you. For God the Father has sent me for that very purpose."

They replied, "What does God want us to do?"

Jesus told them, "This is what God wants you to do: Believe in the one he has sent."

WE MUST BELIEVE

Many sincere seekers for God are puzzled about what he wants them to do. The world's religions are humankind's attempts to answer this question. But Jesus' reply is brief and simple: We must believe on him whom God has sent. Satisfying God does not come from the work we *do* but from whom we *believe*. The first step is accepting that Jesus is

Jesus criticized the people who only followed him for the physical and temporal benefits and not for the satisfying of their spiritual hunger. Many people use religion to gain prestige, comfort, or even political votes. But those are self-centered motives.

who he claims to be. All spiritual development is built on this affirmation. Declare to Jesus that he is "the Messiah, the Son of the living God" (Matthew 16:16), and embark on a life of belief that is satisfying to your Creator.

June 5

Jesus is the true Bread from heaven
John 6:30-40 *(Harmony 99b)*

*T*hey replied, "You must show us a miraculous sign if you want us to believe in you. What will you do for us? After all, our ancestors ate manna while they journeyed through the wilderness! As the Scriptures say, 'Moses gave them bread from heaven to eat.' "

Jesus said, "I assure you, Moses didn't give them bread from heaven. My Father did. And now he offers you the true bread from heaven. The true bread of God is the one who comes down from heaven and gives life to the world."

"Sir," they said, "give us that bread every day of our lives."

Jesus replied, "I am the bread of life. No one who comes to me will ever be hungry again. Those who believe in me will never thirst. But you haven't believed in me even though you have seen me. However, those the Father has given me will come to me, and I will never reject them. For I have come down from heaven to do the will of God who sent me, not to do what I want. And this is the will of God, that I should not lose even one of all those he has given me, but that I should raise them to eternal life at the last day. For it is my Father's will that all who see his Son and believe in him should have eternal life—that I should raise them at the last day."

SPIRITUAL HUNGER
People eat bread to satisfy physical hunger and to sustain physical life. We can satisfy spiritual hunger and sustain spiritual life only by a right relationship with Jesus Christ. No wonder he called himself the Bread of Life. But bread must be eaten to sustain life, and Christ must be invited into our daily walk to sustain spiritual life.

Jesus did not work independently of God the Father but in union with him. His purpose was to do the will of God, not to satisfy human desires.

The Jews disagree that Jesus is from heaven
John 6:41-51 *(Harmony 100a)*

*T*hen the people began to murmur in disagreement because he had said, "I am the bread from heaven." They said, "This is Jesus, the son of Joseph. We know his father and mother. How can he say, 'I came down from heaven'?"

But Jesus replied, "Don't complain about what I said. For people can't come to me unless the Father who sent me draws them to me, and at the last day I will raise them from the dead. As it is written in the Scriptures, 'They will all be taught by God.' Everyone who hears and learns from the Father comes to me. (Not that anyone has ever seen the Father; only I, who was sent from God, have seen him.)

"I assure you, anyone who believes in me already has eternal life. Yes, I am the bread of life! Your ancestors ate manna in the wilderness, but they all died. However, the bread from heaven gives eternal life to everyone who eats it. I am the living bread that came down out of heaven. Anyone who eats this bread will live forever; this bread is my flesh, offered so the world may live."

SATISFACTION

The religious leaders frequently asked Jesus to prove to them why he was better than the prophets they already had. Jesus was referring to the manna that Moses had given their ancestors in the wilderness (see Exodus 16). That bread was physical and temporal. The people had eaten it, and it had sustained them for a day. But they had to get more bread every day, and this bread could not keep them from dying. Jesus, who is much greater than Moses, offers himself as the spiritual bread from heaven that satisfies completely and leads to eternal life. God, not man, plays the most active role in salvation. When someone chooses to believe in Jesus Christ as Savior, he or she does so only in response to the urging of God's Holy Spirit. God does the urging and gives the faith; the person then decides whether or not to believe. Thus, no one can believe in Jesus without God's help. If you know Christ as Savior, thank him for his powerful work in your life.

The religious leaders grumbled because they could not accept Jesus' claim of divinity. They saw him only as a carpenter from Nazareth. They refused to believe that Jesus was God's divine Son, and they could not tolerate his message.

The Jews disagree that Jesus is from heaven
John 6:52-59 *(Harmony 100b)*

*T*hen the people began arguing with each other about what he meant. "How can this man give us his flesh to eat?" they asked.

So Jesus said again, "I assure you, unless you eat the flesh of the Son of Man and drink his blood, you cannot have eternal life within you. But those who eat my flesh and drink my blood have eternal life, and I will raise them at the last day. For my flesh is the true food, and my blood is the true drink. All who eat my flesh and drink my blood remain in me, and I in them. I live by the power of the living Father who sent me; in the same way, those who partake of me will live because of me. I am the true bread from heaven. Anyone who eats this bread will live forever and not die as your ancestors did, even though they ate the manna."

He said these things while he was teaching in the synagogue in Capernaum.

THE LIVING BREAD
How can Jesus give us his flesh as bread to eat? This was a shocking message—to eat flesh and drink blood sounded cannibalistic. The idea of drinking any blood, let alone human blood, was repugnant to the religious leaders because the law forbade it (Leviticus 17:10-11). Jesus was not talking about literal blood, of course; he was saying that his life had to become their own. But they could not accept this concept. The apostle Paul later used the body and blood imagery in talking about Communion (see 1 Corinthians 11:23-26). To eat the living bread means to accept Christ into our lives and become united with him. We are united with Christ in two ways: (1) by believing in his death (the sacrifice of his flesh) and resurrection and (2) by devoting ourselves to living as he requires, depending on his teaching for guidance and trusting in the Holy Spirit for power. If you are united with Christ, he is living through you by his Holy Spirit. In what ways do you reflect Christ to your family and friends?

Those who put their faith in Christ will be resurrected from physical death to everlasting life with God when Christ comes again (see 1 Corinthians 15:52; 1 Thessalonians 4:16).

June 8

Many disciples desert Jesus
John 6:60-65 *(Harmony 101a)*

*E*ven his disciples said, "This is very hard to understand. How can anyone accept it?"

Jesus knew within himself that his disciples were complaining, so he said to them, "Does this offend you? Then what will you think if you see me, the Son of Man, return to heaven again? It is the Spirit who gives eternal life. Human effort accomplishes nothing. And the very words I have spoken to you are spirit and life. But some of you don't believe me." (For Jesus knew from the beginning who didn't believe, and he knew who would betray him.) Then he said, "That is what I meant when I said that people can't come to me unless the Father brings them to me."

WHY TURN AWAY?
Why were Jesus' words so difficult for many of his followers to understand? (1) They may have realized that he wasn't going to be the conquering Messiah-King they expected. (2) He refused to give in to their self-centered requests. (3) He emphasized faith, not works. (4) His teachings were difficult to understand, and some of his words were offensive. As we grow in our faith, we may be tempted to turn away because Jesus' lessons are difficult. Will your response be to give up, ignore certain teachings, or reject Christ? Instead, ask God to show you what the teachings mean and how they apply to your life. Then have the courage to act on God's truth.

The Holy Spirit gives spiritual life; without the work of the Holy Spirit we cannot even see our need for new life (14:17). All spiritual renewal begins and ends with God. He reveals truth to us, lives within us, and then enables us to respond to that truth.

June 9

Many disciples desert Jesus
John 6:66-71 *(Harmony 101b)*

*A*t this point many of his disciples turned away and deserted him. Then Jesus turned to the Twelve and asked, "Are you going to leave, too?"

Simon Peter replied, "Lord, to whom would we go? You alone have the words that give eternal life. We believe them, and we know you are the Holy

One of God."

Then Jesus said, "I chose the twelve of you, but one is a devil." He was speaking of Judas, son of Simon Iscariot, one of the Twelve, who would betray him.

NO OTHER WAY

After many of Jesus' followers had deserted him, he asked the twelve disciples if they were also going to leave. Peter replied, "To whom would we go?" In his straightforward way, Peter answered for all of us—there is no other way. Though there are many philosophies and self-styled authorities, Jesus alone has the words of eternal life. People look everywhere for eternal life and miss Christ, the only source. Many people today turn away; others pretend to follow, going to church for status, approval of family and friends, or business contacts. But there are only two real responses to Jesus—you either accept him or reject him. How have you responded to Christ?

The more the people heard Jesus' real message, the more they divided into two camps—the honest seekers who wanted to understand more, and those who rejected Jesus because they didn't like what they had heard.

June 10

Jesus teaches about inner purity
Mark 7:1-13 (also in Matthew 15:1-9) *(Harmony 102a)*

One day some Pharisees and teachers of religious law arrived from Jerusalem to confront Jesus. They noticed that some of Jesus' disciples failed to follow the usual Jewish ritual of hand washing before eating. (The Jews, especially the Pharisees, do not eat until they have poured water over their cupped hands, as required by their ancient traditions. Similarly, they eat nothing bought from the market unless they have immersed their hands in water. This is but one of many traditions they have clung to—such as their ceremony of washing cups, pitchers, and kettles.) So the Pharisees and teachers of religious law asked him, "Why don't your disciples follow our age-old customs? For they eat without first performing the hand-washing ceremony."

Jesus replied, "You hypocrites! Isaiah was prophesying about you when he said, 'These people honor me with their lips, but their hearts are far away. Their worship is a farce, for they replace God's commands with their own man-made teachings.' For you ignore God's specific laws and substitute your own traditions."

Then he said, "You reject God's laws in order to hold on to your own traditions. For instance, Moses gave you this law from God: 'Honor your father and mother,' and 'Anyone who speaks evil of father or mother must be put to death.' But you say it is all right for people to say to their parents, 'Sorry, I can't help you. For I have vowed to give to God what I could have given to you.' You let them disregard their needy parents. As such, you break the law of God in order to protect your own tradition. And this is only one example. There are many, many others."

HYPOCRISY

Hypocrisy is pretending to be something you are not and have no intention of being. Jesus called the Pharisees hypocrites because they worshiped God for the wrong reasons. Their worship was not motivated by love but by a desire to attain profit, to appear holy, and to increase their status. We become hypocrites when we (1) pay more attention to reputation than to character, (2) carefully follow certain religious practices while allowing our hearts to remain distant from God, and (3) emphasize our virtues but others' sins. Why do you go to church?

The Pharisees added hundreds of their own petty rules and regulations to God's holy laws, and then they tried to force people to follow these rules. These men claimed to know God's will in every detail of life.

June 11

Jesus teaches about inner purity
Mark 7:14-19 (also in Matthew 15:10-17) (Harmony 102b)

Then Jesus called to the crowd to come and hear. "All of you listen," he said, "and try to understand. You are not defiled by what you eat; you are defiled by what you say and do!"

Then Jesus went into a house to get away from the crowds, and his disciples asked him what he meant by the statement he had made. "Don't you understand either?" he asked. "Can't you see that what you eat won't defile you? Food doesn't come in contact with your heart, but only passes through the stomach and then comes out again." (By saying this, he showed that every kind of food is acceptable.)

It is idolatry to claim that your interpretation of God's Word is as important as God's Word itself. It is especially dangerous to set up unbiblical standards for others to follow. Instead, look to Christ for guidance about your own behavior, and let him lead others in the details of their lives.

INSIDE OUT

Do we worry more about what is in our diets than what is in our heart and mind? As they interpreted the dietary laws (Leviticus 11), the Jews believed they could be clean before God because of what they refused to eat. But

Jesus pointed out that sin actually begins in the attitudes and intentions of the inner person. Jesus did not degrade the law, but he paved the way for the change made clear in Acts 10:9-29 when God removed the cultural restrictions regarding food. We are not pure because of outward acts—we become pure on the inside as Christ renews our mind and transforms us into his image.

June 12

Jesus teaches about inner purity
Mark 7:20-23 (also in Matthew 15:18-20) *(Harmony 102c)*

*A*nd then he added, "It is the thought-life that defiles you. For from within, out of a person's heart, come evil thoughts, sexual immorality, theft, murder, adultery, greed, wickedness, deceit, eagerness for lustful pleasure, envy, slander, pride, and foolishness. All these vile things come from within; they are what defile you and make you unacceptable to God."

A SINGLE THOUGHT

An evil action begins with a single thought. Allowing our minds to dwell on lust, envy, hatred, or revenge will lead to sin. Don't defile yourself by focusing on evil. What we put into our minds determines what comes out in our words and actions. The apostle Paul tells us to fix our thoughts on what is true, honorable, right, pure, lovely, admirable, excellent, and praiseworthy (Philippians 4:8). Do you have problems with impure thoughts and daydreams? Examine what you are putting into your mind through television, books, conversations, movies, and magazines. Replace harmful input with wholesome material. Above all, read God's Word and pray. Ask God to help you focus your mind on what is good and pure. It takes practice, but it can be done.

There is a downward spiral. First, people reject a command of God; next, they make up their own ideas about God. Then they allow evil thoughts to lead them into evil actions. Finally, they grow to hate God. Only Christ can break this progression and help people escape the downward spiral.

Jesus sends a demon out of a girl
Mark 7:24-30 (also in Matthew 15:21-28) *(Harmony 103)*

*T*hen Jesus left Galilee and went north to the region of Tyre. He tried to keep it secret that he was there, but he couldn't. As usual, the news of his arrival spread fast. Right away a woman came to him whose little girl was possessed by an evil spirit. She had heard about Jesus, and now she came and fell at his feet. She begged him to release her child from the demon's control.

Since she was a Gentile, born in Syrian Phoenicia, Jesus told her, "First I should help my own family, the Jews. It isn't right to take food from the children and throw it to the dogs."

She replied, "That's true, Lord, but even the dogs under the table are given some crumbs from the children's plates."

"Good answer!" he said. "And because you have answered so well, I have healed your daughter." And when she arrived home, her little girl was lying quietly in bed, and the demon was gone.

AVAILABLE TO ALL

Jesus' words do not contradict the truth that God's message is for all people (Psalm 22:27; Isaiah 56:7; Matthew 28:19; Romans 15:9-12). Remember, when Jesus said these words, he was in Gentile territory on a mission to Gentile people. He ministered to Gentiles on many other occasions also. Jesus was simply telling the woman that Jews were to have the first opportunity to accept him as the Messiah because God wanted them to present the message of salvation to the rest of the world (see Genesis 12:3). Jesus was not rejecting the Syrophoenician woman. He may have wanted to test her faith, or he may have wanted to use the situation as another opportunity to teach that faith is available to all kinds of people. Ironically, many Jews would lose God's spiritual healing because of their rejection of Jesus, while many Gentiles, whom the Jews rejected, would find salvation because of their recognition of Jesus. Whom do you know who seems to be beyond the gospel? Don't count them out. Continue to pray that God will bring others to faith, and look for ways to tell them about God's love.

Dog was a term the Jews commonly applied to Gentiles because the Jews considered these heathen people no more likely than dogs to receive God's blessing. Jesus was not degrading the woman by using this term; he was reflecting the Jews' attitude so as to contrast it with his own.

June 14

The crowd marvels at Jesus' healings
Mark 7:31-37 (also in Matthew 15:29-31) *(Harmony 104)*

*J*esus left Tyre and went to Sidon, then back to the Sea of Galilee and the region of the Ten Towns. A deaf man with a speech impediment was brought to him, and the people begged Jesus to lay his hands on the man to heal him. Jesus led him to a private place away from the crowd. He put his fingers into the man's ears. Then, spitting onto his own fingers, he touched the man's tongue with the spittle. And looking up to heaven, he sighed and commanded, "Be opened!" Instantly the man could hear perfectly and speak plainly!

Jesus told the crowd not to tell anyone, but the more he told them not to, the more they spread the news, for they were completely amazed. Again and again they said, "Everything he does is wonderful. He even heals those who are deaf and mute."

HEALING POWER
A great crowd was brought to Jesus to be healed, and he healed them all. Jesus is still able to heal broken lives, and we can be the ones who bring suffering people to him. Who do you know who needs Christ's healing touch? You can bring them to Jesus by prayer or through explaining to them the reason for the hope that you have (1 Peter 3:15). Then let Christ do the healing.

Jesus asked the people not to talk about this healing because he didn't want to be seen simply as a miracle worker. He didn't want the people to miss his real message. We must not be so concerned about what Jesus can do for us that we forget to listen to his message.

June 15

Jesus feeds four thousand
Mark 8:1-9 (also in Matthew 15:32-39) *(Harmony 105)*

*A*bout this time another great crowd had gathered, and the people ran out of food again. Jesus called his disciples and told them, "I feel sorry for these people. They have been here with me for three days, and they have nothing left to eat. And if I send them home without feeding them, they will faint along the road. For some of them have come a long distance."

"How are we supposed to find enough food for them here in the wilderness?" his disciples asked.

"How many loaves of bread do you have?" he asked.

"Seven," they replied. So Jesus told all the people to sit down on the ground. Then he took the seven loaves, thanked God for them, broke them into pieces, and gave them to his disciples, who distributed the bread to the crowd. A few small fish were found, too, so Jesus also blessed these and told the disciples to pass them out.

They ate until they were full, and when the scraps were picked up, there were seven large baskets of food left over! There were about four thousand people in the crowd that day, and he sent them home after they had eaten.

FOOD FOR THOUGHT

This is a different miracle from the feeding of the five thousand described earlier. At that time, those fed were mostly Jews. This time Jesus was ministering to a non-Jewish crowd in the Gentile region of the Decapolis. Jesus had already fed more than five thousand people with five loaves and two fish. Here, in a similar situation, the disciples were again perplexed. How easily we despair when faced with difficult situations. Like the disciples, we often forget that if God has cared for us in the past, he will do the same now. When facing a perplexing problem or a tough task, remember how God has cared for you and trust him to work faithfully again.

Magadan was located on the west shore of the Sea of Galilee. Also known as Magdala or Dalmanutha (8:10), this was Mary Magdalene's hometown.

June 16

Religious leaders ask for a sign in the sky
Matthew 16:1-4 (also in Mark 8:10-12) *(Harmony 106)*

*O*ne day the Pharisees and Sadducees came to test Jesus' claims by asking him to show them a miraculous sign from heaven.

He replied, "You know the saying, 'Red sky at night means fair weather tomorrow, red sky in the morning means foul weather all day.' You are good at reading the weather signs in the sky, but you can't read the obvious signs of the times! Only an evil, faithless generation would ask for a miraculous sign, but the only sign I will give them is the sign of the prophet Jonah." Then Jesus left them and went away.

MIRACLES

These Jewish leaders said they wanted to see a miracle so that they could believe. But Jesus knew that miracles never convince the skeptical. Jesus had been healing, raising people from the dead, and feeding thousands, and still people wanted him to prove himself. Do you doubt Christ because you haven't *seen* a miracle? Do you expect God to prove himself to you personally before you believe? Jesus says, "Blessed are those who haven't seen me and believe anyway" (John 20:29). We have all the miracles recorded in the Old and New Testaments, two thousand years of church

The Pharisees had tried to explain away Jesus' previous miracles by claiming they happened by luck, coincidence, or evil power. Here they demanded a sign from heaven—something only God could do. Jesus refused their demand because he knew that even this kind of miracle would not convince them. They had already decided not to believe.

history, and the witness of thousands of believers. With all this evidence, those who won't believe are either too proud or too stubborn. If you simply step forward in faith and believe, then you will begin to see the miracles that God can do with your life!

June 17

Jesus warns against wrong teaching
Mark 8:13-21 (also in Matthew 16:5-12) *(Harmony 107)*

So he got back into the boat and left them, and he crossed to the other side of the lake.

But the disciples discovered they had forgotten to bring any food, so there was only one loaf of bread with them in the boat. As they were crossing the lake, Jesus warned them, "Beware of the yeast of the Pharisees and of Herod."

They decided he was saying this because they hadn't brought any bread. Jesus knew what they were thinking, so he said, "Why are you so worried about having no food? Won't you ever learn or understand? Are your hearts too hard to take it in? 'You have eyes—can't you see? You have ears—can't you hear?' Don't you remember anything at all? What about the five thousand men I fed with five loaves of bread? How many baskets of leftovers did you pick up afterward?"

"Twelve," they said.

"And when I fed the four thousand with seven loaves, how many large baskets of leftovers did you pick up?"

"Seven," they said.

"Don't you understand even yet?" he asked them.

How could the disciples experience so many of Jesus' miracles and yet be so slow to comprehend who he was? They had already seen Jesus feed over five thousand people with five loaves and two fish (6:35-44), yet here they doubted whether he could feed another large group.

Sometimes we are also slow to catch on. Although Christ has brought us through trials and temptations in the past, we don't believe that he will do it in the future. Is your heart too closed to take in all that God can do for you? Don't be like the disciples. Remember what Christ has done, and have faith that he will do it again.

Yeast in this passage symbolizes evil. Just as only a small amount of yeast is needed to make a batch of bread rise, so the hard-heartedness of the religious and political leaders could permeate and contaminate the entire society and make it rise up against Jesus.

June 18

Jesus restores sight to a blind man
Mark 8:22-26 *(Harmony 108)*

*W*hen they arrived at Bethsaida, some people brought a blind man to Jesus, and they begged him to touch and heal the man. Jesus took the blind man by the hand and led him out of the village. Then, spitting on the man's eyes, he laid his hands on him and asked, "Can you see anything now?"

The man looked around. "Yes," he said, "I see people, but I can't see them very clearly. They look like trees walking around."

Then Jesus placed his hands over the man's eyes again. As the man stared intently, his sight was completely restored, and he could see everything clearly. Jesus sent him home, saying, "Don't go back into the village on your way home."

OPEN EYES

Why did Jesus touch the man a second time before he could see? This miracle was not too difficult for Jesus, but he chose to do it in stages, possibly to show the disciples that some healing would be gradual rather than instantaneous or to demonstrate that spiritual truth is not always perceived clearly at first. Before Jesus left, however, the man was healed completely. Sometimes it takes time for us to understand. Christ stays with us, helping us to finally "see" clearly. Trust him to help you when you don't understand.

Jesus took the man out of the village to heal him and then told him not to go back into the village. Jesus had compassion to heal, but he did not want to be seen as merely a miracle worker.

Peter says Jesus is the Messiah
Matthew 16:13-20 (also in Mark 8:27-30; Luke 9:18-20)
(Harmony 109)

hen Jesus came to the region of Caesarea Philippi, he asked his disciples, "Who do people say that the Son of Man is?"

"Well," they replied, "some say John the Baptist, some say Elijah, and others say Jeremiah or one of the other prophets."

Then he asked them, "Who do you say I am?"

Simon Peter answered, "You are the Messiah, the Son of the living God."

Jesus replied, "You are blessed, Simon son of John, because my Father in heaven has revealed this to you. You did not learn this from any human being. Now I say to you that you are Peter, and upon this rock I will build my church, and all the powers of hell will not conquer it. And I will give you the keys of the Kingdom of Heaven. Whatever you lock on earth will be locked in heaven, and whatever you open on earth will be opened in heaven." Then he sternly warned them not to tell anyone that he was the Messiah.

WHO DO YOU SAY HE IS?
The disciples answered Jesus' question with the common view—that Jesus was one of the great prophets come back to life. This belief may have stemmed from Deuteronomy 18:18, where God said he would raise up a prophet from among the people. Peter, however, confessed Jesus as divine and as the promised and long-awaited Messiah. It is not enough to know what others say about Jesus: You must know, understand, and accept for yourself that he is the Messiah. You must move from curiosity to commitment, from admiration to adoration. If Jesus were to ask you this question, how would you answer? Is he your Lord and Messiah?

The rock on which Jesus would build his church has been identified as: (1) Jesus himself (his work of salvation by dying for us on the cross); (2) Peter (the first great leader of the church at Jerusalem); (3) the confession of faith that Peter gave and that all subsequent true believers would give.

Jesus predicts his death the first time
Mark 8:31–9:1 (also in Matthew 16:21-28; Luke 9:21-27)
(Harmony 110)

*T*hen Jesus began to tell them that he, the Son of Man, would suffer many terrible things and be rejected by the leaders, the leading priests, and the teachers of religious law. He would be killed, and three days later he would rise again. As he talked about this openly with his disciples, Peter took him aside and told him he shouldn't say things like that.

Jesus turned and looked at his disciples and then said to Peter very sternly, "Get away from me, Satan! You are seeing things merely from a human point of view, not from God's."

Then he called his disciples and the crowds to come over and listen. "If any of you wants to be my follower," he told them, "you must put aside your selfish ambition, shoulder your cross, and follow me. If you try to keep your life for yourself, you will lose it. But if you give up your life for my sake and for the sake of the Good News, you will find true life. And how do you benefit if you gain the whole world but lose your own soul in the process? Is anything worth more than your soul? If a person is ashamed of me and my message in these adulterous and sinful days, I, the Son of Man, will be ashamed of that person when I return in the glory of my Father with the holy angels."

Jesus went on to say, "I assure you that some of you standing here right now will not die before you see the Kingdom of God arrive in great power!"

LOST AND FOUND
Many people spend all their energy seeking pleasure. Jesus said, however, that a world of pleasure centered on possessions, position, or power is ultimately worthless. Whatever you have on earth is only temporary; it cannot be exchanged for your soul. If you work hard at getting what you want, you might eventually have a "pleasurable" life, but in the end you will find it hollow and empty. We should be willing to lose our lives for the sake of the gospel, not because our lives are useless, but because nothing—not even life itself—can compare to what we gain with Christ. Jesus wants us to *choose* to follow him rather than to lead a life of sin and self-satisfaction. He wants us to stop trying to control our own destiny and to let him direct us. This makes good sense because, as the Creator, Christ knows better than we do what real life is about. He asks for submission, not self-hatred; he asks us only to lose our self-centered determination to be in charge.

In this moment Peter was not considering God's purposes but was speaking out of his own natural human desires and feelings. Peter wanted Christ to be king but not the suffering servant prophesied in Isaiah 53. He was ready to receive the glory of following the Messiah but not the persecution.

June 21

Jesus is transfigured on the mountain
Luke 9:28-31 (also in Matthew 17:1-3; Mark 9:2-4)
(Harmony 111a)

*A*bout eight days later Jesus took Peter, James, and John to a mountain to pray. And as he was praying, the appearance of his face changed, and his clothing became dazzling white. Then two men, Moses and Elijah, appeared and began talking with Jesus. They were glorious to see. And they were speaking of how he was about to fulfill God's plan by dying in Jerusalem.

THE INNER CIRCLE
When Jesus said that some of his disciples would see the Kingdom of God arrive (9:27), he may have been referring to the three disciples who would see the Transfiguration. We don't know why Jesus singled out Peter, James, and John for this special revelation of his glory and purity. Perhaps they were the ones most ready to understand and accept this great truth. These three disciples were the inner circle of the group of twelve. They were among the first to hear Jesus' call (Mark 1:16-19). They headed the Gospel lists of disciples (Mark 3:16-17). And they were present at certain healings where others were excluded (Luke 8:51). God calls different people to certain areas of service for him. Some are more visible than others, but all are needed to accomplish his work in the world. Are you doing what God called you to do?

Moses and Elijah were the two greatest prophets in the Old Testament. Moses represents the law, or the old covenant. He wrote the Pentateuch and predicted the coming of a great prophet (Deuteronomy 18:15-19). Elijah represents the prophets who foretold the coming of the Messiah (Malachi 4:5-6). Moses' and Elijah's presence with Jesus confirmed Jesus' messianic mission—to fulfill God's law and the words of God's prophets.

June 22

Jesus is transfigured on the mountain
Luke 9:32-36 (also in Matthew 17:4-13; Mark 9:5-13)
(Harmony 111b)

*P*eter and the others were very drowsy and had fallen asleep. Now they woke up and saw Jesus' glory and the two men standing with him. As Moses and Elijah were starting to leave, Peter, not even knowing what he was saying, blurted out, "Master, this is wonderful! We will make three shrines—one for you, one for Moses, and one for Elijah." But even as he was saying this, a cloud came over them; and terror gripped them as it covered them.

Then a voice from the cloud said, "This is my Son, my Chosen One. Listen to him." When the voice died away, Jesus was there alone. They didn't tell anyone what they had seen until long after this happened.

GOD'S SON

The Transfiguration revealed Christ's divine nature. God's voice exalted Jesus above Moses and Elijah as the long-awaited Messiah with full divine authority. Moses represented the law, and Elijah, the prophets. Their appearance showed Jesus as the fulfillment of both the Old Testament law and the prophetic promises.

Jesus was not a reincarnation of Elijah or Moses. He was not merely one of the prophets. As God's only Son, he far surpasses them in authority and power. Many voices try to tell us how to live and how to know God personally. Some of these are helpful; many are not. We must first listen to the Bible and then evaluate all other authorities in light of God's revelation.

Jesus told Peter, James, and John not to speak about what they had seen because they would not fully understand it until Jesus had risen from the dead. Then they would realize that only through dying could Jesus show his power over death and his authority to be King of all. The disciples could not be powerful witnesses for God until they had grasped this truth.

June 23

Jesus heals a demon-possessed boy
Mark 9:14-29 (also in Matthew 17:14-21; Luke 9:37-43)
(Harmony 112)

At the foot of the mountain they found a great crowd surrounding the other disciples, as some teachers of religious law were arguing with them. The crowd watched Jesus in awe as he came toward them, and then they ran to greet him. "What is all this arguing about?" he asked.

One of the men in the crowd spoke up and said, "Teacher, I brought my son for you to heal him. He can't speak because he is possessed by an evil spirit that won't let him talk. And whenever this evil spirit seizes him, it throws him violently to the ground and makes him foam at the mouth and grind his teeth and become rigid. So I asked your disciples to cast out the evil spirit, but they couldn't do it."

Jesus said to them, "You faithless people! How long must I be with you until you believe? How long must I put up with you? Bring the boy to me." So they brought the boy. But when the evil spirit saw Jesus, it threw the child into a violent convulsion, and he fell to the ground, writhing and foaming at the mouth. "How long has this been happening?" Jesus asked the boy's father.

He replied, "Since he was very small. The evil spirit often makes him fall into the fire or into water, trying to kill him. Have mercy on us and help us. Do something if you can."

"What do you mean, 'If I can'?" Jesus asked. "Anything is possible if a person believes."

The father instantly replied, "I do believe, but help me not to doubt!"

When Jesus saw that the crowd of onlookers was growing, he rebuked the evil spirit. "Spirit of deafness and muteness," he said, "I command you to come out of this child and never enter him again!" Then the spirit screamed and threw the boy into another violent convulsion and left him. The boy lay there motionless, and he appeared to be dead. A murmur ran through the crowd, "He's dead." But Jesus took him by the hand and helped him to his feet, and he stood up.

Afterward, when Jesus was alone in the house with his disciples, they asked him, "Why couldn't we cast out that evil spirit?"

Jesus replied, "This kind can be cast out only by prayer."

ANYTHING WITH FAITH

Why couldn't the disciples drive out the evil spirit that had caused the boy to be mute? They had special authority to do so, but perhaps their faith was faltering. Mark tells this story to show that the battle with Satan is a difficult, ongoing struggle.

Jesus did not mean that we can automatically obtain anything we want if we just think positively. Jesus meant that anything is *possible* if we believe, because nothing is too difficult for God. We cannot have everything we pray for as if by magic; but with faith, we can have everything we need to serve him. The attitude of trust and confidence that the Bible calls *belief* or *faith* (Hebrews 11:1, 6) is not something we can obtain without help. Faith is a gift from God (Ephesians 2:8-9). No matter how much faith we have, we never reach the point of being self-sufficient. Faith is not stored away like money in the bank. Growing in faith is a constant process of daily renewing our trust in Jesus.

June 24

Jesus predicts his death the second time
Mark 9:30-32 (also in Matthew 17:22-23; Luke 9:44-45)
(Harmony 113)

*L*eaving that region, they traveled through Galilee. Jesus tried to avoid all publicity in order to spend more time with his disciples and teach them. He said to them, "The Son of Man is going to be betrayed. He will be killed, but three days later he will rise from the dead." But they didn't understand what he was saying, and they were afraid to ask him what he meant.

CALLED TO BELIEVE

Once again Jesus predicted his death (see also Matthew 16:21); but more important, he told of his resurrection. Unfortunately, the disciples heard only the first part of Jesus' words and became discouraged. They couldn't understand why Jesus wanted to go back to Jerusalem where he would walk right into trouble.

The disciples didn't fully comprehend the purpose of Jesus' death and resurrection until Pentecost (Acts 2). The disciples didn't understand why Jesus kept talking about his death because they expected him to set up a political kingdom. His death, they thought, would dash their hopes. They didn't know that Jesus' death and resurrection would make his Kingdom possible. We shouldn't get upset at ourselves for being slow to understand everything about Jesus. After all, the disciples were with him, saw his miracles, heard his words, and still had difficulty understanding. Despite their questions and doubts, however, they believed. We should do no less.

At times, Jesus limited his public ministry in order to train his disciples in depth. He knew the importance of equipping them to carry on when he returned to heaven. Leaving Caesarea Philippi, Jesus began his last tour through the region of Galilee.

June 25

Peter finds the coin in the fish's mouth
Matthew 17:24-27 (Harmony 114)

*O*n their arrival in Capernaum, the tax collectors for the Temple tax came to Peter and asked him, "Doesn't your teacher pay the Temple tax?"

"Of course he does," Peter replied. Then he went into the house to talk to Jesus about it.

But before he had a chance to speak, Jesus asked him, "What do you think, Peter? Do kings tax their own people or the foreigners they have conquered?"

"They tax the foreigners," Peter replied.

"Well, then," Jesus said, "the citizens are free! However, we don't want to offend them, so go down to the lake and throw in a line. Open the mouth of the first fish you catch, and you will find a coin. Take the coin and pay the tax for both of us."

GOOD AMBASSADORS

As usual, Peter answered a question without really knowing the answer, putting Jesus and the disciples in an awkward position. Jesus used this situation, however, to emphasize his kingly role. Just as kings pay no taxes and collect none from their family, Jesus, the King, owed no taxes. But he supplied the tax payment for both himself and Peter rather than offend those who didn't understand his kingship. As God's people, we are foreigners on earth because our loyalty is always to our real King—Jesus. Still we have to cooperate with the authorities and be responsible citizens. An ambassador to another country keeps the local laws in order to represent well the one who sent him. We are Christ's ambassadors (2 Corinthians 5:20). Are you being a good foreign ambassador for him to this world?

All Jewish males had to pay a Temple tax to support Temple upkeep (Exodus 30:11-16). Tax collectors set up booths to collect these taxes. Only Matthew records this incident, perhaps because he had been a tax collector himself.

June 26

The disciples argue about who would be the greatest
Mark 9:33-37 (also in Matthew 18:1-6; Luke 9:46-48)
(Harmony 115)

After they arrived at Capernaum, Jesus and his disciples settled in the house where they would be staying. Jesus asked them, "What were you discussing out on the road?" But they didn't answer, because they had been arguing about which of them was the greatest. He sat down and called the twelve disciples over to him. Then he said, "Anyone who wants to be the first must take last place and be the servant of everyone else."

Then he put a little child among them. Taking the child in his arms, he said to them, "Anyone who welcomes a little child like this on my behalf welcomes me, and anyone who welcomes me welcomes my Father who sent me."

THE GREATEST

The disciples, caught up in their constant struggle for personal success, were embarrassed to answer Jesus' question. It is always painful to compare our motives with Christ's. It is not wrong for believers to be industrious or ambitious. But when ambition pushes obedience and service to one side, it becomes sin. Pride or insecurity can cause us to overvalue position and prestige. In God's Kingdom, such motives are destructive. The only safe ambition is directed toward Christ's Kingdom, not our own advancement. It is possible for thoughtless, selfish people to gain a measure of greatness in the world's eyes, but enduring greatness is measured only by God's standards. What do you use as your measure of greatness—personal achievement or unselfish service?

Children are trusting by nature. They trust adults, and through that trust their capacity to trust God grows. God holds parents and other adults who influence young children accountable for how they affect these little ones' ability to trust.

June 27

The disciples forbid another to use Jesus' name
Mark 9:38-42 (also in Luke 9:49-50) *(Harmony 116)*

*J*ohn said to Jesus, "Teacher, we saw a man using your name to cast out demons, but we told him to stop because he isn't one of our group."

"Don't stop him!" Jesus said. "No one who performs miracles in my name will soon be able to speak evil of me. Anyone who is not against us is for us. If anyone gives you even a cup of water because you belong to the Messiah, I assure you, that person will be rewarded.

"But if anyone causes one of these little ones who trusts in me to lose faith, it would be better for that person to be thrown into the sea with a large millstone tied around the neck.

COMMON FAITH, COMMON GOAL

The disciples were jealous of a man who healed in Jesus' name because they were more concerned about their own group's position than about helping to free those troubled by demons. We do the same when we refuse to participate in worthy causes because (1) other people or groups are not affiliated with our denomination, (2) these projects do not involve the kind of people

In 9:40, Jesus was not saying that being indifferent or neutral toward him is as good as being committed. The statement is spoken in a different way in Matthew 12:30: "Anyone who isn't helping me is harming me." In both cases Jesus was pointing out that neutrality toward him is not possible.

with whom we feel most comfortable, (3) others don't do things the way we are used to doing them, or (4) our efforts won't receive enough recognition. Correct theology is important but should never be an excuse to avoid helping people in need. People who are on Jesus' side have the same goal of building up the Kingdom of God, and they should not let their differences hinder them from attaining it. Those who share a common faith in Christ should cooperate. People don't have to be just like us to be following Jesus with us.

June 28

Jesus warns against temptation
Mark 9:43-50 (also in Matthew 18:7-9) *(Harmony 117)*

*I*f your hand causes you to sin, cut it off. It is better to enter heaven with only one hand than to go into the unquenchable fires of hell with two hands. If your foot causes you to sin, cut it off. It is better to enter heaven with only one foot than to be thrown into hell with two feet. And if your eye causes you to sin, gouge it out. It is better to enter the Kingdom of God half blind than to have two eyes and be thrown into hell, 'where the worm never dies and the fire never goes out.'

"For everyone will be purified with fire. Salt is good for seasoning. But if it loses its flavor, how do you make it salty again? You must have the qualities of salt among yourselves and live in peace with each other."

SALTY ENOUGH?
Jesus used salt to illustrate three qualities that should be found in his people: (1) *We should remember God's faithfulness,* just as salt when used with a sacrifice recalled God's covenant with his people (Leviticus 2:13). (2) *We should make a difference in the "flavor" of the world we live in,* just as salt changes meat's flavor (see Matthew 5:13). (3) *We should counteract the moral decay in society,* just as salt preserves food from decay. When we lose this desire to "salt" the earth with the love and message of God, we become useless to him. Think of how you can be salty this week.

Jesus used startling language to stress the importance of cutting sin out of our lives. Painful discipline is required of his true followers. Giving up a relationship, job, or habit that is against God's will may seem just as painful as cutting off a hand. Nothing should stand in the way of faith.

June 29

Jesus warns against looking down on others
Matthew 18:10-14 *(Harmony 118)*

*B*eware that you don't despise a single one of these little ones. For I tell you that in heaven their angels are always in the presence of my heavenly Father.

"If a shepherd has one hundred sheep, and one wanders away and is lost, what will he do? Won't he leave the ninety-nine others and go out into the hills to search for the lost one? And if he finds it, he will surely rejoice over it more than over the ninety-nine that didn't wander away! In the same way, it is not my heavenly Father's will that even one of these little ones should perish.

GUIDANCE

Just as a shepherd is concerned enough about one lost sheep to go search the hills for it, so God is concerned about every human being he has created ("he does not want anyone to perish" [2 Peter 3:9]). You come in contact with children who need Christ at home, at school, in church, and in the neighborhood. Steer them toward Christ by your example, your words, and your acts of kindness.

Certain angels are assigned to watch over children, and they have direct access to God. If their angels have constant access to God, the least we can do is to allow children to approach us easily in spite of our far-too-busy schedules.

June 30

Jesus teaches how to treat a believer who sins
Matthew 18:15-18 *(Harmony 119a)*

*I*f another believer sins against you, go privately and point out the fault. If the other person listens and confesses it, you have won that person back. But if you are unsuccessful, take one or two others with you and go back again, so that everything you say may be confirmed by two or three witnesses. If that person still refuses to listen, take your case to the church. If the church decides you are right, but the other person won't accept it, treat that person as a pagan or a corrupt tax collector. I tell you this: Whatever you prohibit on earth is prohibited in heaven, and whatever you allow on earth is allowed in heaven.

SINNED AGAINST

These are Jesus' guidelines for dealing with those who sin against us. They were meant for (1) Christians, not unbelievers, (2) sins committed against *you* and not others, and (3) conflict resolution in the context of the church, not the community at large. Jesus' words are not a license for a frontal attack on every person who hurts or slights us. They are not a license to start a destructive gossip campaign or to call for a church trial. These guidelines are designed to reconcile those who disagree so that all Christians can live in harmony.

This prohibiting and allowing refers to the decisions of the church in conflicts. Among believers, there is no court higher than the church. Ideally, the church's decisions should be God-guided and based on discernment of his Word. Believers have the responsibility to bring their problems to the church, and the church has the responsibility to use God's guidance in seeking to resolve them.

When someone wrongs us, we often do the opposite of what Jesus recommends. We turn away in hatred or resentment, seek revenge, or engage in gossip. By contrast, we should go to that person *first,* as difficult as that may be. Then we should forgive that person as often as he or she needs it (18:21-22). This will create a much better chance of restoring the relationship.

July 1

Jesus promises to be with us in prayer
Matthew 18:19-20 *(Harmony 119b)*

I also tell you this: If two of you agree down here on earth concerning anything you ask, my Father in heaven will do it for you. For where two or three gather together because they are mine, I am there among them."

PRAYER POWER

Jesus looked ahead to a new day when he would be present with his followers, not physically, but through his Holy Spirit. When two or three of Jesus' followers agree in prayer, Jesus is with them, and the Father listens. Two or more believers, filled with the Holy Spirit, will pray according to God's will, not their own; thus their requests will be granted. Although God is all-powerful and all-knowing, he has chosen to let us help him change the world through our prayers. How this works is a mystery to us because of our limited understanding, but it is a reality. Our earnest prayers will have powerful results (James 5:16). Make prayer a regular part of your life, alone and with other believers.

God is three persons in one—Father, Son, and Holy Spirit. God became a man in Jesus so that Jesus could die for our sins. When Jesus ascended into heaven, his physical presence left the earth, but he promised to send the Holy Spirit so that his spiritual presence would still be among us.

July 2

Jesus tells the parable of the unforgiving debtor
Matthew 18:21-22 *(Harmony 120a)*

T hen Peter came to him and asked, "Lord, how often should I forgive someone who sins against me? Seven times?"
"No!" Jesus replied, "seventy times seven!"

FORGIVEN

When Jesus explained that we should forgive others "seventy times seven," he meant that we shouldn't even keep track of how many times we forgive someone. We should always forgive those who are truly repentant, no matter how many times they ask. As Christians, we should forgive as we have been forgiven. True forgiveness means we treat the one we've forgiven as we would want to be treated. As we understand God's mercy, we will want to be like him. Having received forgiveness, we will pass it on to others. Is there someone you say you have forgiven, but who still needs your kindness?

The rabbis taught that people should forgive those who offended them—but only three times. Peter, trying to be especially generous, asked Jesus if seven (the "perfect" number) was enough times to forgive someone.

July 3

Jesus tells the parable of the unforgiving debtor
Matthew 18:23-35 *(Harmony 120b)*

For this reason, the Kingdom of Heaven can be compared to a king who decided to bring his accounts up to date with servants who had borrowed money from him. In the process, one of his debtors was brought in who owed him millions of dollars. He couldn't pay, so the king ordered that he, his wife, his children, and everything he had be sold to pay the debt. But the man fell down before the king and begged him, 'Oh, sir, be patient with me, and I will pay it all.' Then the king was filled with pity for him, and he released him and forgave his debt.

"But when the man left the king, he went to a fellow servant who owed him a few thousand dollars. He grabbed him by the throat and demanded instant payment. His fellow servant fell down before him and begged for a little more time. 'Be patient and I will pay it,' he pleaded. But his creditor wouldn't wait. He had the man arrested and jailed until the debt could be paid in full.

"When some of the other servants saw this, they were very upset. They went to the king and told him what had happened. Then the king called in the man he had forgiven and said, 'You evil servant! I forgave you that tremendous debt because you pleaded with me. Shouldn't you have mercy on your fellow servant, just as I had mercy on you?' Then the angry king sent the man to prison until he had paid every penny.

"That's what my heavenly Father will do to you if you refuse to forgive your brothers and sisters in your heart."

HARD TO FORGIVE
If we love someone the way Christ loves us, we will be willing to forgive. If we have experienced God's grace, we will want to pass it on to others. Forgiveness involves both attitudes and actions. If you find it difficult to *feel* for-

giving of someone who has hurt you, try *acting* forgiving. Many times right actions can lead to right feelings. Because God has forgiven all our sins, we should not withhold forgiveness from others. Realizing how completely Christ has forgiven us should produce a free and generous attitude of forgiveness toward others. When we don't forgive others, we are setting ourselves outside and above Christ's law of love. Those who are unwilling to forgive have not become one with Christ.

In Bible times, serious consequences came to those who could not pay their debts. A person lending money could seize the borrower who couldn't pay and force him or his family to work until the debt was paid. The debtor could also be thrown into prison, or his family could be sold into slavery to help pay off the debt.

July 4

Jesus' brothers ridicule him
John 7:1-9 *(Harmony 121)*

*A*fter this, Jesus stayed in Galilee, going from village to village. He wanted to stay out of Judea where the Jewish leaders were plotting his death. But soon it was time for the Festival of Shelters, and Jesus' brothers urged him to go to Judea for the celebration. "Go where your followers can see your miracles!" they scoffed. "You can't become a public figure if you hide like this! If you can do such wonderful things, prove it to the world!" For even his brothers didn't believe in him.

Jesus replied, "Now is not the right time for me to go. But you can go anytime, and it will make no difference. The world can't hate you, but it does hate me because I accuse it of sin and evil. You go on. I am not yet ready to go to this festival, because my time has not yet come." So Jesus remained in Galilee.

THE EVIDENCE
Jesus' brothers had a difficult time believing in him. Some of these brothers would eventually become leaders in the church (James, for example), but for several years they were embarrassed by Jesus. After Jesus died and rose again, they finally believed. Today we have every reason to believe because we have the full record of Jesus' miracles, death, and resurrection. We also have the evidence of what the gospel has done in people's lives through the centuries. We have no excuses.

The Festival of Shelters, also called the Feast of Tabernacles, is described in Leviticus 23:33ff. This event occurred in October, about six months after the Passover celebration. The feast commemorated the days when the Israelites wandered in the wilderness and lived in tents (Leviticus 23:43).

July 5

Jesus teaches about the cost of following him
Luke 9:51-56 *(Harmony 122a)*

*A*s the time drew near for his return to heaven, Jesus resolutely set out for Jerusalem. He sent messengers ahead to a Samaritan village to prepare for his arrival. But they were turned away. The people of the village refused to have anything to do with Jesus because he had resolved to go to Jerusalem. When James and John heard about it, they said to Jesus, "Lord, should we order down fire from heaven to burn them up?" But Jesus turned and rebuked them. So they went on to another village.

REVENGE
When James and John were rejected by the Samaritan village, they didn't want to stop at shaking the dust from their feet (9:5). They wanted to retaliate by calling down fire from heaven on the people as Elijah had done on the servants of a wicked king of Israel (2 Kings 1). When others reject or scorn us, we, too, may feel like retaliating. We must remember that judgment belongs to God, and we must not expect him to use his power to carry out our personal vendettas.

After Assyria invaded Israel, the northern kingdom, and resettled it with its own people (2 Kings 17:24-41), the mixed race that developed became known as the Samaritans. "Purebred" Jews hated these "half-breeds"; the Samaritans, in turn, hated the Jews.

July 6

Jesus teaches about the cost of following him
Luke 9:57-62 (also in Matthew 8:18-22) *(Harmony 122b)*

*A*s they were walking along someone said to Jesus, "I will follow you no matter where you go."

But Jesus replied, "Foxes have dens to live in, and birds have nests, but I, the Son of Man, have no home of my own, not even a place to lay my head."

He said to another person, "Come, be my disciple."

The man agreed, but he said, "Lord, first let me return home and bury my father."

Jesus replied, "Let those who are spiritually dead care for their own dead. Your duty is to go and preach the coming of the Kingdom of God."

Another said, "Yes, Lord, I will follow you, but first let me say good-bye to my family."

But Jesus told him, "Anyone who puts a hand to the plow and then looks back is not fit for the Kingdom of God."

CROSS AND CROWN

What does Jesus want from us? Total dedication, not halfhearted commitment. Following Jesus is not always easy or comfortable. Often it means great cost and sacrifice, with no earthly rewards or security. Jesus didn't have a place to call home. You may find that following Christ costs you popularity, friendships, leisure time, or treasured habits. But while the cost of following Christ is high, the value of being Christ's disciple is even higher. Discipleship is an investment that lasts for eternity and yields incredible rewards. We can't pick and choose among Jesus' ideas and follow him selectively; we have to accept the cross along with the crown, judgment as well as mercy. We must count the cost and be willing to abandon everything else that has given us security. Focusing on Jesus, we should allow nothing to distract us from the manner of living that he calls good and true.

Jesus was always direct with those who wanted to follow him. He made sure they counted the cost and set aside any conditions they might have for following him. As God's Son, Jesus did not hesitate to demand complete loyalty. Even family loyalty was not to take priority over the demands of obedience.

July 7

Jesus teaches openly at the Temple
John 7:10-13 *(Harmony 123a)*

*B*ut after his brothers had left for the festival, Jesus also went, though secretly, staying out of public view. The Jewish leaders tried to find him at the festival and kept asking if anyone had seen him. There was a lot of discussion about him among the crowds. Some said, "He's a wonderful man," while others said, "He's nothing but a fraud, deceiving the people." But no one had the courage to speak favorably about him in public, for they were afraid of getting in trouble with the Jewish leaders.

SPEAK UP

Jesus came with the greatest gift ever offered, so why did he often act secretly? The religious leaders hated him, and many would refuse his gift of salvation, no matter what he said or did. The more Jesus taught and worked publicly, the more these leaders would cause trouble for him and his followers. So it was necessary for Jesus to teach and work as quietly as possible.

Many people today have the privilege of teaching, preaching, and worshiping publicly with little persecution. These believers should be grateful and make the most of their opportunities to proclaim the gospel. Although many people talk about Christ in church, when it comes to making a public statement about their faith, they are often embarrassed. Jesus says that he will acknowledge us before God if we acknowledge him before others (Matthew 10:32). Be courageous! Speak up for Christ!

The religious leaders had a great deal of power over the common people. Apparently these leaders couldn't do much to Jesus at this time, but they threatened anyone who might publicly support him. Excommunication from the synagogue was one of the reprisals for believing in Jesus (9:22). To a Jew, this was a severe punishment.

July 8

Jesus teaches openly at the Temple
John 7:14-24 *(Harmony 123b)*

*T*hen, midway through the festival, Jesus went up to the Temple and began to teach. The Jewish leaders were surprised when they heard him. "How does he know so much when he hasn't studied everything we've studied?" they asked.

So Jesus told them, "I'm not teaching my own ideas, but those of God who sent me. Anyone who wants to do the will of God will know whether my teaching is from God or is merely my own. Those who present their own ideas are looking for praise for themselves, but those who seek to honor the one who sent them are good and genuine. None of you obeys the law of Moses! In fact, you are trying to kill me."

The crowd replied, "You're demon possessed! Who's trying to kill you?"

Jesus replied, "I worked on the Sabbath by healing a man, and you were offended. But you work on the Sabbath, too, when you obey Moses' law of circumcision. (Actually, this tradition of circumcision is older than the law of Moses; it goes back to Abraham.) For if the correct time for circumcising your son falls on the Sabbath, you go ahead and do it, so as not to break the law of Moses. So why should I be condemned for making a man completely well on the Sabbath? Think this through and you will see that I am right."

MORE THAN REQUIRED
The Pharisees spent their days trying to achieve holiness by keeping the meticulous rules that they had added to God's laws. Jesus' accusation that they didn't keep Moses' laws stung them deeply. In spite of their pompous pride in themselves and their rules, they did not even fulfill a legalistic religion, for they

were living far below what the law of Moses required. Their plot to commit murder was certainly against the law. Jesus' followers should do *more* than the moral law requires, not by adding to its requirements, but by going beyond and beneath the mere dos and don'ts of the law to the spirit of the law. This means being kind and forgiving, serving others, and showing love.

Have you ever listened to religious speakers and wondered if they were telling the truth? Test them: (1) Their words should agree with, not contradict, the Bible; (2) their words should point to God and his will, not to themselves.

July 9

Jesus teaches openly at the Temple
John 7:25-31 *(Harmony 123c)*

*S*ome of the people who lived there in Jerusalem said among themselves, "Isn't this the man they are trying to kill? But here he is, speaking in public, and they say nothing to him. Can it be that our leaders know that he really is the Messiah? But how could he be? For we know where this man comes from. When the Messiah comes, he will simply appear; no one will know where he comes from."

While Jesus was teaching in the Temple, he called out, "Yes, you know me, and you know where I come from. But I represent one you don't know, and he is true. I know him because I have come from him, and he sent me to you." Then the leaders tried to arrest him; but no one laid a hand on him, because his time had not yet come.

Many among the crowds at the Temple believed in him. "After all," they said, "would you expect the Messiah to do more miraculous signs than this man has done?"

NO NEUTRAL GROUND
Many consider neutrality to be a sign of maturity and objectivity. Maintaining a neutral position toward Christ may be popular, but it is dangerous. People stay undecided about Jesus under the pretense of not wanting to make a hasty or wrong judgment. But Jesus never allowed indecision. He confronted men and women with the unavoidable choice of belief or unbelief. Today those who remain undecided must understand that they remain, by that choice, in opposition to Christ. You can't sit on the fence; whose side are you on?

There was a popular tradition that the Messiah would simply appear. But those who believed this tradition were ignoring the Scriptures that clearly predicted the Messiah's birthplace (Micah 5:2).

Religious leaders attempt to arrest Jesus
John 7:32-44 *(Harmony 124a)*

*W*hen the Pharisees heard that the crowds were murmuring such things, they and the leading priests sent Temple guards to arrest Jesus. But Jesus told them, "I will be here a little longer. Then I will return to the one who sent me. You will search for me but not find me. And you won't be able to come where I am."

The Jewish leaders were puzzled by this statement. "Where is he planning to go?" they asked. "Maybe he is thinking of leaving the country and going to the Jews in other lands, or maybe even to the Gentiles! What does he mean when he says, 'You will search for me but not find me,' and 'You won't be able to come where I am'?"

On the last day, the climax of the festival, Jesus stood and shouted to the crowds, "If you are thirsty, come to me! If you believe in me, come and drink! For the Scriptures declare that rivers of living water will flow out from within." (When he said "living water," he was speaking of the Spirit, who would be given to everyone believing in him. But the Spirit had not yet been given, because Jesus had not yet entered into his glory.)

When the crowds heard him say this, some of them declared, "This man surely is the Prophet." Others said, "He is the Messiah." Still others said, "But he can't be! Will the Messiah come from Galilee? For the Scriptures clearly state that the Messiah will be born of the royal line of David, in Bethlehem, the village where King David was born." So the crowd was divided in their opinion about him. And some wanted him arrested, but no one touched him.

COME AND DRINK

Jesus used the term *living water* in 4:10 to indicate eternal life. Here he used the term to refer to the Holy Spirit. The two go together: When a person trusts Jesus as Savior, the Holy spirit is given as a guarantee of eternal life. Jesus' words, "come and drink," alluded to the theme of many Bible passages that talk about the Messiah's life-giving blessings (Isaiah 12:2-3; 44:3-4; 58:11). In promising to give the Holy Spirit to all who believed, Jesus was claiming to be the Messiah, for that was something only the Messiah could do. The Holy Spirit was first given to Jesus' followers at Pentecost (Acts 2) and is still given today to all who believe in Jesus as Savior. If you know Christ, you have the Holy Spirit living in you and can depend on him for power for living the Christian life.

Although the Romans ruled Palestine, they gave the Jewish religious leaders authority over minor civil and religious affairs. The religious leaders supervised their own Temple guards and gave the officers power to arrest anyone causing a disturbance or breaking any of their ceremonial laws.

Religious leaders attempt to arrest Jesus
John 7:45-52 *(Harmony 124b)*

*T*he Temple guards who had been sent to arrest him returned to the leading priests and Pharisees. "Why didn't you bring him in?" they demanded.

"We have never heard anyone talk like this!" the guards responded.

"Have you been led astray, too?" the Pharisees mocked. "Is there a single one of us rulers or Pharisees who believes in him? These ignorant crowds do, but what do they know about it? A curse on them anyway!"

Nicodemus, the leader who had met with Jesus earlier, then spoke up. "Is it legal to convict a man before he is given a hearing?" he asked.

They replied, "Are you from Galilee, too? Search the Scriptures and see for yourself—no prophet ever comes from Galilee!"

KEEPERS OF THE TRUTH
Nicodemus confronted the Pharisees with their failure to keep their own laws. The Pharisees were losing ground—the Temple guards came back impressed by Jesus (7:46), and one of the Pharisees' own, Nicodemus, was defending him. With their hypocritical motives being exposed and their prestige slowly eroding, they began to move to protect themselves. Pride would interfere with their ability to reason, and soon they would become obsessed with getting rid of Jesus just to save face. What was good and right no longer mattered. It is easy to think that we have the truth and that those who disagree with us do not have any truth at all. But God's truth is available to everyone. Don't copy the Pharisees' self-centered and narrow attitude.

Nicodemus was the Pharisee who visited Jesus at night (John 3). Apparently Nicodemus had become a secret believer. Most of the Pharisees hated Jesus and wanted to kill him, so Nicodemus risked his reputation and high position when he spoke up for Jesus.

Jesus forgives an adulterous woman
John 8:1-11 *(Harmony 125)*

*J*esus returned to the Mount of Olives, but early the next morning he was back again at the Temple. A crowd soon gathered, and he sat down and taught them. As he was speaking, the teachers of religious law and Pharisees brought a woman they had caught in the act of adultery.

They put her in front of the crowd.

"Teacher," they said to Jesus, "this woman was caught in the very act of adultery. The law of Moses says to stone her. What do you say?"

They were trying to trap him into saying something they could use against him, but Jesus stooped down and wrote in the dust with his finger. They kept demanding an answer, so he stood up again and said, "All right, stone her. But let those who have never sinned throw the first stones!" Then he stooped down again and wrote in the dust.

When the accusers heard this, they slipped away one by one, beginning with the oldest, until only Jesus was left in the middle of the crowd with the woman. Then Jesus stood up again and said to her, "Where are your accusers? Didn't even one of them condemn you?"

"No, Lord," she said.

And Jesus said, "Neither do I. Go and sin no more."

THE FIRST STONE

This is a significant statement about judging others. Because Jesus upheld the legal penalty for adultery, stoning, he could not be accused of being against the law. But by saying that only a sinless person could throw the first stone, he highlighted the importance of compassion and forgiveness. When others are caught in sin, are you quick to pass judgment? To do so is to act as though you have never sinned. It is God's role to judge, not ours. Our role is to show forgiveness and compassion. Jesus didn't condemn the woman accused of adultery, but neither did he ignore or condone her sin. He told the woman to leave her life of sin. Jesus stands ready to forgive any sin in your life, but confession and repentance mean a change of heart. With God's help we can accept Christ's forgiveness and stop our wrongdoing.

The Jewish leaders had already disregarded the law by arresting the woman without the man. The law required that both parties to adultery be stoned (Leviticus 20:10; Deuteronomy 22:22). The leaders were using the woman as a trap so they could trick Jesus.

July 13

Jesus is the light of the world
John 8:12 *(Harmony 126a)*

*J*esus said to the people, "I am the light of the world. If you follow me, you won't be stumbling through the darkness, because you will have the light that leads to life."

THE LIGHT OF THE WORLD

What does following Christ mean? As a soldier follows his captain, so we should follow Christ, our Commander. As a slave follows his master, so we should follow Christ, our Lord. As we follow the advice of a trusted counselor, so we should follow Jesus' commands to us in Scripture. As we follow the laws of our nation, so we should follow the laws of the Kingdom of Heaven. When we follow Jesus, the true light, we can avoid walking blindly and falling into sin. He lights the path ahead of us so we can see how to live. He removes the darkness of sin from our lives. Have you allowed the light of Christ to shine into your life? Let Christ guide your life, and you'll never need to stumble in darkness. Is he the light of *your* world?

Jesus was speaking in the part of the Temple where the offerings were put, where candles burned to symbolize the pillar of fire that led the people of Israel through the wilderness (Exodus 13:21-22). In this context, Jesus called himself the light of the world. The pillar of fire represented God's presence, protection, and guidance. Jesus brings God's presence, protection, and guidance.

July 14

Jesus is the light of the world
John 8:13-20 *(Harmony 126b)*

*T*he Pharisees replied, "You are making false claims about yourself!"

Jesus told them, "These claims are valid even though I make them about myself. For I know where I came from and where I am going, but you don't know this about me. You judge me with all your human limitations, but I am not judging anyone. And if I did, my judgment would be correct in every respect because I am not alone—I have with me the Father who sent me. Your own law says that if two people agree about something, their witness is accepted as fact. I am one witness, and my Father who sent me is the other."

"Where is your father?" they asked.

Jesus answered, "Since you don't know who I am, you don't know who my Father is. If you knew me, then you would know my Father, too." Jesus made these statements while he was teaching in the section of the Temple known as the Treasury. But he was not arrested, because his time had not yet come.

The Pharisees thought that Jesus was either a lunatic or a liar. Jesus provided them with a third alternative that he was the Son of God. Because most of the Pharisees refused to consider the third alternative, they never recognized him as Messiah and Lord. If you are seeking to know who Jesus is, do not close any door before looking through it honestly. Only with an open mind will you know the truth that he is Messiah and Lord.

The Pharisees argued that Jesus' claim was legally invalid because he had no other witnesses. Jesus responded that his confirming witness was God himself. Jesus and the Father made two witnesses, the number required by the law (Deuteronomy 19:15).

July 15

Jesus warns of coming judgment
John 8:21-29 *(Harmony 127)*

*L*ater Jesus said to them again, "I am going away. You will search for me and die in your sin. You cannot come where I am going."

The Jewish leaders asked, "Is he planning to commit suicide? What does he mean, 'You cannot come where I am going'?"

Then he said to them, "You are from below; I am from above. You are of this world; I am not. That is why I said that you will die in your sins; for unless you believe that I am who I say I am, you will die in your sins."

"Tell us who you are," they demanded.

Jesus replied, "I am the one I have always claimed to be. I have much to say about you and much to condemn, but I won't. For I say only what I have heard from the one who sent me, and he is true." But they still didn't understand that he was talking to them about his Father.

So Jesus said, "When you have lifted up the Son of Man on the cross, then you will realize that I am he and that I do nothing on my own, but I speak what the Father taught me. And the one who sent me is with me—he has not deserted me. For I always do those things that are pleasing to him."

WHAT DO YOU WANT?

Those questioning Jesus were convinced they understood God's plan. They thought they had a clear idea of exactly what kind of savior they needed, and Jesus did not fit that pattern. Are you trusting Jesus to be your Savior because he knows best, or are you reserving final judgment just in case a "better" option

If the Jewish religious leaders would not believe in Jesus while he was with them, they would run the risk of not having any further opportunity. They would die in their sin because they had rejected the only one who could save them.

comes along? Are you trusting God to graciously meet your needs even when you do not fully understand them, or are you clinging to the belief that you know best what God can do for you? Are you still shopping for a better offer? Only Jesus can give forgiveness and eternal life.

July 16

Jesus speaks about God's true children
John 8:30-33 *(Harmony 128a)*

*T*hen many who heard him say these things believed in him. Jesus said to the people who believed in him, "You are truly my disciples if you keep obeying my teachings. And you will know the truth, and the truth will set you free."

"But we are descendants of Abraham," they said. "We have never been slaves to anyone on earth. What do you mean, 'set free'?"

SET FREE
Sin has a way of enslaving us, controlling us, dominating us, and dictating our actions. Jesus can free us from this slavery that keeps us from becoming what God created us to be. If sin is restraining, mastering, or enslaving us, Jesus can break its power over our life. He frees us from the consequences of sin, from self-deception, and from deception by Satan. He shows us clearly the way to everlasting life with God. Thus, Jesus does not give us freedom to do what we want but freedom to follow God. As we seek to serve God, Jesus' perfect truth frees us to be all that God meant us to be.

To know the truth is to know God's revelation to people. That revelation is Jesus himself. Therefore, Jesus is the truth that makes us free (8:36). He is the source of truth, the perfect standard of what is right.

July 17

Jesus speaks about God's true children
John 8:34-47 *(Harmony 128b)*

*J*esus replied, "I assure you that everyone who sins is a slave of sin. A slave is not a permanent member of the family, but a son is part of the family forever. So if the Son sets you free, you will indeed be free. Yes, I realize that you are descendants of Abraham. And yet some of you are trying to kill me because my message does not find a place in your hearts. I am telling you what I saw when I was with my Father. But you are following the advice of your father."

"Our father is Abraham," they declared.

"No," Jesus replied, "for if you were children of Abraham, you would follow his good example. I told you the truth I heard from God, but you are trying to kill me. Abraham wouldn't do a thing like that. No, you are obeying your real father when you act that way."

They replied, "We were not born out of wedlock! Our true Father is God himself."

Jesus told them, "If God were your Father, you would love me, because I have come to you from God. I am not here on my own, but he sent me. Why can't you understand what I am saying? It is because you are unable to do so! For you are the children of your father the Devil, and you love to do the evil things he does. He was a murderer from the beginning and has always hated the truth. There is no truth in him. When he lies, it is consistent with his character; for he is a liar and the father of lies. So when I tell the truth, you just naturally don't believe me! Which of you can truthfully accuse me of sin? And since I am telling you the truth, why don't you believe me? Anyone whose Father is God listens gladly to the words of God. Since you don't, it proves you aren't God's children."

WHOSE CHILD?
Jesus made a distinction between hereditary children and *true* children. The religious leaders were hereditary children of Abraham (founder of the Jewish nation) and therefore claimed to be children of God. But their actions showed them to be true children of Satan, for they followed the advice of Satan. True children of Abraham (faithful followers of God) would not act as they did. Your church membership and family connections will not make you a true child of God. Your true father is the one you imitate and obey.

The attitudes and actions of these leaders clearly identified them as followers of Satan. They may not have been conscious of this, but their hatred of truth, their lies, and their murderous intentions indicated how much control the Devil had over them.

Jesus states he is eternal
John 8:48-59 *(Harmony 129)*

*T*he people retorted, "You Samaritan devil! Didn't we say all along that you were possessed by a demon?"

"No," Jesus said, "I have no demon in me. For I honor my Father—and you dishonor me. And though I have no wish to glorify myself, God wants to glorify me. Let him be the judge. I assure you, anyone who obeys my teaching will never die!"

The people said, "Now we know you are possessed by a demon. Even Abraham and the prophets died, but you say that those who obey your teaching will never die! Are you greater than our father Abraham, who died? Are you greater than the prophets, who died? Who do you think you are?"

Jesus answered, "If I am merely boasting about myself, it doesn't count. But it is my Father who says these glorious things about me. You say, 'He is our God,' but you do not even know him. I know him. If I said otherwise, I would be as great a liar as you! But it is true—I know him and obey him. Your ancestor Abraham rejoiced as he looked forward to my coming. He saw it and was glad."

The people said, "You aren't even fifty years old. How can you say you have seen Abraham?"

Jesus answered, "The truth is, I existed before Abraham was even born!" At that point they picked up stones to kill him. But Jesus hid himself from them and left the Temple.

THE TRUE SON OF GOD
This is one of the most powerful statements uttered by Jesus. When he said that he existed before Abraham was born, he undeniably proclaimed his divinity. This claim demands a response. It cannot be ignored. The Jewish leaders tried to stone Jesus for blasphemy because he claimed equality with God. But Jesus *is* God. How have you responded to Jesus, the Son of God?

In accordance with the law in Leviticus 24:16, the religious leaders were ready to stone Jesus for claiming to be God. They well understood what Jesus was claiming, and because they didn't believe him, they charged him with blasphemy.

Jesus sends out seventy messengers
Luke 10:1-16 *(Harmony 130)*

*T*he Lord now chose seventy-two other disciples and sent them on ahead in pairs to all the towns and villages he planned to visit. These were his instructions to them: "The harvest is so great, but the workers are so few. Pray to the Lord who is in charge of the harvest, and ask him to send out more workers for his fields. Go now, and remember that I am sending you out as lambs among wolves. Don't take along any money, or a traveler's bag, or even an extra pair of sandals. And don't stop to greet anyone on the road.

"Whenever you enter a home, give it your blessing. If those who live there are worthy, the blessing will stand; if they are not, the blessing will return to you. When you enter a town, don't move around from home to home. Stay in one place, eating and drinking what they provide you. Don't hesitate to accept hospitality, because those who work deserve their pay.

"If a town welcomes you, eat whatever is set before you and heal the sick. As you heal them, say, 'The Kingdom of God is near you now.' But if a town refuses to welcome you, go out into its streets and say, 'We wipe the dust of your town from our feet as a public announcement of your doom. And don't forget the Kingdom of God is near!' The truth is, even wicked Sodom will be better off than such a town on the judgment day.

"What horrors await you, Korazin and Bethsaida! For if the miracles I did in you had been done in wicked Tyre and Sidon, their people would have sat in deep repentance long ago, clothed in sackcloth and throwing ashes on their heads to show their remorse. Yes, Tyre and Sidon will be better off on the judgment day than you. And you people of Capernaum, will you be exalted to heaven? No, you will be brought down to the place of the dead."

Then he said to the disciples, "Anyone who accepts your message is also accepting me. And anyone who rejects you is rejecting me. And anyone who rejects me is rejecting God who sent me."

NO UNEMPLOYMENT

Far more than twelve people had been following Jesus. Here Jesus designated a group of seventy to prepare a number of towns for Jesus' later visit. Jesus was sending thirty-five teams of two to reach the multitudes. These teams were not to try to do the job without help; rather, they were to ask God for more workers. Some people, as soon as they

Jesus gave two rules for the disciples to follow as they traveled: They were to eat what was set before them—that is, they were to accept hospitality without being picky—and they were to heal the sick. Because of the healings, people would be willing to listen to the gospel.

understand the gospel, want to go to work immediately contacting unsaved people. This story suggests a different approach: Begin by mobilizing people to pray. And before praying for unsaved people, pray that other concerned disciples will join you in reaching out to them. In Christian service there is no unemployment. God has work enough for everyone. Don't just sit back and watch others work—look for ways to help with the harvest.

July 20

The seventy messengers return
Luke 10:17-20 *(Harmony 131a)*

When the seventy-two disciples returned, they joyfully reported to him, "Lord, even the demons obey us when we use your name!"

"Yes," he told them, "I saw Satan falling from heaven as a flash of lightning! And I have given you authority over all the power of the enemy, and you can walk among snakes and scorpions and crush them. Nothing will injure you. But don't rejoice just because evil spirits obey you; rejoice because your names are registered as citizens of heaven."

CITIZENS
The disciples had seen tremendous results as they ministered in Jesus' name and with his authority. They were elated by the victories they had witnessed, and Jesus shared their enthusiasm. He helped them get their priorities right, however, by reminding them of their most important victory—that their names were written in heaven. This honor was more important than any of their accomplishments. As we see God's wonders at work in and through us, we should not lose sight of the greatest wonder of all—our heavenly citizenship.

Some interpreters believe this verse refers to Satan's original fall and explain that Satan's pride led to all the evil we see on earth today. To Jesus' disciples, who were thrilled with their power over evil spirits ("snakes and scorpions"), he may have been giving this stern warning: "Yours is the kind of pride that led to Satan's downfall. Be careful!"

The seventy messengers return
Luke 10:21-24 *(Harmony 131b)*

*T*hen Jesus was filled with the joy of the Holy Spirit and said, "O Father, Lord of heaven and earth, thank you for hiding the truth from those who think themselves so wise and clever, and for revealing it to the childlike. Yes, Father, it pleased you to do it this way.

"My Father has given me authority over everything. No one really knows the Son except the Father, and no one really knows the Father except the Son and those to whom the Son chooses to reveal him."

Then when they were alone, he turned to the disciples and said, "How privileged you are to see what you have seen. I tell you, many prophets and kings have longed to see and hear what you have seen and heard, but they could not."

EQUALLY AVAILABLE

Jesus thanked God that spiritual truth was for everyone and not just for the elite. Many of life's rewards seem to go to the intelligent, the rich, the good-looking, or the powerful, but the Kingdom of God is equally available to all, regardless of position or abilities. We come to Jesus, not through strength or brains, but through childlike trust. Jesus is not opposed to engaging in scholarly pursuits; he is opposed to spiritual pride (being wise in one's own eyes). Christ's mission was to reveal God the Father to people. His words brought difficult ideas down to earth. He explained God's love through parables, teachings, and, most of all, his life. By examining Jesus' actions, principles, and attitudes, we can understand God more clearly. Join Jesus in thanking God that we all have equal access to him. Trust in God's grace, not in your personal qualifications, for your citizenship in the Kingdom.

Old Testament men of God such as David and the prophet Isaiah made many God-inspired predictions that Jesus fulfilled. As Peter later wrote, these prophets wondered what their words meant and when they would be fulfilled (1 Peter 1:10-13). In Jesus' words, they "longed to see and hear what you have seen and heard"—the coming of God's Kingdom.

July 22

Jesus tells the parable of the Good Samaritan
Luke 10:25-28 *(Harmony 132a)*

*O*ne day an expert in religious law stood up to test Jesus by asking him this question: "Teacher, what must I do to receive eternal life?"

Jesus replied, "What does the law of Moses say? How do you read it?"

The man answered, "'You must love the Lord your God with all your heart, all your soul, all your strength, and all your mind.' And, 'Love your neighbor as yourself.'"

NOT SO DIFFERENT

Jesus would answer the lawyer's question by telling the parable of the Good Samaritan. There was deep hatred between Jews and Samaritans. The Jews saw themselves as pure descendants of Abraham, while the Samaritans were a mixed race produced when Jews from the northern kingdom intermarried with other peoples after Israel's exile. To this lawyer, the person least likely to act correctly would be the Samaritan. In fact, he could not bear to say *Samaritan* in answer to Jesus' question. The lawyer's attitude betrayed his lack of the very thing that he had earlier said the law commanded—love. In our churches today, it's our natural inclination to feel uncomfortable around people who are different from us and to gravitate toward those who are similar to us. But when we allow our differences to separate us from our fellow believers, we are disregarding clear biblical teaching. Make a point to seek out and appreciate people who are not just like you and your friends. You may find that you have a lot in common with them.

This lawyer was quoting Deuteronomy 6:5 and Leviticus 19:18. He correctly understood that the law demanded total devotion to God and love for one's neighbor.

July 23

Jesus tells the parable of the Good Samaritan
Luke 10:29-37 *(Harmony 132b)*

*R*ight!" Jesus told him. "Do this and you will live!"

The man wanted to justify his actions, so he asked Jesus, "And who is my neighbor?"

Jesus replied with an illustration: "A Jewish man was traveling on a trip from Jerusalem to Jericho, and he was attacked by bandits. They stripped him of his clothes and money, beat him up, and left him half dead beside the road.

"By chance a Jewish priest came along; but when he saw the man lying there, he crossed to the other side of the road and passed him by. A Temple assistant walked over and looked at him lying there, but he also passed by on the other side.

"Then a despised Samaritan came along, and when he saw the man, he felt deep pity. Kneeling beside him, the Samaritan soothed his wounds with medicine and bandaged them. Then he put the man on his own donkey and took him to an inn, where he took care of him. The next day he handed the innkeeper two pieces of silver and told him to take care of the man. 'If his bill runs higher than that,' he said, 'I'll pay the difference the next time I am here.'

"Now which of these three would you say was a neighbor to the man who was attacked by bandits?" Jesus asked.

The man replied, "The one who showed him mercy."

Then Jesus said, "Yes, now go and do the same."

GOOD NEIGHBOR

The lawyer treated the wounded man as a topic for discussion; the thieves, as an object to exploit; the priest, as a problem to avoid; and the Levite, as an object of curiosity. Only the Samaritan treated him as a person to love. From the parable we learn three principles about loving our neighbor: (1) Lack of love is often easy to justify, even though it is never right; (2) our neighbor is anyone of any race, creed, or social background who is in need; and (3) love means acting to meet the person's need. Wherever you live there are needy people close by. There is no good reason for refusing to help.

That Jesus would use as an example the road between Jerusalem and Jericho on which the man was attacked would have rung true to his audience. This road was rocky, surrounded with crags to hide bandits, and had a reputation for being dangerous to lone travelers.

July 24

Jesus visits Mary and Martha
Luke 10:38-42 *(Harmony 133)*

*A*s Jesus and the disciples continued on their way to Jerusalem, they came to a village where a woman named Martha welcomed them into her home. Her sister, Mary, sat at the Lord's feet, listening to what he taught. But Martha was worrying over the big dinner she was preparing. She came to Jesus and said, "Lord, doesn't it seem unfair to you that my sister just sits here while I do all the work? Tell her to come and help me."

But the Lord said to her, "My dear Martha, you are so upset over all these details! There is really only one thing worth being concerned about. Mary has discovered it—and I won't take it away from her."

SERVING WHOM?

Mary and Martha both loved Jesus. On this occasion they were both serving him. But Martha thought Mary's style of serving was inferior to hers. She didn't realize that in her desire to serve, she was actually neglecting her guest. Jesus did not blame Martha for being concerned about preparing dinner. He was only asking her to set priorities. It is possible for service to Christ to degenerate into mere busywork that is no longer full of devotion to God. Are you so busy doing things *for* Jesus that you're not spending any time *with* him? Don't let your service become self-serving.

After returning to Jerusalem for the Festival of Shelters (John 7:2), Jesus visited his friends Mary, Martha, and Lazarus, who lived in the tiny village of Bethany, just outside Jerusalem on the Mount of Olives.

July 25

Jesus teaches his disciples about prayer
Luke 11:1-4 *(Harmony 134a)*

*O*nce when Jesus had been out praying, one of his disciples came to him as he finished and said, "Lord, teach us to pray, just as John taught his disciples."

He said, "This is how you should pray: "Father, may your name be honored. May your Kingdom come soon. Give us our food day by day. And forgive us our sins just as we forgive those who have sinned against us. And don't let us yield to temptation."

PRAISING, FORGIVING

Notice the order in this prayer. First Jesus praised God; then he made his requests. Praising God first puts us in the right frame of mind to tell him about our needs. Too often our prayers are more like shopping lists than conversations. When Jesus taught his disciples to pray, he made forgiveness the cornerstone of their relationship with God. God has forgiven our sins; we must now forgive those who have wronged us. To remain unforgiving shows we have not understood that we ourselves deeply need to be forgiven. Think of

God's provision is daily, not all at once. We cannot store it up and then cut off communication with God. And we dare not be self-satisfied. If you are running low on strength, consider how long you have been away from the Source.

some people who have wronged you. Have you forgiven them? How will God deal with you if he treats you as you treat others?

July 26

Jesus teaches his disciples about prayer
Luke 11:5-10 *(Harmony 134b)*

*T*hen, teaching them more about prayer, he used this illustration: "Suppose you went to a friend's house at midnight, wanting to borrow three loaves of bread. You would say to him, 'A friend of mine has just arrived for a visit, and I have nothing for him to eat.' He would call out from his bedroom, 'Don't bother me. The door is locked for the night, and we are all in bed. I can't help you this time.' But I tell you this—though he won't do it as a friend, if you keep knocking long enough, he will get up and give you what you want so his reputation won't be damaged.

"And so I tell you, keep on asking, and you will be given what you ask for. Keep on looking, and you will find. Keep on knocking, and the door will be opened. For everyone who asks, receives. Everyone who seeks, finds. And the door is opened to everyone who knocks."

PERSISTENCE

Have you ever grown tired of praying for something or someone? Our vigilance is an expression of our faith that God answers our prayers. Faith shouldn't die if the answers come slowly, for the delay may be God's way of working his will in our lives. When you feel tired of praying, know that God is present, always listening, always answering—maybe not in ways you had hoped but in ways that he knows are best. Persistence, or boldness, in prayer overcomes our insensitivity, not God's. To practice persistence does more to change our heart and mind than his, and it helps us understand and express the intensity of our need. Persistence in prayer helps us recognize God's work. Are you waiting for God's timing? Trust his judgment for your best interests.

Everyone who asks, receives if their requests are made in faith. To ask in faith is to ask with confidence that God will align our desires with his purposes.

July 27

Jesus teaches his disciples about prayer
Luke 11:11-13 *(Harmony 134c)*

*Y*ou fathers—if your children ask for a fish, do you give them a snake instead? Or if they ask for an egg, do you give them a scorpion? Of course not! If you sinful people know how to give good gifts to your children, how much more will your heavenly Father give the Holy Spirit to those who ask him."

GOD'S GIFT

Even though good fathers make mistakes, they treat their children well. How much better our perfect heavenly Father treats his children! The most important gift he could ever give us is the Holy Spirit (Acts 2:1-4), whom he promised to give all believers after his death, resurrection, and return to heaven (John 15:26). At Pentecost (Acts 2:4), the Holy Spirit was made available to all who believe in Jesus. We receive the Holy Spirit when we receive Jesus Christ. Pray with an attitude of positive expectancy. Your heavenly Father wants the very best for you.

God is the perfect Father. Although some people's fathers may not have been very good examples, God can be depended on to always do what is best for his children.

July 28

Jesus answers hostile accusations
Luke 11:14-26 *(Harmony 135a)*

*O*ne day Jesus cast a demon out of a man who couldn't speak, and the man's voice returned to him. The crowd was amazed, but some said, "No wonder he can cast out demons. He gets his power from Satan, the prince of demons!" Trying to test Jesus, others asked for a miraculous sign from heaven to see if he was from God.

He knew their thoughts, so he said, "Any kingdom at war with itself is doomed. A divided home is also doomed. You say I am empowered by the prince of demons. But if Satan is fighting against himself by empowering me to cast out his demons, how can his kingdom survive? And if I am empowered by the prince of demons, what about your own followers? They cast out demons, too, so they will judge you for what you have said. But if I am casting out demons by the power of God, then the Kingdom of God has arrived among you. For when Satan, who is completely armed, guards his palace, it is safe—until someone who is stronger attacks and overpowers him, strips him of his weapons, and carries off his belongings.

"Anyone who isn't helping me opposes me, and anyone who isn't working with me is actually working against me.

"When an evil spirit leaves a person, it goes into the desert, searching for rest. But when it finds none, it says, 'I will return to the person I came from.' So it returns and finds that its former home is all swept and clean. Then the spirit finds seven other spirits more evil than itself, and they all enter the person and live there. And so that person is worse off than before."

EMPTIED, FILLED

Jesus was illustrating an unfortunate human tendency—our desire to reform often does not last long. In Israel's history, almost as soon as a good king would pull down idols, a bad king would set them up again. It is not enough to be emptied of evil; we must then be filled with the power of the Holy Spirit to accomplish God's new purpose in our lives. If we are controlled by the Holy Spirit, we will produce the kind of fruit that pleases God (as described in Galatians 5:22-23). We do not need to fear the Spirit's control. He does not possess us against our will or treat us as robots.

Regardless of how great Satan's power is, Jesus is stronger still. Satan, who had controlled the kingdom of this world for thousands of years, was now being controlled and overpowered by Jesus and the Kingdom of Heaven. He will bind Satan and dispose of him for eternity (see Revelation 20:2, 10).

July 29

Jesus answers hostile accusations
Luke 11:27-28 *(Harmony 135b)*

*A*s he was speaking, a woman in the crowd called out, "God bless your mother—the womb from which you came, and the breasts that nursed you!"

He replied, "But even more blessed are all who hear the word of God and put it into practice."

OBEY FIRST

Jesus was speaking to people who put extremely high value on family ties. Their genealogies were important guarantees that they were part of God's chosen people. A

This woman was complimenting Jesus by complimenting his mother. Jesus, however, implied that he wanted obedience far more than compliments.

man's value came from his ancestors, and a woman's value came from the sons she bore. Jesus' response to the woman meant that a person's obedience to God is more important than his or her place on the family tree. Consistent obedience is even more important than the honor of bearing a respected son. How do you rate your obedience? God is more than willing to give you the power to obey him with all your heart.

July 30

Jesus warns against unbelief
Luke 11:29-32 *(Harmony 136)*

*A*s the crowd pressed in on Jesus, he said, "These are evil times, and this evil generation keeps asking me to show them a miraculous sign. But the only sign I will give them is the sign of the prophet Jonah. What happened to him was a sign to the people of Nineveh that God had sent him. What happens to me will be a sign that God has sent me, the Son of Man, to these people.

"The queen of Sheba will rise up against this generation on judgment day and condemn it, because she came from a distant land to hear the wisdom of Solomon. And now someone greater than Solomon is here—and you refuse to listen to him. The people of Nineveh, too, will rise up against this generation on judgment day and condemn it, because they repented at the preaching of Jonah. And now someone greater than Jonah is here—and you refuse to repent.

LIABLE TO JUDGMENT

The people of Nineveh, the capital of Assyria, repented when Jonah preached to them—and Jonah did not even care about them. The heathen queen of Sheba praised the God of Israel when she heard Solomon's wisdom, and Solomon was full of faults. By contrast, Jesus, the perfect Son of God, had come to people that he loved dearly—but they rejected him. Thus, God's chosen people made themselves more liable to judgment than either a notoriously wicked nation or a powerful heathen queen. The Ninevites and the queen of Sheba had turned to God with far less evidence than Jesus was giving his listeners—and far less than we have today. We have eyewitness reports of the risen Jesus, the continuing power of the Holy Spirit unleashed at Pentecost, easy access to the Bible, and knowledge of two thousand years of

God had sent Jonah to announce judgment to the Gentiles (non-Jews). Jesus was affirming that he, too, had been sent by God. Matthew 12:40 adds another piece of evidence: Jesus would die and then rise after three days, just as Jonah was in the belly of the great fish for three days and was rescued.

Christ's acts through his church. With the knowledge and insight available to us, our response to Christ ought to be even more complete and wholehearted. What spiritual resources do you have? How do you use them to increase your knowledge of Christ?

July 31

Jesus teaches about the light within
Luke 11:33-36 *(Harmony 137)*

*N*o one lights a lamp and then hides it or puts it under a basket. Instead, it is put on a lampstand to give light to all who enter the room. Your eye is a lamp for your body. A pure eye lets sunshine into your soul. But an evil eye shuts out the light and plunges you into darkness. Make sure that the light you think you have is not really darkness. If you are filled with light, with no dark corners, then your whole life will be radiant, as though a floodlight is shining on you."

SEEING THE LIGHT
The lamp is Christ; the eye represents spiritual understanding and insight. A lustful eye is less sensitive and can blot out the light of Christ's presence. If you have a hard time seeing God at work in the world and in your life, check your vision. Are any sinful desires blinding you to Christ? If so, what can you do? Our world is filled with impurity. We can stay pure in an impure environment by reading God's Word and doing what it says (Psalm 119:9).

Lust is more than inappropriate sexual desire. It can be an unnatural or greedy desire for anything (such as sports, knowledge, possessions, or power).

August 1

Jesus criticizes the religious leaders
Luke 11:37-44 *(Harmony 138a)*

As Jesus was speaking, one of the Pharisees invited him home for a meal. So he went in and took his place at the table. His host was amazed to see that he sat down to eat without first performing the ceremonial washing required by Jewish custom. Then the Lord said to him, "You Pharisees are so careful to clean the outside of the cup and the dish, but inside you are still filthy—full of greed and wickedness! Fools! Didn't God make the inside as well as the outside? So give to the needy what you greedily possess, and you will be clean all over.

"But how terrible it will be for you Pharisees! For you are careful to tithe even the tiniest part of your income, but you completely forget about justice and the love of God. You should tithe, yes, but you should not leave undone the more important things.

"How terrible it will be for you Pharisees! For how you love the seats of honor in the synagogues and the respectful greetings from everyone as you walk through the markets! Yes, how terrible it will be for you. For you are like hidden graves in a field. People walk over them without knowing the corruption they are stepping on."

GENEROSITY

The Pharisees loved to think of themselves as "clean," but their stinginess toward God and the poor proved that they were not as clean as they thought. How do you use the resources God has entrusted to you? Are you generous in meeting the needs around you? Your generosity reveals much about the purity of your heart. It is easy to rationalize not helping others because we have already given to the church, but a person who follows Jesus should give to those in need. While tithing is important to the life of the church, we also need to be compassionate. Where we can help, we should help.

This washing was done not for health reasons, but as a symbol of washing away any contamination from touching anything unclean. Not only did the Pharisees make a public show of their washing, but they also commanded everyone else to follow a practice originally intended only for the priests.

August 2

Jesus criticizes the religious leaders
Luke 11:45-54 *(Harmony 138b)*

*T*eacher," said an expert in religious law, "you have insulted us, too, in what you just said."

"Yes," said Jesus, "how terrible it will be for you experts in religious law! For you crush people beneath impossible religious demands, and you never lift a finger to help ease the burden. How terrible it will be for you! For you build tombs for the very prophets your ancestors killed long ago. Murderers! You agree with your ancestors that what they did was right. You would have done the same yourselves. This is what God in his wisdom said about you: 'I will send prophets and apostles to them, and they will kill some and persecute the others.'

"And you of this generation will be held responsible for the murder of all God's prophets from the creation of the world—from the murder of Abel to the murder of Zechariah, who was killed between the altar and the sanctuary. Yes, it will surely be charged against you.

"How terrible it will be for you experts in religious law! For you hide the key to knowledge from the people. You don't enter the Kingdom yourselves, and you prevent others from entering."

As Jesus finished speaking, the Pharisees and teachers of religious law were furious. From that time on they grilled him with many hostile questions, trying to trap him into saying something they could use against him.

TRULY CLEAN

Jesus criticized the Pharisees and the teachers of religious law harshly because they (1) cleaned their outsides but not their insides, (2) remembered to give a tenth of even their garden herbs, but neglected justice, (3) loved praise and attention, (4) loaded people down with burdensome religious demands, (5) would not accept the truth about Jesus, and (6) prevented others from believing the truth as well. They went wrong by focusing on outward appearances and ignoring the inner condition of their hearts. We do the same when our service comes from a desire to be seen rather than from a pure heart and out of a love for others. People may sometimes be fooled, but God isn't. Don't be a Christian on the outside only. Bring your inner life under God's control, and your outer life will naturally reflect him.

God's prophets have been persecuted and murdered throughout history. But this generation was rejecting more than a human prophet—they were rejecting God himself—the one to whom all their history and prophecy were pointing.

August 3

Jesus speaks against hypocrisy
Luke 12:1-3 *(Harmony 139a)*

*M*eanwhile, the crowds grew until thousands were milling about and crushing each other. Jesus turned first to his disciples and warned them, "Beware of the yeast of the Pharisees—beware of their hypocrisy. The time is coming when everything will be revealed; all that is secret will be made public. Whatever you have said in the dark will be heard in the light, and what you have whispered behind closed doors will be shouted from the housetops for all to hear!"

KEEPING UP APPEARANCES
As Jesus watched the huge crowds waiting to hear him, he warned his disciples against hypocrisy—trying to appear good when one's heart is far from God. The Pharisees could not keep their attitudes hidden forever. Their selfishness would act like yeast, and soon they would expose themselves for what they really were—power-hungry impostors, not devoted religious leaders. It is easy to be angry at the blatant hypocrisy of the Pharisees, but each of us must resist the temptation to settle for the appearance of respectability when our heart is far from God.

The Pharisees' hypocrisy was evidenced by the burdens they added to God's law. To the commandment to remember the Sabbath (Exodus 20:8), they had added instructions regarding how far a person could walk on the Sabbath. Healing a person was considered unlawful work on the Sabbath, although rescuing a trapped animal was permitted. No wonder Jesus condemned their additions to the law.

August 4

Jesus speaks against hypocrisy
Luke 12:4-7 *(Harmony 139b)*

*D*ear friends, don't be afraid of those who want to kill you. They can only kill the body; they cannot do any more to you. But I'll tell you whom to fear. Fear God, who has the power to kill people and then throw them into hell.

"What is the price of five sparrows? A couple of pennies? Yet God does not forget a single one of them. And the very hairs on your head are all numbered. So don't be afraid; you are more valuable to him than a whole flock of sparrows."

FEAR?

Fear of opposition or ridicule can weaken our witness for Christ. Often we cling to peace and comfort, even at the cost of our walk with God. Jesus reminds us here that we should fear God, who controls eternity, and not mere temporal consequences. Our true value is God's estimate of our worth, not our peers'. Other people evaluate and categorize us according to how we perform, what we achieve, and how we look. But God cares for us, as he does for all of his creatures, because we belong to him. So we can face life without fear.

To "fear" God means to honor and respect him as the almighty, sovereign God, the ruler of the universe. We don't have to be afraid and run from him, because he loves us. But we must submit to his authority and obey him.

August 5

Jesus speaks against hypocrisy
Luke 12:8-12 *(Harmony 139c)*

*A*nd I assure you of this: If anyone acknowledges me publicly here on earth, I, the Son of Man, will openly acknowledge that person in the presence of God's angels. But if anyone denies me here on earth, I will deny that person before God's angels. Yet those who speak against the Son of Man may be forgiven, but anyone who speaks blasphemies against the Holy Spirit will never be forgiven.

"And when you are brought to trial in the synagogues and before rulers and authorities, don't worry about what to say in your defense, for the Holy Spirit will teach you what needs to be said even as you are standing there."

DENY OR CONFESS?

We deny Jesus when we (1) hope no one will think we are Christians, (2) decide *not* to speak up for what is right, (3) are silent about our relationship with God, (4) blend into society, (5) accept our culture's non-Christian values. By contrast, we confess him when we (1) live moral, upright, Christ-honoring lives, (2) look for opportunities to share our faith with others, (3) help others in need, (4) take a stand for justice, (5) love others, (6) acknowledge our loyalty to Christ, (7) use our lives and resources to carry out his desires rather than our own.

Jesus said that blasphemy against the Holy Spirit is unforgivable. It involves attributing to Satan the work that the Holy Spirit accomplishes; thus, it is deliberate and ongoing rejection of the Holy Spirit's work and even of God himself.

August 6

Jesus tells the parable of the rich fool
Luke 12:13-21 *(Harmony 140)*

*T*hen someone called from the crowd, "Teacher, please tell my brother to divide our father's estate with me."

Jesus replied, "Friend, who made me a judge over you to decide such things as that?" Then he said, "Beware! Don't be greedy for what you don't have. Real life is not measured by how much we own."

And he gave an illustration: "A rich man had a fertile farm that produced fine crops. In fact, his barns were full to overflowing. So he said, 'I know! I'll tear down my barns and build bigger ones. Then I'll have room enough to store everything. And I'll sit back and say to myself, My friend, you have enough stored away for years to come. Now take it easy! Eat, drink, and be merry!'

"But God said to him, 'You fool! You will die this very night. Then who will get it all?'

"Yes, a person is a fool to store up earthly wealth but not have a rich relationship with God."

THE GOOD LIFE

Jesus is pointing to a higher issue—a correct attitude toward the accumulation of wealth. Life is more than material goods; far more important is our relationship with God. Jesus says that the good life has nothing to do with being wealthy, so be on guard against greed (desire for what we don't have). This is the exact opposite of what society usually says.

The rich man in Jesus' story died before he could begin to use what was stored in his big barns. Planning for retirement—preparing for life before death—is wise, but neglecting life after death is disastrous.

Advertisers spend millions of dollars to entice us to think that if we buy more and more of their products, we will be happier, more fulfilled, more comfortable. How do you respond to the constant pressure to buy? Learn to tune out expensive enticements and concentrate instead on the truly good life—living in a relationship with God and doing his work.

August 7

Jesus warns about worry
Luke 12:22-31 *(Harmony 141a)*

*T*hen turning to his disciples, Jesus said, "So I tell you, don't worry about everyday life—whether you have enough food to eat or clothes to wear. For life consists of far more than food and clothing. Look at the ravens. They don't need to plant or harvest or put food in barns because God feeds them. And you are far more valuable to him than any birds! Can all your worries add a single moment to your life? Of course not! And if worry can't do little things like that, what's the use of worrying over bigger things?

"Look at the lilies and how they grow. They don't work or make their clothing, yet Solomon in all his glory was not dressed as beautifully as they are. And if God cares so wonderfully for flowers that are here today and gone tomorrow, won't he more surely care for you? You have so little faith! And don't worry about food—what to eat and drink. Don't worry whether God will provide it for you. These things dominate the thoughts of most people, but your Father already knows your needs. He will give you all you need from day to day if you make the Kingdom of God your primary concern.

AT THE CENTER
Seeking the Kingdom of God means making Jesus the Lord and King of your life. He must control every area—your work, play, plans, relationships. Is the Kingdom only one of your many concerns, or is it central to all you do? Are you holding back any areas of your life from God's control? As Lord and Creator, he wants to help provide what you need as well as guide how you use what he provides.

Worry is pointless because it can't meet any of our needs; worry is foolish because the Creator of the universe loves us and knows what we need. He promises to meet all our real needs, but not necessarily all our desires.

August 8

Jesus warns about worry
Luke 12:32-34 *(Harmony 141b)*

*S*o don't be afraid, little flock. For it gives your Father great happiness to give you the Kingdom.

"Sell what you have and give to those in need. This will store up treasure for you in heaven! And the purses of heaven have no holes in them. Your treasure will be safe—no thief can steal it and no moth can destroy it. Wherever your treasure is, there your heart and thoughts will also be."

TREASURE HUNT

Money seen as an end in itself quickly traps us and cuts us off from both God and the needy. The key to using money wisely is to see how much we can use for God's purposes, not how much we can accumulate for ourselves. Does God's love touch your wallet? Does your money free you to help others? Where

God does not command all believers to sell everything they have. What he wants is believers who hold their possessions loosely, willing to sell or give away in order to help someone else.

do you put your time, money, and energy? What do you think about most? Consider how you should change the way you use your resources in order to reflect Kingdom values more accurately.

August 9

Jesus warns about preparing for his coming
Luke 12:35-40 *(Harmony 142a)*

*B*e dressed for service and well prepared, as though you were waiting for your master to return from the wedding feast. Then you will be ready to open the door and let him in the moment he arrives and knocks. There will be special favor for those who are ready and waiting for his return. I tell you, he himself will seat them, put on an apron, and serve them as they sit and eat! He may come in the middle of the night or just before dawn. But whenever he comes, there will be special favor for his servants who are ready!

"Know this: A homeowner who knew exactly when a burglar was coming would not permit the house to be broken into. You must be ready all the time, for the Son of Man will come when least expected."

GETTING READY

Christ's return at an unexpected time is not a trap, a trick by which God hopes to catch us off guard. In fact, God is delaying his return so more people will have the opportunity to follow him (see 2 Peter 3:9). Now is the time to live out our beliefs and to reflect God's love as we relate to others.

Jesus repeatedly said that he would leave this world but would return at some future time (see Matthew 24; 25; John 14:1-3). He also said that a Kingdom is being prepared for his followers.

People who are ready for their Lord's return are (1) not hypocritical but sincere (12:1); (2) not fearful but ready to witness (12:4-9); (3) not worried but trusting (12:25-26); (4) not greedy but generous (12:34); (5) not lazy but diligent (12:37). May your life be more like Christ's so that when he comes, you will be ready to greet him joyfully.

August 10

Jesus warns about preparing for his coming
Luke 12:41-48 *(Harmony 142b)*

*P*eter asked, "Lord, is this illustration just for us or for everyone?" And the Lord replied, "I'm talking to any faithful, sensible servant to whom the master gives the responsibility of managing his household and feeding his family. If the master returns and finds that the servant has done a good job, there will be a reward. I assure you, the master will put that servant in charge of all he owns. But if the servant thinks, 'My master won't be back for a while,' and begins oppressing the other servants, partying, and getting drunk—well, the master will return unannounced and unexpected. He will tear the servant apart and banish him with the unfaithful. The servant will be severely punished, for though he knew his duty, he refused to do it.

"But people who are not aware that they are doing wrong will be punished only lightly. Much is required from those to whom much is given, and much more is required from those to whom much more is given."

FUTURE REWARD
Jesus promises a reward for those who have been faithful to him. While we sometimes experience immediate and material rewards for our obedience to God, this is not always the case. If it were so, we would be tempted to boast about our achievements and do good only for what we get. Jesus said that if we look for rewards now, we will lose them later (see Mark 8:36). Our heavenly rewards will be the most accurate reflection of what we have done on earth, and they will be far greater than we can imagine.

Watchful and faithful leaders will be given increased opportunities and responsibilities. The more resources, talents, and understanding we have, the more we are responsible to use them effectively. God will not hold us responsible for gifts he has not given us, but all of us have been given gifts and enough duties to keep us busy until Jesus comes.

August 11

Jesus warns about coming division
Luke 12:49-53 *(Harmony 143)*

I have come to bring fire to the earth, and I wish that my task were already completed! There is a terrible baptism ahead of me, and I am under a heavy burden until it is accomplished. Do you think I have come to bring peace to the earth? No, I have come to bring strife and division! From now on families will be split apart, three in favor of me, and two against—or the other way around. There will be a division between father and son, mother and daughter, mother-in-law and daughter-in-law."

TAKING A RISK

By these strange and unsettling words, Jesus revealed that his claims would result in conflict. They demand a personal response, so families may be torn apart when some choose to follow him and others refuse. There is no middle ground with Jesus. A decision must be made to trust Jesus as your Savior and commit your life to him, which may result in severing relationships. Are you willing to risk your family's disapproval in order to gain eternal life?

The "baptism" to which Jesus referred was his coming crucifixion. Jesus was dreading the physical pain, of course, but even worse would be the spiritual pain of complete separation from God that would accompany his death for the sins of the world.

August 12

Jesus warns about the future crisis
Luke 12:54-59 *(Harmony 144)*

T hen Jesus turned to the crowd and said, "When you see clouds beginning to form in the west, you say, 'Here comes a shower.' And you are right. When the south wind blows, you say, 'Today will be a scorcher.' And it is. You hypocrites! You know how to interpret the appearance of the earth and the sky, but you can't interpret these present times.

"Why can't you decide for yourselves what is right? If you are on the way to court and you meet your accuser, try to settle the matter before it reaches the judge, or you may be sentenced and handed over to an officer and thrown in jail. And if that happens, you won't be free again until you have paid the last penny."

KINGDOM SIGNS

Jesus was announcing the coming of God's Kingdom and warning his listeners of its importance. Like a rainstorm on a sunny day, there were signs that the Kingdom would soon arrive. But Jesus' hearers, though skilled at interpreting weather signs, were intentionally ignoring the signs of the times. Jesus' question could be asked of many today: "Why can't you decide for yourselves what is right?" Have you taken Jesus at his word? See for yourself the truth of his words.

For most of recorded history, the world's principal occupation was farming. The farmer depended directly on the weather for his livelihood. He needed just the right amounts of sun and rain—not too much, not too little—to make his living, and he grew skilled at interpreting natural signs.

August 13

Jesus calls the people to repent
Luke 13:1-5 *(Harmony 145a)*

*A*bout this time Jesus was informed that Pilate had murdered some people from Galilee as they were sacrificing at the Temple in Jerusalem. "Do you think those Galileans were worse sinners than other people from Galilee?" he asked. "Is that why they suffered? Not at all! And you will also perish unless you turn from your evil ways and turn to God. And what about the eighteen men who died when the Tower of Siloam fell on them? Were they the worst sinners in Jerusalem? No, and I tell you again that unless you repent, you will also perish."

TOUGH QUESTIONS

Pilate may have killed the Galileans because he thought they were rebelling against Rome; those killed by the Tower of Siloam may have been working for the Romans on an aqueduct there. The Pharisees, who were opposed to using force to deal with Rome, would have said that the Galileans deserved to die for rebelling. The Zealots, a group of anti-Roman terrorists, would have said the aqueduct workers deserved to die for cooperating. Jesus said

Whether a person is killed in a tragic accident or miraculously survives is not a measure of righteousness. Everyone has to die; that's part of being human. But people don't need to stay dead. Jesus promises that those who believe in him will not perish but have eternal life (John 3:16).

that neither the Galileans nor the workers should be blamed for their calamity. And instead of blaming others, everyone should look to his or her own day of judgment. Death may come at any time. Being a believer doesn't shield you from death or even from tragic death. Are you ready to die? Do you know for sure that you'll be with the Savior?

August 14

Jesus calls the people to repent
Luke 13:6-9 *(Harmony 145b)*

*T*hen Jesus used this illustration: "A man planted a fig tree in his garden and came again and again to see if there was any fruit on it, but he was always disappointed. Finally, he said to his gardener, 'I've waited three years, and there hasn't been a single fig! Cut it down. It's taking up space we can use for something else.'

"The gardener answered, 'Give it one more chance. Leave it another year, and I'll give it special attention and plenty of fertilizer. If we get figs next year, fine. If not, you can cut it down.'"

NO FRUIT
In the Old Testament, a fruitful tree was often used as a symbol of godly living (see, for example, Psalm 1:3 and Jeremiah 17:7-8). Jesus pointed out what would happen to the other kind of tree—the kind that took valuable time and space and still produced nothing for the patient gardener. This was one way Jesus warned his listeners that God would not tolerate forever their lack of productivity. (Luke 3:9 records John the Baptist's version of the same message.) Have you been enjoying God's special treatment without giving anything in return? If so, respond to the Gardener's patient care, and begin to bear the fruit God has created you to produce.

Fig trees were plentiful in Israel. In this parable, the fig tree also represents the nation of Israel. The fruitless fig tree would be cut down; Israel would be cut off from God's blessing for refusing God's Son.

August 15

Jesus heals the handicapped woman
Luke 13:10-17 *(Harmony 146)*

*O*ne Sabbath day as Jesus was teaching in a synagogue, he saw a woman who had been crippled by an evil spirit. She had been bent double for eighteen years and was unable to stand up straight. When Jesus saw her, he called her over and said, "Woman, you are healed of your sickness!" Then he touched her, and instantly she could stand straight. How she praised and thanked God!

But the leader in charge of the synagogue was indignant that Jesus had healed her on the Sabbath day. "There are six days of the week for working," he said to the crowd. "Come on those days to be healed, not on the Sabbath."

But the Lord replied, "You hypocrite! You work on the Sabbath day! Don't you untie your ox or your donkey from their stalls on the Sabbath and lead them out for water? Wasn't it necessary for me, even on the Sabbath day, to free this dear woman from the bondage in which Satan has held her for eighteen years?" This shamed his enemies. And all the people rejoiced at the wonderful things he did.

THE LETTER OF THE LAW
Why was healing considered work? The religious leaders saw healing as part of a doctor's profession, and practicing one's profession on the Sabbath was prohibited. The synagogue ruler could not see beyond the law to Jesus' compassion in healing this handicapped woman. Jesus shamed him and the other leaders by pointing out their hypocrisy. The Pharisees hid behind their own set of laws to avoid love's obligations. We, too, can use the letter of the law to rationalize away our obligation to care for others (for example, by tithing regularly and then refusing to help a needy neighbor). But people's needs are more important than rules and regulations. Take time to help others, even if doing so might compromise your public image.

In our fallen world, disease and disability are common. Their causes are many and often multiple—inadequate nutrition, contact with a source of infection, a lowered immune system, and even direct attack by Satan. Whatever the immediate cause of our illness, we can trace its original source to Satan, the author of all the evil in our world. The good news is that Jesus is more powerful than any devil or disease.

August 16

Jesus teaches about the Kingdom of God
Luke 13:18-21 *(Harmony 147)*

*T*hen Jesus said, "What is the Kingdom of God like? How can I illustrate it? It is like a tiny mustard seed planted in a garden; it grows and becomes a tree, and the birds come and find shelter among its branches."

He also asked, "What else is the Kingdom of God like? It is like yeast used by a woman making bread. Even though she used a large amount of flour, the yeast permeated every part of the dough."

The general expectation among Jesus' hearers was that the Messiah would come as a great king and leader, freeing the nation from Rome and restoring Israel's former glory. But Jesus said his Kingdom was beginning quietly. Like the tiny mustard seed that grows into an enormous tree, or the spoonful of yeast that makes the bread dough double in size, the Kingdom of God would eventually push outward until the whole world was changed. You are a part of that Kingdom because people have continued to spread the gospel since the days of Christ. What are you doing to continue the growth of the Kingdom?

The mustard plant grows to be quite large; in fact, one of the largest plants in Palestine. And yet its seeds are the tiniest. Jesus' audience easily understood his illustration.

August 17

Jesus heals the man who was born blind
John 9:1-5 *(Harmony 148a)*

*A*s Jesus was walking along, he saw a man who had been blind from birth. "Teacher," his disciples asked him, "why was this man born blind? Was it a result of his own sins or those of his parents?"

"It was not because of his sins or his parents' sins," Jesus answered. "He was born blind so the power of God could be seen in him. All of us must quickly carry out the tasks assigned us by the one who sent me, because there is little time left before the night falls and all work comes to an end. But while I am still here in the world, I am the light of the world."

SUFFERING

A common belief in Jewish culture was that calamity or suffering was the result of some great sin. But Christ used this man's suffering to teach about faith and to glorify God. We live in a fallen world where good behavior is not always rewarded and bad behavior not always punished. Therefore, innocent people sometimes suffer. If God took suffering away whenever we asked, we would follow him for comfort and convenience, not out of love and devotion. Regardless of the reasons for our suffering, Jesus has the power to help us deal with it. When you suffer from a disease, trag-

In chapter 9, we see four different reactions to Jesus. The neighbors revealed surprise and skepticism; the Pharisees showed disbelief and prejudice; the parents believed but kept quiet for fear of excommunication; and the healed man showed consistent, growing faith.

edy, or disability, try not to ask why this happened to you. Instead, ask God to give you strength for the trial and a clearer perspective on what is happening.

August 18

Jesus heals the man who was born blind
John 9:6-12 *(Harmony 148b)*

*T*hen he spit on the ground, made mud with the saliva, and smoothed the mud over the blind man's eyes. He told him, "Go and wash in the pool of Siloam" (Siloam means Sent). So the man went and washed, and came back seeing!

His neighbors and others who knew him as a blind beggar asked each other, "Is this the same man—that beggar?" Some said he was, and others said, "No, but he surely looks like him!"

And the beggar kept saying, "I am the same man!"

They asked, "Who healed you? What happened?"

He told them, "The man they call Jesus made mud and smoothed it over my eyes and told me, 'Go to the pool of Siloam and wash off the mud.' I went and washed, and now I can see!"

"Where is he now?" they asked.

"I don't know," he replied.

STEPS OF FAITH

Jesus' miracles were meant to strengthen people's faith and lead them to believe in him as the Messiah. Christ's miracles were significant, not just because of their power, but because of their purpose—to help, to heal, and to point people to God. This man's simple act of faith in going to wash, as Jesus instructed, resulted in his restored sight. Faith is a step between promise and assurance. Miracles seem so out of reach for our feeble faith. But every miracle, large or small, begins with an act of obedience. We may not see the solution until we take the first step of faith.

The pool of Siloam was built by Hezekiah. His workers constructed an underground tunnel from a spring outside the city walls to carry water into the city. Thus, the people could always get water without fear of being attacked. This was especially important during times of siege (see 2 Kings 20:20; 2 Chronicles 32:30).

August 19

Religious leaders question the blind man
John 9:13-23 *(Harmony 149a)*

*T*hen they took the man to the Pharisees. Now as it happened, Jesus had healed the man on a Sabbath. The Pharisees asked the man all about it. So he told them, "He smoothed the mud over my eyes, and when it was washed away, I could see!"

Some of the Pharisees said, "This man Jesus is not from God, for he is working on the Sabbath." Others said, "But how could an ordinary sinner do such miraculous signs?" So there was a deep division of opinion among them.

Then the Pharisees once again questioned the man who had been blind and demanded, "This man who opened your eyes—who do you say he is?"

The man replied, "I think he must be a prophet."

The Jewish leaders wouldn't believe he had been blind, so they called in his parents. They asked them, "Is this your son? Was he born blind? If so, how can he see?"

His parents replied, "We know this is our son and that he was born blind, but we don't know how he can see or who healed him. He is old enough to speak for himself. Ask him." They said this because they were afraid of the Jewish leaders, who had announced that anyone saying Jesus was the Messiah would be expelled from the synagogue. That's why they said, "He is old enough to speak for himself. Ask him."

SABBATH REST

The Jewish Sabbath, Saturday, was the weekly holy day of rest. The Pharisees had made a long list of specific dos and don'ts regarding the Sabbath. Kneading the clay and healing the man were considered work and therefore were forbidden. Jesus may have purposely made the clay in order to emphasize his teaching about the Sabbath—that it is right to care for others' needs even if it involves working on a day of rest. The Sabbath had two purposes: It was a time to *rest* and a time to *remember* what God had done. We need rest. Without time out from the bustle, life loses its meaning. In our day, as in Moses' day, taking time out is not easy. Your Sabbath rest may be different from others'; to you gardening might be restful while someone else would consider it work. Don't get bogged down in laws and judging. God created a Sabbath for you. He reminds us that without Sabbaths we will forget the purpose for all of our

While the Pharisees conducted investigations and debated about Jesus, people were being healed and lives were being changed. The Pharisees' skepticism was based not on insufficient evidence, but on jealousy of Jesus' popularity and his influence on the people.

activity and lose the balance crucial to a faithful life. Make sure that your Sabbath provides a time of both refreshment and remembrance of God.

August 20

Religious leaders question the blind man
John 9:24-34 *(Harmony 149b)*

So for the second time they called in the man who had been blind and told him, "Give glory to God by telling the truth, because we know Jesus is a sinner."

"I don't know whether he is a sinner," the man replied. "But I know this: I was blind, and now I can see!"

"But what did he do?" they asked. "How did he heal you?"

"Look!" the man exclaimed. "I told you once. Didn't you listen? Why do you want to hear it again? Do you want to become his disciples, too?"

Then they cursed him and said, "You are his disciple, but we are disciples of Moses. We know God spoke to Moses, but as for this man, we don't know anything about him."

"Why, that's very strange!" the man replied. "He healed my eyes, and yet you don't know anything about him! Well, God doesn't listen to sinners, but he is ready to hear those who worship him and do his will. Never since the world began has anyone been able to open the eyes of someone born blind. If this man were not from God, he couldn't do it."

"You were born in sin!" they answered. "Are you trying to teach us?" And they threw him out of the synagogue.

SPREAD THE NEWS
By now the man who had been blind had heard the same questions over and over. He did not know how or why he was healed, but he knew that his life had been miraculously changed, and he was not afraid to tell the truth. You don't need to know all the answers in order to share Christ with others. It is important to tell them how he has changed your life. Then trust that God will use your words to help others believe in him, too.

The man's new faith was severely tested by some of the authorities. He was cursed and evicted from the synagogue—a horrible punishment for a Jew.

August 21

Jesus teaches about spiritual blindness
John 9:35-41 *(Harmony 150)*

*W*hen Jesus heard what had happened, he found the man and said, "Do you believe in the Son of Man?"

The man answered, "Who is he, sir, because I would like to."

"You have seen him," Jesus said, "and he is speaking to you!"

"Yes, Lord," the man said, "I believe!" And he worshiped Jesus.

Then Jesus told him, "I have come to judge the world. I have come to give sight to the blind and to show those who think they see that they are blind."

The Pharisees who were standing there heard him and asked, "Are you saying we are blind?"

"If you were blind, you wouldn't be guilty," Jesus replied. "But you remain guilty because you claim you can see.

GETTING TO KNOW HIM

The longer this man experienced his new life through Christ, the more confident he became in the one who had healed him. He gained not only physical sight but also spiritual sight as he recognized Jesus, first as a prophet (9:17), then as his Lord. When you turn to Christ, you begin to see him differently. The longer you walk with him, the better you will understand who he is. Peter tells us to "grow in the special favor and knowledge of our Lord and Savior Jesus Christ" (2 Peter 3:18). If you want to know more about Jesus, keep walking with him.

People lose a vital ability when they can no longer see their own sinfulness. The results are broken relationships, authority out of control, blindness to the needy, and forgetfulness toward God. Spiritual blindness is a matter of life and death.

August 22

Jesus is the good shepherd
John 10:1-10 *(Harmony 151a)*

I assure you, anyone who sneaks over the wall of a sheepfold, rather than going through the gate, must surely be a thief and a robber! For a shepherd enters through the gate. The gatekeeper opens the gate for him, and the sheep hear his voice and come to him. He calls his own sheep by name and leads them out. After he has gathered his own flock, he walks ahead of them, and they follow him because they recognize his voice. They won't follow a stranger; they will run from him because they don't recognize his voice."

Those who heard Jesus use this illustration didn't understand what he meant, so he explained it to them. "I assure you, I am the gate for the sheep," he said. "All others who came before me were thieves and robbers. But the true sheep did not listen to them. Yes, I am the gate. Those who come in through me will be saved. Wherever they go, they will find green pastures. The thief's purpose is to steal and kill and destroy. My purpose is to give life in all its fullness."

THE GOOD SHEPHERD
The New Testament calls Jesus the good shepherd (John 10:11); the great Shepherd (Hebrews 13:20); and the Head Shepherd (1 Peter 5:4). Sheep are completely dependent on the shepherd for provision, guidance, and protection. As the Lord is the good shepherd, so we are his sheep—not frightened, passive animals, but obedient followers, wise enough to follow one who will lead us in the right places and in right ways. When we allow the good shepherd to guide us, we have contentment. When we choose to sin, however, we go our own way and cannot blame God for the environment we create for ourselves. Rebelling against the shepherd's leading is actually rebelling against our own best interests. Remember this the next time you are tempted to go your own way rather than the shepherd's way.

At night, sheep were often gathered into a sheepfold to protect them from thieves, weather, and wild animals. The sheepfolds were caves, sheds, or open areas surrounded by walls made of stones or branches. The shepherd often slept in the fold to protect the sheep.

August 23

Jesus is the good shepherd
John 10:11-16 *(Harmony 151b)*

I am the good shepherd. The good shepherd lays down his life for the sheep. A hired hand will run when he sees a wolf coming. He will leave the sheep because they aren't his and he isn't their shepherd. And so the wolf attacks them and scatters the flock. The hired hand runs away because he is merely hired and has no real concern for the sheep.

"I am the good shepherd; I know my own sheep, and they know me, just as my Father knows me and I know the Father. And I lay down my life for the sheep. I have other sheep, too, that are not in this sheepfold. I must bring them also, and they will listen to my voice; and there will be one flock with one shepherd."

PAST, PRESENT, AND FUTURE

A hired man tends the sheep for money, while the shepherd does it for love. The shepherd owns the sheep and is committed to them. Jesus is not merely doing a job; he is committed to love us and even lay down his life for us. False teachers and false prophets do not have this commitment. Jesus *did* die for us. He has *once and for all* paid the penalty for our sins by his own sacrificial death, and he can be depended on to restore our broken relationship with God. We are released from sin's domination over us when we commit ourselves to Christ, trusting completely in what he has done for us. No one can add to what Jesus did to save us; our past, present, and future sins are all forgiven, and Jesus is with the Father as a sign that our sins are forgiven. If you are a Christian, remember that Christ has paid the price for your sins once and for all.

The "other sheep" were non-Jews. Jesus came to save Gentiles as well as Jews. This is an insight into Christ's worldwide mission—to die for the sins of the world. People tend to want to restrict God's blessings to their own group, but Jesus refuses to be limited by the fences we build.

August 24

Jesus is the good shepherd
John 10:17-21 *(Harmony 151c)*

*T*he Father loves me because I lay down my life that I may have it back again. No one can take my life from me. I lay down my life voluntarily. For I have the right to lay it down when I want to and also the power to take it again. For my Father has given me this command."

When he said these things, the people were again divided in their opinions about him. Some of them said, "He has a demon, or he's crazy. Why listen to a man like that?" Others said, "This doesn't sound like a man possessed by a demon! Can a demon open the eyes of the blind?"

If Jesus had been merely a man, his claims to be God would have proved him insane. But his miracles proved his words true—he really is God. The Jewish leaders could not see beyond their own prejudices, and they looked at Jesus only from a human perspective—Jesus confined in a human box. But Jesus was not limited by their restricted vision.

LAYING IT DOWN

Jesus is God; thus, he could say that he would both lay down his life *and* take it back again. Jesus' death and resurrection, as part of God's plan for the salvation of the world, were under God's full control. No one could kill Jesus without his consent. It was important that Jesus die on the cross to take the punishment for sin, but it was also important that he rise from the dead. The resurrection of Christ is the center of the Christian faith. Because Christ rose from the dead as he promised, we know that what he said is true—he is God. Because he rose, we have certainty that our sins are forgiven. Because he rose, he lives and represents us to God. Because he rose and defeated death, we know we will also be raised.

August 25

Religious leaders surround Jesus at the Temple
John 10:22-30 *(Harmony 152a)*

*I*t was now winter, and Jesus was in Jerusalem at the time of Hanukkah. He was at the Temple, walking through the section known as Solomon's Colonnade. The Jewish leaders surrounded him and asked, "How long are you going to keep us in suspense? If you are the Messiah, tell us plainly."

Jesus replied, "I have already told you, and you don't believe me. The proof is what I do in the name of my Father. But you don't believe me because you are not part of my flock. My sheep recognize my voice; I know them, and they follow me.

I give them eternal life, and they will never perish. No one will snatch them away from me, for my Father has given them to me, and he is more powerful than anyone else. So no one can take them from me. The Father and I are one."

ON WHOSE TERMS?

The statement "the Father and I are one" is the clearest statement of Jesus' divinity he ever made. Jesus and his Father are not the same person, but they are one in essence and nature. Thus, Jesus was not merely a good teacher—he was God. His claim to be God was unmistakable. The religious leaders wanted to kill him because their laws said that anyone claiming to be God should die. Nothing could persuade them that Jesus' claim was true. Jesus tried to correct their mistaken ideas, but they clung to the wrong idea of what kind of Messiah God would send. Such blindness still keeps people away from Jesus. They want him on their own terms; they do not want him if it means changing their whole lives. Have you accepted Jesus on his terms?

Hanukkah (also called the Feast of Lights) commemorates the cleansing of the Temple under Judas Maccabeus in 165 B.C. after Antiochus Epiphanes had defiled it a few years earlier by sacrificing a pig on the altar of burnt offering. The feast is celebrated toward the end of December.

Religious leaders surround Jesus at the Temple
John 10:31-42 *(Harmony 152b)*

*O*nce again the Jewish leaders picked up stones to kill him. Jesus said, "At my Father's direction I have done many things to help the people. For which one of these good deeds are you killing me?"

They replied, "Not for any good work, but for blasphemy, because you, a mere man, have made yourself God."

Jesus replied, "It is written in your own law that God said to certain leaders of the people, 'I say, you are gods!' And you know that the Scriptures cannot be altered. So if those people, who received God's message, were called 'gods,' why do you call it blasphemy when the Holy One who was sent into the world by the Father says, 'I am the Son of God'? Don't believe me unless I carry out my Father's work. But if I do his work, believe in what I have done, even if you don't believe me. Then you will realize that the Father is in me, and I am in the Father."

Once again they tried to arrest him, but he got away and left them. He went beyond the Jordan River to stay near the place where John was first baptizing. And many followed him. "John didn't do miracles," they remarked to one another, "but all his predictions about this man have come true." And many believed in him there.

OUR ONLY SOURCE

"Scriptures cannot be altered"—what the Bible says is true. If we accept Christ as Lord, we also must accept his testimony to the Bible as God's Word. The whole Bible is God's inspired Word. Because it is inspired and trustworthy, we should *read* it and *apply* it to our lives. The Bible is our standard for testing everything else that claims to be true. It is our safeguard against false teaching and our source of guidance for how we should live. It is our only source of knowledge about how we can be saved. God wants to show you what is true and equip you to live for him. How much time do you spend in God's Word? Read it regularly to discover God's truth and to become confident in your life and faith. Develop a plan for reading the whole Bible, not just the familiar passages.

The Jewish leaders attempted to carry out the directive found in Leviticus 24:16 regarding those who blaspheme (claim to be God). They intended to stone Jesus.

Jesus teaches about entering the Kingdom
Luke 13:22-30 *(Harmony 153)*

*J*esus went through the towns and villages, teaching as he went, always pressing on toward Jerusalem. Someone asked him, "Lord, will only a few be saved?"

He replied, "The door to heaven is narrow. Work hard to get in, because many will try to enter, but when the head of the house has locked the door, it will be too late. Then you will stand outside knocking and pleading, 'Lord, open the door for us!' But he will reply, 'I do not know you.' You will say, 'But we ate and drank with you, and you taught in our streets.' And he will reply, 'I tell you, I don't know you. Go away, all you who do evil.'

"And there will be great weeping and gnashing of teeth, for you will see Abraham, Isaac, Jacob, and all the prophets within the Kingdom of God, but you will be thrown out. Then people will come from all over the world to take their places in the Kingdom of God. And note this: Some who are despised now will be greatly honored then; and some who are greatly honored now will be despised then."

THE FEAST

There will be many surprises in God's Kingdom. Some who are despised now will be greatly honored then; some influential people here will be left outside the gates. Many "great" people on this earth (in God's eyes) are virtually ignored by the rest of the world. What matters to God is not a person's earthly popularity, status, wealth, heritage, or power, but his or her commitment to Christ. How do your values match what the Bible tells you to value? Put God first in your life , and you will join people from all over the world who will take their places at the feast in the Kingdom of Heaven.

This is the second time Luke reminds us that Jesus was intentionally going to Jerusalem (the other time is in 9:51). Jesus knew he was on his way to die, but he continued preaching to large crowds. The prospect of death did not deter Jesus from his mission.

August 28

Jesus grieves over Jerusalem
Luke 13:31-35 *(Harmony 154)*

A few minutes later some Pharisees said to him, "Get out of here if you want to live, because Herod Antipas wants to kill you!"

Jesus replied, "Go tell that fox that I will keep on casting out demons and doing miracles of healing today and tomorrow; and the third day I will accomplish my purpose. Yes, today, tomorrow, and the next day I must proceed on my way. For it wouldn't do for a prophet of God to be killed except in Jerusalem!

"O Jerusalem, Jerusalem, the city that kills the prophets and stones God's messengers! How often I have wanted to gather your children together as a hen protects her chicks beneath her wings, but you wouldn't let me. And now look, your house is left to you empty. And you will never see me again until you say, 'Bless the one who comes in the name of the Lord!'"

GOD'S TIMING
The Pharisees weren't interested in protecting Jesus from danger—they were trying to trap him. The Pharisees urged Jesus to leave because they wanted to stop him from going to Jerusalem, not because they feared Herod. But Jesus' life, work, and death were not to be determined by Herod or the Pharisees. His life was planned and directed by God himself, and his mission would unfold in God's time and according to God's plan. When you are following God's will, you must do whatever he calls you to do without letting any obstacles get in your way. God will make sure that his will is accomplished.

Jerusalem, the city of God, symbolized the entire nation. It was Israel's largest city and the nation's spiritual and political capital. Jews from around the world visited it frequently. But Jerusalem had a history of rejecting God's prophets (1 Kings 19:10; 2 Chronicles 24:19; Jeremiah 2:30; 26:20-23), and it would reject the Messiah just as it had rejected his forerunners.

August 29

Jesus heals a man with dropsy
Luke 14:1-6 *(Harmony 155)*

O ne Sabbath day Jesus was in the home of a leader of the Pharisees. The people were watching him closely, because there was a man there whose arms and legs were swollen. Jesus asked the Pharisees and experts in religious law, "Well, is it permitted in the law to heal people on the Sabbath day, or not?" When they refused to answer, Jesus touched the sick man and healed him and sent him away. Then he turned to them and asked, "Which of you doesn't work on the Sabbath? If your son or your cow falls into a pit, don't you proceed at once to get him out?" Again they had no answer.

UNAFRAID
Earlier Jesus had been invited to a Pharisee's home for discussion (7:36). This time a prominent Pharisee invited Jesus to his home specifically to trap him into saying or doing something for which he could be arrested. It may be surprising to see Jesus on the Pharisees' turf after he had denounced them so many times. But Jesus was not afraid to face the Pharisees, even though he knew that their purpose was to trick him into breaking their laws. Jesus was not afraid of confrontation; neither should his followers be. We can trust God to help us have the right words and to accomplish his will through us.

Luke, the physician, identified this man's disease—he was suffering from an abnormal accumulation of fluid in bodily tissues and cavities, sometimes called dropsy.

August 30

Jesus teaches about seeking honor
Luke 14:7-14 *(Harmony 156)*

*W*hen Jesus noticed that all who had come to the dinner were trying to sit near the head of the table, he gave them this advice: "If you are invited to a wedding feast, don't always head for the best seat. What if someone more respected than you has also been invited? The host will say, 'Let this person sit here instead.' Then you will be embarrassed and will have to take whatever seat is left at the foot of the table!

"Do this instead—sit at the foot of the table. Then when your host sees you, he will come and say, 'Friend, we have a better place than this for you!' Then you will be honored in front of all the other guests. For the proud will be humbled, but the humble will be honored."

Then he turned to his host. "When you put on a luncheon or a dinner," he said, "don't invite your friends, brothers, relatives, and rich neighbors. For they will repay you by inviting you back. Instead, invite the poor, the crippled, the lame, and the blind. Then at the resurrection of the godly, God will reward you for inviting those who could not repay you."

REALISTIC EVALUATION

How can we humble ourselves? Some people try to give the appearance of humility in order to manipulate others. Others think that humility means putting themselves down. Truly humble people only compare themselves with Christ, realize their sinfulness, and understand their limitations. On the other hand, they also recognize their gifts and strengths and are willing to use them as Christ directs. Healthy self-esteem is important because some of us think too little of ourselves. On the other hand, some of us overestimate ourselves. The key to an honest and accurate evaluation is knowing the basis of our self-worth—our identity in Christ. Apart from him, we aren't capable of very much by eternal standards; in him, we are valuable and capable of worthy service. Evaluating yourself by the worldly standards of success and achievement can cause you to think too much about your worth in the eyes of others and thus miss your true value in God's eyes. Humility is not self-degradation; it is realistic assessment and commitment to serve.

Jesus taught two lessons here. First, he spoke to the guests, telling them not to seek places of honor. Service is more important in God's Kingdom than status. Second, he told the host not to be exclusive about whom he invites. God opens his Kingdom to everyone.

August 31

Jesus tells the parable of the great feast
Luke 14:15-24 *(Harmony 157)*

*H*earing this, a man sitting at the table with Jesus exclaimed, "What a privilege it would be to have a share in the Kingdom of God!"

Jesus replied with this illustration: "A man prepared a great feast and sent out many invitations. When all was ready, he sent his servant around to notify the guests that it was time for them to come. But they all began making excuses. One said he had just bought a field and wanted to inspect it, so he asked to be excused. Another said he had just bought five pair of oxen and wanted to try them out. Another had just been married, so he said he couldn't come.

"The servant returned and told his master what they had said. His master was angry and said, 'Go quickly into the streets and alleys of the city and invite the poor, the crippled, the lame, and the blind.' After the servant had done this, he reported, 'There is still room for more.' So his master said, 'Go out into the country lanes and behind the hedges and urge anyone you find to come, so that the house will be full. For none of those I invited first will get even the smallest taste of what I had prepared for them.'"

ACCEPT THE INVITATION

It was customary to send two invitations to a party—the first to announce the event; the second to tell the guests that everything was ready. The guests in Jesus' story insulted the host by making excuses when they received the second invitation. In Jesus' story, many people turned down the invitation to the banquet because the timing was inconvenient. We, too, can resist or delay responding to God's invitation, and our excuses may sound reasonable—work duties, family responsibilities, financial needs, and so forth. Nevertheless, God's invitation is the most important event in our life, no matter how inconveniently it may be timed. What are your favorite excuses? Jesus reminds us that the time will come when God will pull his invitation and offer it to others—then it will be too late to get into the banquet.

In Israel's history, God's first invitation came from Moses and the prophets; the second came from his Son. The religious leaders accepted the first invitation. They believed that God had called them to be his people, but they insulted God by refusing to accept his Son.

September 1

Jesus teaches about the cost of being a disciple
Luke 14:25-27 *(Harmony 158a)*

*G*reat crowds were following Jesus. He turned around and said to them, "If you want to be my follower you must love me more than your own father and mother, wife and children, brothers and sisters—yes, more than your own life. Otherwise, you cannot be my disciple. And you cannot be my disciple if you do not carry your own cross and follow me.

TOTAL SUBMISSION
Jesus' audience was well aware of what it meant to carry one's own cross. When the Romans led a criminal to his execution site, he was forced to carry the cross on which he would die. This showed his submission to Rome and warned observers that they had better submit, too. Jesus spoke this teaching to get the crowds to think through their enthusiasm for him. He encouraged those whose commitment was superficial either to go deeper or to turn back. Following Christ means total submission to him—perhaps even to the point of death. Jesus wants more than enthusiasm—he wants total dedication. Have you dedicated your life to Jesus?

To love Jesus far more than even one's family means that, ultimately, Jesus is the focus of one's life. Loved ones should never be allowed to pull a person away from Christ.

September 2

Jesus teaches about the cost of being a disciple
Luke 14:28-35 *(Harmony 158b)*

*B*ut don't begin until you count the cost. For who would begin construction of a building without first getting estimates and then checking to see if there is enough money to pay the bills? Otherwise, you might complete only the foundation before running out of funds. And then how everyone would laugh at you! They would say, 'There's the person who started that building and ran out of money before it was finished!'

"Or what king would ever dream of going to war without first sitting down with his counselors and discussing whether his army of ten thousand is strong enough to defeat the twenty thousand soldiers who are marching against him? If he is not able, then while the enemy is still far away, he will send a delegation to discuss terms of peace. So no one can become my disciple without giving up everything for me.

"Salt is good for seasoning. But if it loses its flavor, how do you make it salty again? Flavorless salt is good neither for the soil nor for fertilizer. It is thrown away. Anyone who is willing to hear should listen and understand!"

STAY SALTY
Salt can lose its flavor. When it gets wet and then dries, nothing is left but a tasteless residue. Many Christians blend into the world and avoid the cost of standing up for Christ. But Jesus says if Christians lose their distinctive saltiness, they become worthless. Just as salt flavors and preserves food, we are to preserve the good in the world, help keep it from spoiling, and bring new flavor to life. Being "salty" requires careful planning, willing sacrifice, and unswerving commitment to represent Christ in the world. How salty are you?

What are the costs of the Christian life? Christians may face loss of social status or wealth. They may have to give up control over their money, their time, or their career. They may be hated, separated from their family, and even put to death. Following Christ does not mean a trouble-free life.

September 3

Jesus tells the parable of the lost sheep
Luke 15:1-7 *(Harmony 159)*

*T*ax collectors and other notorious sinners often came to listen to Jesus teach. This made the Pharisees and teachers of religious law complain that he was associating with such despicable people—even eating with them!

So Jesus used this illustration: "If you had one hundred sheep, and one of them strayed away and was lost in the wilderness, wouldn't you leave the ninety-nine others to go and search for the lost one until you found it? And then you would joyfully carry it home on your shoulders. When you arrived, you would call together your friends and neighbors to rejoice with you because your lost sheep was found. In the same way, heaven will be happier over one lost sinner who returns to God than over ninety-nine others who are righteous and haven't strayed away!"

GUILT BY ASSOCIATION

Why were the Pharisees and scribes bothered that Jesus associated with these people? The religious leaders were always careful to stay "clean" according to Old Testament law. In fact, they went well beyond the law in their avoidance of certain people and situations and in their ritual washings. By contrast, Jesus took their concept of "cleanness" lightly. He risked defilement by touching those who had leprosy and by neglecting to wash in the Pharisees' prescribed manner, and he showed complete disregard for their sanctions against associating with certain classes of people. He came to offer salvation to sinners, to show that God loves them. Jesus didn't worry about the accusations. Instead, he continued going to those who needed him, regardless of the effect on his reputation. What keeps you from people who need Christ? Jesus associated with sinners because he wanted to bring the lost sheep—people considered beyond hope—the gospel of God's Kingdom. Before you were a believer, God sought you; and his love is still seeking those who are yet lost.

It may seem foolish for the shepherd to leave ninety-nine sheep to go search for just one. But the shepherd knew that the ninety-nine would be safe in the sheepfold, whereas the lost sheep was in danger. God's love for each individual is so great that he seeks each one out and rejoices when he or she is "found."

September 4

Jesus tells the parable of the lost coin
Luke 15:8-10 *(Harmony 160)*

*O*r suppose a woman has ten valuable silver coins and loses one. Won't she light a lamp and look in every corner of the house and sweep every nook and cranny until she finds it? And when she finds it, she will call in her friends and neighbors to rejoice with her because she has found her lost coin. In the same way, there is joy in the presence of God's angels when even one sinner repents."

EXTRAORDINARY LOVE

We may be able to understand a God who would forgive sinners who come to him for mercy. But a God who tenderly searches for sinners and then joyfully forgives them must possess an extraordinary love! That is what prompted Jesus to come to earth to search for lost people and save them. God has extraordinary love for you. If you feel far from God, don't despair. He is searching for

Palestinian women received ten silver coins as a wedding gift. Besides their monetary value, these coins held sentimental value like that of a wedding ring, and to lose one would be extremely distressing. Just as a woman would rejoice at finding her lost coin or ring, so the angels rejoice over a repentant sinner.

you. Each individual is precious to God. He grieves over every loss and rejoices whenever one of his children is found and brought into the Kingdom.

September 5

Jesus tells the parable of the lost son
Luke 15:11-24 *(Harmony 161a)*

*T*o illustrate the point further, Jesus told them this story: "A man had two sons. The younger son told his father, 'I want my share of your estate now, instead of waiting until you die.' So his father agreed to divide his wealth between his sons.

"A few days later this younger son packed all his belongings and took a trip to a distant land, and there he wasted all his money on wild living. About the time his money ran out, a great famine swept over the land, and he began to starve. He persuaded a local farmer to hire him to feed his pigs. The boy became so hungry that even the pods he was feeding the pigs looked good to him. But no one gave him anything.

"When he finally came to his senses, he said to himself, 'At home even the hired men have food enough to spare, and here I am, dying of hunger! I will go home to my father and say, "Father, I have sinned against both heaven and you, and I am no longer worthy of being called your son. Please take me on as a hired man."'

"So he returned home to his father. And while he was still a long distance away, his father saw him coming. Filled with love and compassion, he ran to his son, embraced him, and kissed him. His son said to him, 'Father, I have sinned against both heaven and you, and I am no longer worthy of being called your son.'

"But his father said to the servants, 'Quick! Bring the finest robe in the house and put it on him. Get a ring for his finger, and sandals for his feet. And kill the calf we have been fattening in the pen. We must celebrate with a feast, for this son of mine was dead and has now returned to life. He was lost, but now he is found.' So the party began."

The younger son, like many who are rebellious and immature, wanted to be free to live as he pleased, and he had to hit bottom before he came to his senses. It often takes great sorrow and tragedy to cause people to look to the only one who can help them. Are you trying to live life your own way, selfishly pushing aside any responsibility or commitment that gets in your way? Stop and look before you hit bottom. You will save yourself and your family much grief.

In the two preceding stories, the seeker actively looked for the coin and the sheep, which could not return by themselves. In this story, the father watched and waited. He was dealing with a human being with a will of his own, but he was ready to greet his son if he returned. In the same way, God's love is constant and patient and welcoming.

September 6

Jesus tells the parable of the lost son
Luke 15:25-32 *(Harmony 161b)*

*M*eanwhile, the older son was in the fields working. When he returned home, he heard music and dancing in the house, and he asked one of the servants what was going on. 'Your brother is back,' he was told, 'and your father has killed the calf we were fattening and has prepared a great feast. We are celebrating because of his safe return.'

"The older brother was angry and wouldn't go in. His father came out and begged him, but he replied, 'All these years I've worked hard for you and never once refused to do a single thing you told me to. And in all that time you never gave me even one young goat for a feast with my friends. Yet when this son of yours comes back after squandering your money on prostitutes, you celebrate by killing the finest calf we have.'

"His father said to him, 'Look, dear son, you and I are very close, and everything I have is yours. We had to celebrate this happy day. For your brother was dead and has come back to life! He was lost, but now he is found!'"

In the story of the lost son, the father's response is contrasted with the older brother's. The father forgave because he was filled with love. The son refused to forgive because he was bitter about the injustice of the situation. His resentment rendered him just as lost to the father's love as his younger brother had been. Don't let anything keep

In Jesus' story the older brother represented the Pharisees, who were angry and resentful that sinners were being welcomed into God's Kingdom. How easy it is to resent God's gracious forgiveness of others whom we consider to be far worse sinners than we are.

you from forgiving others. If you are refusing to forgive people, you are missing a wonderful opportunity to experience joy and share it with others. Make your joy grow: Forgive somebody who has hurt you.

September 7

Jesus tells the parable of the shrewd accountant
Luke 16:1-12 *(Harmony 162a)*

*J*esus told this story to his disciples: "A rich man hired a manager to handle his affairs, but soon a rumor went around that the manager was thoroughly dishonest. So his employer called him in and said, 'What's this I hear about your stealing from me? Get your report in order, because you are going to be dismissed.'

"The manager thought to himself, 'Now what? I'm through here, and I don't have the strength to go out and dig ditches, and I'm too proud to beg. I know just the thing! And then I'll have plenty of friends to take care of me when I leave!'

"So he invited each person who owed money to his employer to come and discuss the situation. He asked the first one, 'How much do you owe him?' The man replied, 'I owe him eight hundred gallons of olive oil.' So the manager told him, 'Tear up that bill and write another one for four hundred gallons.'

"'And how much do you owe my employer?' he asked the next man. 'A thousand bushels of wheat,' was the reply. 'Here,' the manager said, 'take your bill and replace it with one for only eight hundred bushels.'

"The rich man had to admire the dishonest rascal for being so shrewd. And it is true that the citizens of this world are more shrewd than the godly are. I tell you, use your worldly resources to benefit others and make friends. In this way, your generosity stores up a reward for you in heaven.

"Unless you are faithful in small matters, you won't be faithful in large ones. If you cheat even a little, you won't be honest with greater responsibilities. And if you are untrustworthy about worldly wealth, who will trust you with the true riches of heaven? And if you are not faithful with other people's money, why should you be trusted with money of your own?"

MONEY MATTERS MATTER
Our use of money is a good test of the lordship of Christ in our lives. (1) Let us use our resources wisely because they belong to God, and not to us. (2) Money can be used for good or evil; let us use ours for good. (3) Money has a lot of power, so we must use it carefully and thoughtfully. (4) We must use our material goods in a way that will foster faith and obedience (see 12:33-34). Our

integrity often meets its match in money matters. God calls us to be honest in small details so that in time we can be trusted with greater responsibility and wealth. Heaven's riches are far more valuable than earthly wealth. But if we are not trustworthy with our money here (no matter how much or little we have), we will be unfit to handle the vast riches of God's Kingdom.

If we use our money to help those in need or to help others find Christ, our earthly investment will bring eternal benefit. When we obey God, the unselfish use of possessions will follow.

September 8

Jesus tells the parable of the shrewd accountant
Luke 16:13-18 *(Harmony 162b)*

*N*o one can serve two masters. For you will hate one and love the other, or be devoted to one and despise the other. You cannot serve both God and money."

The Pharisees, who dearly loved their money, naturally scoffed at all this. Then he said to them, "You like to look good in public, but God knows your evil hearts. What this world honors is an abomination in the sight of God.

"Until John the Baptist began to preach, the laws of Moses and the messages of the prophets were your guides. But now the Good News of the Kingdom of God is preached, and eager multitudes are forcing their way in. But that doesn't mean that the law has lost its force in even the smallest point. It is stronger and more permanent than heaven and earth.

"Anyone who divorces his wife and marries someone else commits adultery, and anyone who marries a divorced woman commits adultery."

MASTER MONEY
Money has the power to take God's place in your life. It can become your master. How can you tell if you are a slave to money? (1) Do you think and worry about it frequently? (2) Do you give up doing what you should do or would like to do in order to make more money? (3) Do you spend a great deal of time caring for your possessions? (4) Is it difficult for you to give money away? (5) Are you in debt?

Money is a hard master and a deceptive one. Wealth promises power and control, but often it cannot deliver. Great fortunes can be

John the Baptist's ministry was the dividing line between the Old and New Testaments (John 1:15-18). With the arrival of Jesus came the realization of all the prophets' hopes. Jesus emphasized that his Kingdom fulfilled the law (the Old Testament); it did not cancel it (Matthew 5:17). His was not a new system but the culmination of the old.

made—and lost—overnight, and no amount of money can provide health, happiness, or eternal life. How much better it is to let God be your Master. His servants have peace of mind and security, both now and forever. Heaven's riches are far more valuable than earthly wealth.

September 9

Jesus tells about the rich man and the beggar
Luke 16:19-31 *(Harmony 163)*

*J*esus said, "There was a certain rich man who was splendidly clothed and who lived each day in luxury. At his door lay a diseased beggar named Lazarus. As Lazarus lay there longing for scraps from the rich man's table, the dogs would come and lick his open sores. Finally, the beggar died and was carried by the angels to be with Abraham. The rich man also died and was buried, and his soul went to the place of the dead. There, in torment, he saw Lazarus in the far distance with Abraham.

"The rich man shouted, 'Father Abraham, have some pity! Send Lazarus over here to dip the tip of his finger in water and cool my tongue, because I am in anguish in these flames.'

"But Abraham said to him, 'Son, remember that during your lifetime you had everything you wanted, and Lazarus had nothing. So now he is here being comforted, and you are in anguish. And besides, there is a great chasm separating us. Anyone who wanted to cross over to you from here is stopped at its edge, and no one there can cross over to us.'

"Then the rich man said, 'Please, Father Abraham, send him to my father's home. For I have five brothers, and I want him to warn them about this place of torment so they won't have to come here when they die.'

"But Abraham said, 'Moses and the prophets have warned them. Your brothers can read their writings anytime they want to.'

"The rich man replied, 'No, Father Abraham! But if someone is sent to them from the dead, then they will turn from their sins.'

"But Abraham said, 'If they won't listen to Moses and the prophets, they won't listen even if someone rises from the dead.'"

HOARD OR HELP?

The Pharisees considered wealth to be a proof of a person's righteousness. Jesus startled them with this story where a diseased beggar is rewarded and a rich man is punished. The rich man did not go to hell because of his wealth but because he was self-centered. He refused to feed Lazarus, take him in, or care for him. He was hardhearted in spite of his great blessings. The amount of money we have is not as important as the way we use it. What is your attitude toward your money and possessions? Do you hoard them selfishly, or do you use them to help others?

The rich man thought that his five brothers would surely believe a messenger who had been raised from the dead. But Jesus said that if they did not believe Moses and the prophets, who spoke constantly of the duty to care for the poor, not even a resurrection would convince them.

September 10

Jesus tells about forgiveness and faith
Luke 17:1-4 *(Harmony 164a)*

*O*ne day Jesus said to his disciples, "There will always be temptations to sin, but how terrible it will be for the person who does the tempting. It would be better to be thrown into the sea with a large millstone tied around the neck than to face the punishment in store for harming one of these little ones. I am warning you! If another believer sins, rebuke him; then if he repents, forgive him. Even if he wrongs you seven times a day and each time turns again and asks forgiveness, forgive him."

POINTING OUT SIN

To rebuke does not mean to point out every sin we see; it means to bring sin to a person's attention with the purpose of restoring him or her to God and to fellow humans. When you feel you must rebuke another Christian for a sin, check your attitudes before you speak. Do you love the person? Are you willing to forgive? Unless rebuke is tied to forgiveness, it will not help the sinning person. It's too easy to point out someone else's faults or sins. If we feel we must admonish someone, we should be sure we are confronting that person in love and forgiveness, not because we are annoyed, inconvenienced, or seeking to blame him or her.

Jesus may have been directing this warning at the religious leaders who taught their converts their own hypocritical ways (see Matthew 23:15). They were perpetuating an evil system. A person who teaches others has a solemn responsibility (James 3:1).

Jesus tells about forgiveness and faith
Luke 17:5-10 *(Harmony 164b)*

One day the apostles said to the Lord, "We need more faith; tell us how to get it."

"Even if you had faith as small as a mustard seed," the Lord answered, "you could say to this mulberry tree, 'May God uproot you and throw you into the sea,' and it would obey you!

"When a servant comes in from plowing or taking care of sheep, he doesn't just sit down and eat. He must first prepare his master's meal and serve him his supper before eating his own. And the servant is not even thanked, because he is merely doing what he is supposed to do. In the same way, when you obey me you should say, 'We are not worthy of praise. We are servants who have simply done our duty.'"

SEED FAITH

The disciples' request was genuine; they wanted the faith necessary for such radical forgiveness. But Jesus didn't directly answer their question because the amount of faith is not as important as its genuineness. Faith is total dependence on God and a willingness to do his will. Faith is not something we use to put on a show for others; it is complete and humble obedience to God's will, readiness to do whatever he calls us to do. A mustard seed is small, but it is alive and growing.

If we have obeyed God, we have only done our duty and should regard it as a privilege. Obedience is not something extra we do; it is our duty. However, Jesus is not rendering our service as meaningless or useless, nor is he doing away with rewards. He is attacking unwarranted self-esteem and spiritual pride.

Like a tiny seed, a small amount of genuine faith in God will take root and grow. Almost invisible at first, it will begin to spread, first under the ground and then visibly. Although each change will be gradual and imperceptible, soon this faith will have produced major results that will uproot and destroy competing loyalties. We don't need more faith; a tiny seed of faith is enough, if it is alive and growing. The amount of faith isn't as important as the right kind of faith—faith in our all-powerful God. Ask God to increase your faith and to give you the strength to act on the faith you have.

Lazarus becomes ill and dies
John 11:1-16 *(Harmony 165)*

A man named Lazarus was sick. He lived in Bethany with his sisters, Mary and Martha. This is the Mary who poured the expensive perfume on the Lord's feet and wiped them with her hair. Her brother, Lazarus, was sick. So the two sisters sent a message to Jesus telling him, "Lord, the one you love is very sick."

But when Jesus heard about it he said, "Lazarus's sickness will not end in death. No, it is for the glory of God. I, the Son of God, will receive glory from this." Although Jesus loved Martha, Mary, and Lazarus, he stayed where he was for the next two days and did not go to them. Finally after two days, he said to his disciples, "Let's go to Judea again."

But his disciples objected. "Teacher," they said, "only a few days ago the Jewish leaders in Judea were trying to kill you. Are you going there again?"

Jesus replied, "There are twelve hours of daylight every day. As long as it is light, people can walk safely. They can see because they have the light of this world. Only at night is there danger of stumbling because there is no light." Then he said, "Our friend Lazarus has fallen asleep, but now I will go and wake him up."

The disciples said, "Lord, if he is sleeping, that means he is getting better!" They thought Jesus meant Lazarus was having a good night's rest, but Jesus meant Lazarus had died.

Then he told them plainly, "Lazarus is dead. And for your sake, I am glad I wasn't there, because this will give you another opportunity to believe in me. Come, let's go see him."

Thomas, nicknamed the Twin, said to his fellow disciples, "Let's go, too—and die with Jesus."

WAITING ON GOD
Jesus loved this family and often stayed with them. He knew their pain but did not respond immediately. His delay had a specific purpose. God's timing, especially his delays, may make us think he is not answering or is not answering the way we want. But he will meet all our needs according to his perfect schedule and purpose (Philippians 4:19). If Jesus had been with Lazarus during the final moments of Lazarus's sickness, Jesus might have healed Lazarus rather than let him die. But Lazarus died so that Jesus' power over death could be shown to

The raising of Lazarus was an essential display of Jesus' power, and the resurrection from the dead is a crucial belief of Christian faith. Jesus not only raised himself from the dead (10:18), but he has the power to raise others.

his disciples and others. Any trial a believer faces can ultimately bring glory to God because God can bring good out of any bad situation (Genesis 50:20; Romans 8:28). When trouble comes, do you grumble, complain, and blame God, or do you see your problems as opportunities to honor him?

September 13

Jesus comforts Mary and Martha
John 11:17-26 *(Harmony 166a)*

*W*hen Jesus arrived at Bethany, he was told that Lazarus had already been in his grave for four days. Bethany was only a few miles down the road from Jerusalem, and many of the people had come to pay their respects and console Martha and Mary on their loss. When Martha got word that Jesus was coming, she went to meet him. But Mary stayed at home. Martha said to Jesus, "Lord, if you had been here, my brother would not have died. But even now I know that God will give you whatever you ask."

Jesus told her, "Your brother will rise again."

"Yes," Martha said, "when everyone else rises, on resurrection day."

Jesus told her, "I am the resurrection and the life. Those who believe in me, even though they die like everyone else, will live again. They are given eternal life for believing in me and will never perish. Do you believe this, Martha?"

HIS AWESOME POWER
Their brother was growing very sick, so Mary and Martha called for Jesus to help. They believed in his ability to help because they had seen his miracles. We, too, know of Jesus' miracles, both from Scripture and through changed lives we have seen. When we need extraordinary help, Jesus offers extraordinary resources. We should not hesitate to ask him for assistance. Jesus has power over life and death as well as power to forgive sins because he is the Creator of life (see 14:6). He who *is* life can surely restore life. Whoever believes in Christ has a spiritual life that death cannot conquer or diminish in any way. When we realize Christ's power and how wonderful his offer to us really is, how can we help but commit our lives to him! To those of us who believe, what wonderful assurance and certainty we have: "I will live again, and you will, too" (14:19).

The village of Bethany is located about two miles east of Jerusalem on the road to Jericho. It was near enough to Jerusalem for Jesus and the disciples to be in danger, but far enough away so as not to attract attention prematurely.

Jesus comforts Mary and Martha
John 11:27-36 *(Harmony 166b)*

*Y*es, Lord," she told him. "I have always believed you are the Messiah, the Son of God, the one who has come into the world from God." Then she left him and returned to Mary. She called Mary aside from the mourners and told her, "The Teacher is here and wants to see you." So Mary immediately went to him.

Now Jesus had stayed outside the village, at the place where Martha met him. When the people who were at the house trying to console Mary saw her leave so hastily, they assumed she was going to Lazarus's grave to weep. So they followed her there. When Mary arrived and saw Jesus, she fell down at his feet and said, "Lord, if you had been here, my brother would not have died."

When Jesus saw her weeping and saw the other people wailing with her, he was moved with indignation and was deeply troubled. "Where have you put him?" he asked them.

They told him, "Lord, come and see." Then Jesus wept. The people who were standing nearby said, "See how much he loved him."

JESUS CARES

When Jesus saw the weeping and wailing, he too wept openly. Perhaps he empathized with their grief, or perhaps he was troubled at their unbelief. In either case, Jesus showed that he cares enough for us to weep with us in our sorrow. John stresses that we have a God who cares. This portrait contrasts with the popular Greek concept that God had no emotions and no messy involvement with humans. Here we see many of Jesus' emotions—compassion, indignation, sorrow, even frustration. He often expressed deep emotion, and we must never be afraid to reveal our true feelings to him. He understands them, for he experienced them. Be honest, and don't try to hide anything from your Savior. He cares.

Martha is best known for being too busy to sit down and talk with Jesus (Luke 10:38-42). But here we see her as a woman of deep faith. Her statement of faith is exactly the response that Jesus wants from us.

Jesus raises Lazarus from the dead
John 11:37-44 *(Harmony 167)*

*B*ut some said, "This man healed a blind man. Why couldn't he keep Lazarus from dying?"

And again Jesus was deeply troubled. Then they came to the grave. It was a cave with a stone rolled across its entrance. "Roll the stone aside," Jesus told them.

But Martha, the dead man's sister, said, "Lord, by now the smell will be terrible because he has been dead for four days."

Jesus responded, "Didn't I tell you that you will see God's glory if you believe?" So they rolled the stone aside. Then Jesus looked up to heaven and said, "Father, thank you for hearing me. You always hear me, but I said it out loud for the sake of all these people standing here, so they will believe you sent me." Then Jesus shouted, "Lazarus, come out!" And Lazarus came out, bound in graveclothes, his face wrapped in a headcloth. Jesus told them, "Unwrap him and let him go!"

TRAGEDIES INTO TRIUMPHS

Lazarus came back to life, but he would die again physically. Yet, because he believed in Jesus, he would be raised again to eternal life. We know this because Jesus Christ came back to life. All Christians, including those living when Christ returns, will live with Christ forever. Therefore, we need not despair when loved ones die or world events take a tragic turn. God will turn our tragedies to triumphs, our poverty to riches, our pain to glory, and our defeat to victory. All believers throughout history will stand reunited in God's very presence, safe and secure. Comfort and reassure each other with this great hope.

Tombs at this time were usually caves carved in the limestone rock of a hillside. A tomb was often large enough for people to walk inside. Several bodies would be placed in one tomb. After burial, a large stone would be rolled across the entrance to the tomb.

Religious leaders plot to kill Jesus
John 11:45-53 *(Harmony 168a)*

*M*any of the people who were with Mary believed in Jesus when they saw this happen. But some went to the Pharisees and told them what Jesus had done. Then the leading priests and Pharisees called the high council together to discuss the situation. "What are we going to do?" they asked each other. "This man certainly performs many miraculous signs. If we leave him alone, the whole nation will follow him, and then the Roman army will come and destroy both our Temple and our nation."

And one of them, Caiaphas, who was high priest that year, said, "How can you be so stupid? Why should the whole nation be destroyed? Let this one man die for the people."

This prophecy that Jesus should die for the entire nation came from Caiaphas in his position as high priest. He didn't think of it himself; he was inspired to say it. It was a prediction that Jesus' death would be not for Israel only, but for the gathering together of all the children of God scattered around the world.

So from that time on the Jewish leaders began to plot Jesus' death.

HARD HEARTS
Even when confronted point-blank with the power of Jesus' deity, some refused to believe. These eyewitnesses not only rejected Jesus; they also plotted his murder. They were so hardened that they preferred to reject God's Son rather than admit that they were wrong. When we judge others, we automatically consider ourselves to be better. Beware of pride. If allowed to grow, it can lead to enormous sin.

The Jewish leaders knew that if they didn't stop Jesus, the Romans would discipline them. Rome gave partial freedom to the Jews as long as they were quiet and obedient. Jesus' miracles often caused a disturbance. The leaders feared that Rome's displeasure would bring additional hardship to their nation.

September 17

Religious leaders plot to kill Jesus
John 11:54-57 *(Harmony 168b)*

*A*s a result, Jesus stopped his public ministry among the people and left Jerusalem. He went to a place near the wilderness, to the village of Ephraim, and stayed there with his disciples.

It was now almost time for the celebration of Passover, and many people from the country arrived in Jerusalem several days early so they could go through the cleansing ceremony before the Passover began. They wanted to see Jesus, and as they talked in the Temple, they asked each other, "What do you think? Will he come for the Passover?" Meanwhile, the leading priests and Pharisees had publicly announced that anyone seeing Jesus must report him immediately so they could arrest him.

> **QUIET TIME**
> Lazarus's return to life became the last straw for the religious leaders who were bent on killing Jesus. So Jesus stopped his public ministry and took his disciples away from Jerusalem to Ephraim, a town several miles to the north. Jesus needed time to talk to his disciples and teach them many things before he died. He wanted to get away from the conflict in Jerusalem so the disciples could rest and concentrate on his words for them. At times all of us need to get away from the busyness of our daily routines, resting and listening to God. Set aside a certain time each day when you can quietly listen and talk to God.

Passover was a holiday designed to celebrate Israel's deliverance from Egypt and to remind the people what God had done. Many Jews came to Jerusalem to celebrate this holy day.

September 18

Jesus heals ten lepers
Luke 17:11-19 *(Harmony 169)*

*A*s Jesus continued on toward Jerusalem, he reached the border between Galilee and Samaria. As he entered a village there, ten lepers stood at a distance, crying out, "Jesus, Master, have mercy on us!"

He looked at them and said, "Go show yourselves to the priests." And as they went, their leprosy disappeared.

One of them, when he saw that he was healed, came back to Jesus, shouting, "Praise God, I'm healed!" He fell face down on the ground at Jesus' feet, thanking him for what he had done. This man was a Samaritan.

Jesus asked, "Didn't I heal ten men? Where are the other nine? Does only this foreigner return to give glory to God?" And Jesus said to the man, "Stand up and go. Your faith has made you well."

GRATEFUL BELIEVERS

Jesus healed all ten lepers, but only one returned to thank him. It is possible to receive God's great gifts with an ungrateful spirit—nine of the ten men did so. Only the thankful man, however, learned that his faith had played a role in his healing; and only grateful Christians grow in understanding God's grace. God does not demand that we thank him, but he is pleased when we do so. And he uses our responsiveness to teach us more about himself.

Not only was this man a leper, he was also a Samaritan—a race despised by the Jews as idolatrous half-breeds. Once again Luke is pointing out that God's grace is for everybody.

September 19

Jesus teaches about the coming of the Kingdom of God
Luke 17:20-21 *(Harmony 170a)*

One day the Pharisees asked Jesus, "When will the Kingdom of God come?"

Jesus replied, "The Kingdom of God isn't ushered in with visible signs. You won't be able to say, 'Here it is!' or 'It's over there!' For the Kingdom of God is among you."

THE KINGDOM WITHIN

The Pharisees asked when God's Kingdom would come, not knowing that it had already arrived. The Kingdom of God is not like an earthly kingdom with geographical boundaries. Instead, it begins with the work of God's Spirit in people's lives and in relationships. When Jesus ascended into heaven, God's Kingdom would remain in the hearts of all believers through the presence of the Holy Spirit. Still today we must resist looking to institutions or programs for evidence of the progress of God's Kingdom. Instead, we should look for what God is doing in people's hearts.

Some versions say, "the Kingdom of God is within you." The Kingdom within them emphasized that it would begin with spiritual change within. The Kingdom among them emphasized that he, the King, was in their midst.

September 20

Jesus teaches about the coming of the Kingdom of God
Luke 17:22-37 *(Harmony 170b)*

*L*ater he talked again about this with his disciples. "The time is coming when you will long to share in the days of the Son of Man, but you won't be able to," he said. "Reports will reach you that the Son of Man has returned and that he is in this place or that. Don't believe such reports or go out to look for him. For when the Son of Man returns, you will know it beyond all doubt. It will be as evident as the lightning that flashes across the sky. But first the Son of Man must suffer terribly and be rejected by this generation.

"When the Son of Man returns, the world will be like the people were in Noah's day. In those days before the flood, the people enjoyed banquets and parties and weddings right up to the time Noah entered his boat and the flood came to destroy them all.

"And the world will be as it was in the days of Lot. People went about their daily business—eating and drinking, buying and selling, farming and building—until the morning Lot left Sodom. Then fire and burning sulfur rained down from heaven and destroyed them all. Yes, it will be 'business as usual' right up to the hour when the Son of Man returns. On that day a person outside the house must not go into the house to pack. A person in the field must not return to town. Remember what happened to Lot's wife! Whoever clings to this life will lose it, and whoever loses this life will save it. That night two people will be asleep in one bed; one will be taken away, and the other will be left. Two women will be grinding flour together at the mill; one will be taken, the other left."

"Lord, where will this happen?" the disciples asked.

Jesus replied, "Just as the gathering of vultures shows there is a carcass nearby, so these signs indicate that the end is near."

IT MAY BE TODAY

Life will be going on as usual on the day Christ returns. There will be no warning. Most people will be going about their everyday tasks, indifferent to the demands of God. They will be as surprised by Christ's return as the people in Noah's day were by the Flood (Genesis 6–8) or the people in Lot's day by the destruction of Sodom (Genesis 19). We don't know the time of Christ's return, but we do know that he is *Many will claim to be the Messiah, and many will claim that Jesus has returned—and people will believe them. Jesus warns us never to take such reports seriously, no matter how convincing they may sound. When Jesus returns, his power and presence will be evident to everyone.*

coming. He may come today, tomorrow, or centuries in the future. Whenever Christ returns, we must be morally and spiritually ready. Live as if Jesus were returning today.

September 21

Jesus tells the parable of the persistent widow
Luke 18:1-8 *(Harmony 171)*

*O*ne day Jesus told his disciples a story to illustrate their need for constant prayer and to show them that they must never give up. "There was a judge in a certain city," he said, "who was a godless man with great contempt for everyone. A widow of that city came to him repeatedly, appealing for justice against someone who had harmed her. The judge ignored her for a while, but eventually she wore him out. 'I fear neither God nor man,' he said to himself, 'but this woman is driving me crazy. I'm going to see that she gets justice, because she is wearing me out with her constant requests!'"

Then the Lord said, "Learn a lesson from this evil judge. Even he rendered a just decision in the end, so don't you think God will surely give justice to his chosen people who plead with him day and night? Will he keep putting them off? I tell you, he will grant justice to them quickly! But when I, the Son of Man, return, how many will I find who have faith?"

CONSTANT PRAYER
To repeat our prayers until the answer comes does not mean endless repetition or painfully long prayer sessions. Constant prayer means keeping our requests constantly before God as we live for him day by day, believing he will answer. When we live by faith, we are not to give up. God may delay answering, but his delays always have good reasons. As we persist in prayer we grow in character, faith, and hope.

Widows and orphans were among the most vulnerable of all God's people, and both Old Testament prophets and New Testament apostles insisted that these needy people be properly cared for. See, for example, Exodus 22:22-24; Isaiah 1:17; 1 Timothy 5:3; James 1:27.

September 22

Jesus tells the parable of two men who prayed
Luke 18:9-14 *(Harmony 172)*

*T*hen Jesus told this story to some who had great self-confidence and scorned everyone else: "Two men went to the Temple to pray. One was a Pharisee, and the other was a dishonest tax collector. The proud Pharisee stood by himself and prayed this prayer: 'I thank you, God, that I am not a sinner like everyone else, especially like that tax collector over there! For I never cheat, I don't sin, I don't commit adultery, I fast twice a week, and I give you a tenth of my income.'

"But the tax collector stood at a distance and dared not even lift his eyes to heaven as he prayed. Instead, he beat his chest in sorrow, saying, 'O God, be merciful to me, for I am a sinner.' I tell you, this sinner, not the Pharisee, returned home justified before God. For the proud will be humbled, but the humble will be honored."

PRIDE'S TRAP
The Pharisee did not go to the Temple to pray to God but to announce to all within earshot how good he was. The tax collector went recognizing his sin and begging for mercy. Self-righteousness is dangerous. It leads to pride, causes a person to despise others, and prevents him or her from learning anything from God. The tax collector's prayer should be our prayer because we all need God's mercy every day. Don't let pride in your achievements cut you off from God.

The people who lived near Jerusalem often went to the Temple to pray. The Temple was the center of their worship.

September 23

Jesus teaches about marriage and divorce
Matthew 19:1-12 (also in Mark 10:1-12) *(Harmony 173)*

*A*fter Jesus had finished saying these things, he left Galilee and went southward to the region of Judea and into the area east of the Jordan River. Vast crowds followed him there, and he healed their sick.

Some Pharisees came and tried to trap him with this question: "Should a man be allowed to divorce his wife for any reason?"

"Haven't you read the Scriptures?" Jesus replied. "They record that from the beginning 'God made them male and female.' And he said, 'This explains why a man leaves his father and mother and is joined to his wife, and the two are united into one.' Since they are no longer two but one, let no one separate them, for God has joined them together."

"Then why did Moses say a man could merely write an official letter of divorce and send her away?" they asked.

Jesus replied, "Moses permitted divorce as a concession to your hard-hearted wickedness, but it was not what God had originally intended. And I tell you this, a man who divorces his wife and marries another commits adultery—unless his wife has been unfaithful."

Jesus' disciples then said to him, "Then it is better not to marry!"

"Not everyone can accept this statement," Jesus said. "Only those whom God helps. Some are born as eunuchs, some have been made that way by others, and some choose not to marry for the sake of the Kingdom of Heaven. Let anyone who can, accept this statement."

COMMITTED TO PERMANENCE

God allowed divorce as a concession to people's sinfulness. Divorce was not approved, but it was instituted to protect the injured party in a bad situation. Unfortunately, the Pharisees used Deuteronomy 24:1 as a proof text for divorce. Jesus explained that this was not God's intent; instead, God wants married people to consider their marriage permanent. Don't enter marriage with the option of getting out. Your marriage is more likely to be happy if from the outset you are committed to permanence. Don't be hard-hearted like these Pharisees, but be hardheaded in your determination, with God's help, to stay together.

Women were often treated as property. Marriage and divorce were regarded as transactions similar to buying and selling land. But Jesus condemned this attitude, clarifying God's original intention—that marriage bring oneness (Genesis 2:24).

September 24

Jesus blesses little children
Mark 10:13-16 (also in Matthew 19:13-15; Luke 18:15-17)
(Harmony 174)

*O*ne day some parents brought their children to Jesus so he could touch them and bless them, but the disciples told them not to bother him. But when Jesus saw what was happening, he was very displeased with his disciples. He said to them, "Let the children come to me. Don't stop them! For the Kingdom of God belongs to such as these. I assure you, anyone who doesn't have their kind of faith will never get into the

Kingdom of God." Then he took the children into his arms and placed his hands on their heads and blessed them.

WELCOME THE CHILDREN

It was customary for a mother to bring her children to a rabbi for a blessing, and that is why these mothers gathered around Jesus. The disciples, however, thought the children were unworthy of the Master's time—less important than whatever else he was doing. But Jesus welcomed them because little children have the kind of faith and trust needed to enter God's Kingdom. It is important that we introduce our children to Jesus and that we ourselves approach him with childlike attitudes of acceptance, faith, and trust.

Jesus didn't mean that heaven is only for children but that people need childlike attitudes of trust in God. The receptiveness of little children was a great contrast to the stubbornness of the religious leaders who let their education and sophistication stand in the way of the simple faith needed to believe in Jesus.

September 25

Jesus speaks to the rich young man
Mark 10:17-31 (also in Matthew 19:16-30; Luke 18:18-30)
(Harmony 175)

As he was starting out on a trip, a man came running up to Jesus, knelt down, and asked, "Good Teacher, what should I do to get eternal life?"

"Why do you call me good?" Jesus asked. "Only God is truly good. But as for your question, you know the commandments: 'Do not murder. Do not commit adultery. Do not steal. Do not testify falsely. Do not cheat. Honor your father and mother.' "

"Teacher," the man replied, "I've obeyed all these commandments since I was a child."

Jesus felt genuine love for this man as he looked at him. "You lack only one thing," he told him. "Go and sell all you have and give the money to the poor, and you will have treasure in heaven. Then come, follow me." At this, the man's face fell, and he went sadly away because he had many possessions.

Jesus looked around and said to his disciples, "How hard it is for rich people to get into the Kingdom of God!" This amazed them. But Jesus said again, "Dear children, it is very hard to get into the Kingdom of God. It is easier for a camel to go through the eye of a needle than for a rich person to enter the Kingdom of God!"

The disciples were astounded. "Then who in the world can be saved?" they asked.

Jesus looked at them intently and said, "Humanly speaking, it is impossible. But not with God. Everything is possible with God."

Then Peter began to mention all that he and the other disciples had left behind. "We've given up everything to follow you," he said.

And Jesus replied, "I assure you that everyone who has given up house or brothers or sisters or mother or father or children or property, for my sake and for the Good News, will receive now in return, a hundred times over, houses, brothers, sisters, mothers, children, and property—with persecutions. And in the world to come they will have eternal life. But many who seem to be important now will be the least important then, and those who are considered least here will be the greatest then."

GIVING, GAINING

Peter and the other disciples had paid a high price—leaving their homes and jobs—to follow Jesus. But Jesus reminded Peter that following him has its benefits as well as its sacrifices. Any believer who has had to give up something to follow Christ will be paid back in this life as well as in the next. For example, if you must give up a secure job, you will find that God offers a secure relationship with himself now and forever. If you must give up your family's approval, you will gain the love of the family of God. The disciples had begun to pay the price of following Jesus, and Jesus said they would be rewarded. Don't dwell on what you have given up; think about what you have gained, and give thanks for it. You can never outgive God.

Jesus does not ask that all believers sell everything they have. However, because money represents power, authority, and success, often it is difficult for wealthy people to realize their need and their powerlessness to save themselves. The rich in talent or intelligence suffer the same difficulty. The person who has everything on earth can still lack what is most important— eternal life.

September 26

Jesus tells the parable of the workers paid equally
Matthew 20:1-16 *(Harmony 176)*

*F*or the Kingdom of Heaven is like the owner of an estate who went out early one morning to hire workers for his vineyard. He agreed to pay the normal daily wage and sent them out to work.

"At nine o'clock in the morning he was passing through the marketplace and saw some people standing around doing nothing. So he hired them, telling them he would pay them whatever was right at the end of the day. At noon and again around three o'clock he did the same thing. At five o'clock that evening he was in town again and saw some more people standing around. He asked them, 'Why haven't you been working today?'

"They replied, 'Because no one hired us.'

"The owner of the estate told them, 'Then go on out and join the others in my vineyard.'

"That evening he told the foreman to call the workers in and pay them, beginning with the last workers first. When those hired at five o'clock were paid, each received a full day's wage. When those hired earlier came to get their pay, they assumed they would receive more. But they, too, were paid a day's wage. When they received their pay, they protested, 'Those people worked only one hour, and yet you've paid them just as much as you paid us who worked all day in the scorching heat.'

"He answered one of them, 'Friend, I haven't been unfair! Didn't you agree to work all day for the usual wage? Take it and go. I wanted to pay this last worker the same as you. Is it against the law for me to do what I want with my money? Should you be angry because I am kind?'

"And so it is, that many who are first now will be last then; and those who are last now will be first then."

WHO DESERVES IT?

This parable is not about rewards but about salvation. It is strong teaching about *grace*, God's generosity. We shouldn't begrudge those who turn to God in the last moments of life because, in reality, *no one* deserves eternal life.

Jesus further clarified the membership rules of the Kingdom of Heaven: Entrance is by God's grace alone. In this parable, God is the landowner, and believers are the laborers.

Many people we don't expect to see in the Kingdom will be there. The criminal who repented as he was dying (Luke 23:40-43) will be there along with people who have believed and served God for many years. Do you resent God's gracious acceptance of the despised, the outcast, and the sinners who have turned to him for forgiveness? Are you ever jealous of what God has given to another person? Instead, focus on God's gracious benefits to you, and be thankful for what you have.

September 27

Jesus predicts his death for the third time
Luke 18:31-34 (also in Matthew 20:17-19; Mark 10:32-34)
(Harmony 177)

*G*athering the twelve disciples around him, Jesus told them, "As you know, we are going to Jerusalem. And when we get there, all the predictions of the ancient prophets concerning the Son of Man will come true. He will be handed over to the Romans to be mocked, treated shamefully, and spit upon. They will whip him and kill him, but on the third day he will rise again."

But they didn't understand a thing he said. Its significance was hidden from them, and they failed to grasp what he was talking about.

NO ACCIDENT
Jesus' death and resurrection should have come as no surprise to the disciples. Here he clearly explained to them what would happen to him. Unfortunately, they didn't really hear what he was saying. Jesus said he was the Messiah, but they thought the Messiah would be a conquering king. He spoke to them of resurrection, but they heard only his words about death. Because Jesus often spoke in parables, the disciples may have thought that his words on death and resurrection were another parable that they weren't astute enough to understand. The Gospels include Jesus' predictions of his death and resurrection to show that these events were God's plan from the beginning. We can trust that all other biblical predictions about the future for believers will also come true.

Some predictions about what would happen to Jesus are found in Psalm 41:9 (betrayal); Psalm 22:16-18 and Isaiah 53:4-7 (crucifixion); Psalm 16:10 (resurrection). Even though Jesus spoke plainly, the disciples would not grasp the significance of his words until they saw the risen Christ face to face.

September 28

Jesus teaches about serving others
Mark 10:35-45 (also in Matthew 20:20-28) (Harmony 178)

*T*hen James and John, the sons of Zebedee, came over and spoke to him. "Teacher," they said, "we want you to do us a favor."

"What is it?" he asked.

"In your glorious Kingdom, we want to sit in places of honor next to you," they said, "one at your right and the other at your left."

But Jesus answered, "You don't know what you are asking! Are you able to drink from the bitter cup of sorrow I am about to drink? Are you able to be baptized with the baptism of suffering I must be baptized with?"

"Oh yes," they said, "we are able!"

And Jesus said, "You will indeed drink from my cup and be baptized with my baptism, but I have no right to say who will sit on the thrones next to mine. God has prepared those places for the ones he has chosen."

When the ten other disciples discovered what James and John had asked, they were indignant. So Jesus called them together and said, "You know that in this world kings are tyrants, and officials lord it over the people beneath them. But among you it should be quite different. Whoever wants to be a leader among you must be your servant, and whoever wants to be first must be the slave of all. For even I, the Son of Man, came here not to be served but to serve others, and to give my life as a ransom for many."

TRUE LEADERS

James and John wanted the highest positions in Jesus' Kingdom, but Jesus told them that true greatness comes in serving others. Jesus described leadership from a new perspective. Instead of using people, we are to serve them. Jesus' mission was to serve others and to give his life away. A real leader has a servant's heart. Most businesses, organizations, and institutions measure greatness by high personal achievement. In Christ's Kingdom, however, service is the way to get ahead. The desire to be on top will hinder, not help. Rather than seeking to have your needs met, look for ways that you can minister to the needs of others. Servant leaders appreciate others' worth and realize that they're not above any job. If you see something that needs to be done, don't wait to be asked. Take the initiative, and do it like a faithful servant.

A ransom was the price paid to release a slave from bondage. Jesus often told his disciples that he must die, but here he told them why—to redeem all people from the bondage of sin and death. The disciples thought that as long as Jesus was alive, he could save them. But Jesus revealed that only his death would save them and the world.

September 29

Jesus heals a blind beggar

Mark 10:46-52 (also in Matthew 20:29-34; Luke 18:35-43)
(Harmony 179)

*A*nd so they reached Jericho. Later, as Jesus and his disciples left town, a great crowd was following. A blind beggar named Bartimaeus (son of Timaeus) was sitting beside the road as Jesus was going by. When Bartimaeus heard that Jesus from Nazareth was nearby, he began to shout out, "Jesus, Son of David, have mercy on me!"

"Be quiet!" some of the people yelled at him.

But he only shouted louder, "Son of David, have mercy on me!"

When Jesus heard him, he stopped and said, "Tell him to come here."

So they called the blind man. "Cheer up," they said. "Come on, he's calling you!" Bartimaeus threw aside his coat, jumped up, and came to Jesus.

"What do you want me to do for you?" Jesus asked.

"Teacher," the blind man said, "I want to see!"

And Jesus said to him, "Go your way. Your faith has healed you." And instantly the blind man could see! Then he followed Jesus down the road.

CALL OUT

Beggars often waited along the roads near cities, because that was where they were able to be seen by the most people. Usually disabled in some way, beggars were unable to earn a living. Medical help was not available for their problems, and people tended to ignore their obligation to care for the needy (Leviticus 25:35-38). Thus, beggars had little hope of escaping their degrading way of life. But this blind beggar took hope in the Messiah. He shamelessly cried out for Jesus' attention, and Jesus said that his faith had healed him. No matter how desperate your situation may seem, if you call out to Jesus in faith, he will help you.

The blind man called Jesus "Son of David," a title for the Messiah (Isaiah 11:1-3). This means that he understood Jesus to be the long-awaited Messiah. A poor and blind beggar could see that Jesus was the Messiah, while the religious leaders who saw his miracles were blinded to his identity and refused to recognize him as the Messiah.

Jesus brings salvation to Zacchaeus's home
Luke 19:1-7 *(Harmony 180a)*

*J*esus entered Jericho and made his way through the town. There was a man there named Zacchaeus. He was one of the most influential Jews in the Roman tax-collecting business, and he had become very rich. He tried to get a look at Jesus, but he was too short to see over the crowds. So he ran ahead and climbed a sycamore tree beside the road, so he could watch from there.

When Jesus came by, he looked up at Zacchaeus and called him by name. "Zacchaeus!" he said. "Quick, come down! For I must be a guest in your home today."

Zacchaeus quickly climbed down and took Jesus to his house in great excitement and joy. But the crowds were displeased. "He has gone to be the guest of a notorious sinner," they grumbled.

LOVING THE UNLOVABLE

Tax collectors were among the most unpopular people in Israel. Jews by birth, they chose to work for Rome and were considered traitors. Besides, it was common knowledge that tax collectors were making themselves rich by gouging their fellow Jews. No wonder the people muttered when Jesus went home with the tax collector Zacchaeus. But despite the fact that Zacchaeus was both a cheater and a turncoat, Jesus loved him; and in response, the little tax collector was converted. In every society certain groups of people are considered "untouchable" because of their political views, their immoral behavior, or their lifestyle. We should not give in to social pressure to avoid these people. Jesus loves them, and they need to hear the Good News.

To finance their great world empire, the Romans levied heavy taxes on all nations under their control. The Jews opposed these taxes because they went to support a secular government and its heathen gods, but they were still forced to pay.

October 1

Jesus brings salvation to Zacchaeus's home
Luke 19:8-10 *(Harmony 180b)*

*M*eanwhile, Zacchaeus stood there and said to the Lord, "I will give half my wealth to the poor, Lord, and if I have overcharged people on their taxes, I will give them back four times as much!"

Jesus responded, "Salvation has come to this home today, for this man has shown himself to be a son of Abraham. And I, the Son of Man, have come to seek and save those like him who are lost."

A CHANGED LIFE

Judging from the crowd's reaction to him, Zacchaeus must have been a very crooked tax collector. But after he met Jesus, he realized that his life needed straightening out. By giving to the poor and making restitution—with generous interest—to those he had cheated, Zacchaeus demonstrated inward change by outward action. It is not enough to follow Jesus in your head or heart alone. Intellectual assent—agreement with a set of Christian teachings—is incomplete faith. True faith transforms our lives. If our lives remain unchanged, we don't truly believe the truths we claim to believe. You must show your faith by changed behavior. Has your faith resulted in action? What changes do you need to make?

When Jesus said Zacchaeus was a son of Abraham and yet was lost, he must have shocked his hearers in at least two ways. They would not have liked to acknowledge that this unpopular tax collector was a fellow son of Abraham, and they would not have wished to admit that sons of Abraham could be lost. But a person is not saved by a good heritage or condemned by a bad one; faith is more important than genealogy.

October 2

Jesus tells the parable of the king's ten servants
Luke 19:11-27 (Harmony 181)

*T*he crowd was listening to everything Jesus said. And because he was nearing Jerusalem, he told a story to correct the impression that the Kingdom of God would begin right away. He said, "A nobleman was called away to a distant empire to be crowned king and then return. Before he left, he called together ten servants and gave them ten pounds of silver to invest for him while he was gone. But his people hated him and sent a delegation after him to say they did not want him to be their king.

"When he returned, the king called in the servants to whom he had given the money. He wanted to find out what they had done with the money and what their profits were. The first servant reported a tremendous gain—ten times as much as the original amount! 'Well done!' the king exclaimed. 'You are a trustworthy servant. You have been faithful with the little I entrusted to you, so you will be governor of ten cities as your reward.'

"The next servant also reported a good gain—five times the original amount. 'Well done!' the king said. 'You can be governor over five cities.'

"But the third servant brought back only the original amount of money and said, 'I hid it and kept it safe. I was afraid because you are a hard man to deal with, taking what isn't yours and harvesting crops you didn't plant.'

"'You wicked servant!' the king roared. 'Hard, am I? If you knew so much about me and how tough I am, why didn't you deposit the money in the bank so I could at least get some interest on it?' Then turning to the others standing nearby, the king ordered, 'Take the money from this servant, and give it to the one who earned the most.'

"'But, master,' they said, 'that servant has enough already!'

"'Yes,' the king replied, 'but to those who use well what they are given, even more will be given. But from those who are unfaithful, even what little they have will be taken away. And now about these enemies of mine who didn't want me to be their king—bring them in and execute them right here in my presence.' "

This story showed Jesus' followers what they were to do during the time between Jesus' departure and his second coming. Because we live in that time period, it applies directly to us. We have been given excellent resources to build and expand God's Kingdom. Jesus expects us to use these talents so that they multiply and the Kingdom grows. He asks each of us to account for what we do with his gifts. While awaiting the coming of the Kingdom of God in glory, we must do Christ's work. Like the king in this story, God has given you gifts to use for the benefit of his Kingdom.

The king punished the one man because (1) he didn't share his master's interest in the kingdom; (2) he didn't trust his master's intentions; (3) his only concern was for himself, and (4) he did nothing to use the money. Some people on earth are loyal to God while others refuse to acknowledge his lordship. Each will receive rewards or punishment.

Do you want the Kingdom to grow? Do you trust God to govern it fairly? Are you as concerned for others' welfare as you are for your own? Are you willing to use faithfully what he has entrusted to you?

October 3

A woman anoints Jesus with perfume
Mark 14:3-9 (also in Matthew 26:6-13; John 12:1-11)
(Harmony 182)

*M*eanwhile, Jesus was in Bethany at the home of Simon, a man who had leprosy. During supper, a woman came in with a beautiful jar of expensive perfume. She broke the seal and poured the perfume over his head. Some of those at the table were indignant. "Why was this expensive perfume wasted?" they asked. "She could have sold it for a small fortune and given the money to the poor!" And they scolded her harshly.

But Jesus replied, "Leave her alone. Why berate her for doing such a good thing to me? You will always have the poor among you, and you can help them whenever you want to. But I will not be here with you much longer. She has done what she could and has anointed my body for burial ahead of time. I assure you, wherever the Good News is preached throughout the world, this woman's deed will be talked about in her memory."

TRUE WORSHIP
This perfume was made from pure nard, a fragrant ointment imported from the mountains of India. The amount Mary used was worth a year's wages. This act and Jesus' response to it do not teach us to ignore the poor so we

can spend money extravagantly for Christ. This was a unique act for a specific occasion—an anointing that anticipated Jesus' burial and a public declaration of faith in him as Messiah. Jesus was praising Mary for her unselfish act of worship. The essence of worshiping Christ is to regard him with the utmost love, respect, and devotion, and to be willing to sacrifice to him what is most precious.

John specifically mentions Judas as being indignant (John 12:4-5). Judas's indignation over Mary's act of worship was based not on concern for the poor but on greed. Because Judas was the treasurer of Jesus' ministry and had embezzled funds (John 12:6), he no doubt wanted the perfume sold so that he could benefit from the proceeds.

October 4

Jesus rides into Jerusalem on a donkey
Luke 19:28-35 (also in Matthew 21:1-7; Mark 11:1-7; John 12:12-19) *(Harmony 183a)*

*A*fter telling this story, Jesus went on toward Jerusalem, walking ahead of his disciples. As they came to the towns of Bethphage and Bethany, on the Mount of Olives, he sent two disciples ahead. "Go into that village over there," he told them, "and as you enter it, you will see a colt tied there that has never been ridden. Untie it and bring it here. If anyone asks what you are doing, just say, 'The Lord needs it.' "

So they went and found the colt, just as Jesus had said. And sure enough, as they were untying it, the owners asked them, "Why are you untying our colt?"

And the disciples simply replied, "The Lord needs it." So they brought the colt to Jesus and threw their garments over it for him to ride on.

PEACEABLE KING

Jesus came, not as a warring king on a horse or in a chariot, but as a gentle and peaceable king on a donkey's colt, just as Zechariah 9:9 had predicted. After Jesus' resurrection, the disciples would understand for the first time many of the prophecies that they had missed along the way. Jesus' words and actions would take on new meaning and make more sense. In retrospect, the disciples saw how Jesus had led them into a deeper and better understanding of his truth. Reflect on the events leading up to where you are now spiritually. How has God led you to this point? As

Jesus began his last week on earth by riding into Jerusalem on a donkey under a canopy of palm branches, with crowds hailing him as their king. The great Passover festival was about to begin, and Jews had come to Jerusalem from all over the Roman world during this weeklong celebration. On Palm Sunday we celebrate Jesus' triumphal entry into Jerusalem.

you grow older you will look back and see God's involvement more clearly than you do now. Stop right now and thank God for what he has done for you and how he led you to himself.

October 5

Jesus rides into Jerusalem on a donkey
Matthew 21:8-11 (also in Mark 11:8-11; Luke 19:36-44)
(Harmony 183b)

*M*ost of the crowd spread their coats on the road ahead of Jesus, and others cut branches from the trees and spread them on the road. He was in the center of the procession, and the crowds all around him were shouting, "Praise God for the Son of David! Bless the one who comes in the name of the Lord! Praise God in highest heaven!"

The entire city of Jerusalem was stirred as he entered. "Who is this?" they asked.

And the crowds replied, "It's Jesus, the prophet from Nazareth in Galilee."

THE WRONG IDEA
The people who were praising God for giving them a king had the wrong idea about Jesus. They expected him to be a national leader who would restore their nation to its former glory, and thus they were deaf to the words of their prophets and blind to Jesus' real mission. When it became apparent that Jesus was not going to fulfill their hopes, many people turned against him. The Jewish leaders rejected their King (Luke 19:47). They rejected God's offer of salvation in Jesus Christ when they were visited by God himself, and soon their nation would suffer. God did not turn away from the Jewish people who obeyed him, however, and he continues to offer salvation to the people he loves, both Jews and Gentiles. Eternal life is within your reach— accept it while the opportunity is still offered.

Upon approaching Jerusalem, Jesus wept and prophesied the city's destruction due to its rejection of him (see Luke 19:41-44). About forty years after Jesus made this prediction, his words came true. In A.D. 66, the Jews revolted against Roman control. Three years later Titus, son of the emperor Vespasian, was sent to crush the rebellion. Roman soldiers laid siege to Jerusalem, and in A.D. 70 they entered the city and burned it. Six hundred thousand Jews were killed during Titus's onslaught.

Jesus clears the Temple again
Mark 11:12-19 (also in Matthew 21:12-17; Luke 19:45-48)
(Harmony 184)

*T*he next morning as they were leaving Bethany, Jesus felt hungry. He noticed a fig tree a little way off that was in full leaf, so he went over to see if he could find any figs on it. But there were only leaves because it was too early in the season for fruit. Then Jesus said to the tree, "May no one ever eat your fruit again!" And the disciples heard him say it.

When they arrived back in Jerusalem, Jesus entered the Temple and began to drive out the merchants and their customers. He knocked over the tables of the money changers and the stalls of those selling doves, and he stopped everyone from bringing in merchandise. He taught them, "The Scriptures declare, 'My Temple will be called a place of prayer for all nations,' but you have turned it into a den of thieves."

When the leading priests and teachers of religious law heard what Jesus had done, they began planning how to kill him. But they were afraid of him because the people were so enthusiastic about Jesus' teaching. That evening Jesus and the disciples left the city.

The leaders had several reasons for wanting to get rid of Jesus, mostly the fact that he had damaged their business in the Temple by driving the merchants out, preaching against injustice, and favoring the poor over the rich. Also, his great popularity was in danger of attracting Rome's attention.

WHEN TO GET ANGRY
This is the second time Jesus cleared the Temple (see John 2:13-17). Merchants and money changers had set up their booths in the court of the Gentiles in the Temple, crowding out the Gentiles who had come from all over the civilized world to worship God. The merchants sold sacrificial animals at high prices, taking advantage of those who had come long distances. The money changers exchanged all international currency for the special Temple coins—the only money the merchants would accept. They often deceived foreigners who didn't know the exchange rates. Their commercialism in God's house frustrated people's attempts at worship. This, of course, greatly angered Jesus, but he did not sin in his anger. Christians should be upset about sin and injustice and should take a stand against them. Unfortunately, believers are often passive about these important issues and get angry instead over personal insults and petty irritations.

October 7

Jesus explains why he must die
John 12:20-25 *(Harmony 185a)*

*S*ome Greeks who had come to Jerusalem to attend the Passover paid a visit to Philip, who was from Bethsaida in Galilee. They said, "Sir, we want to meet Jesus." Philip told Andrew about it, and they went together to ask Jesus.

Jesus replied, "The time has come for the Son of Man to enter into his glory. The truth is, a kernel of wheat must be planted in the soil. Unless it dies it will be alone—a single seed. But its death will produce many new kernels—a plentiful harvest of new lives. Those who love their life in this world will lose it. Those who despise their life in this world will keep it for eternal life."

LOVE AND HATE

This is a beautiful picture of the necessary sacrifice of Jesus. Unless a grain of wheat is buried in the ground, it will not become a blade of wheat producing many more seeds. Jesus had to die to pay the penalty for our sin, but also to show his power over death. Jesus calls us to be so committed to living for Christ that we "hate" our lives by comparison. This does not mean that we long to die or that we are careless or destructive with the life God has given but that we are willing to die if doing so will glorify Christ. We must disown the tyrannical rule of our own self-centeredness. By laying aside our striving for advantage, security, and pleasure, we can serve God lovingly and freely. Releasing control of our lives and transferring that control to Christ bring eternal life and genuine joy.

These Greeks probably were converts to the Jewish faith. They may have gone to Philip because, though he was a Jew, he had a Greek name.

October 8

Jesus explains why he must die
John 12:26-36 *(Harmony 185b)*

*A*ll those who want to be my disciples must come and follow me, because my servants must be where I am. And if they follow me, the Father will honor them. Now my soul is deeply troubled. Should I pray, 'Father, save me from what lies ahead'? But that is the very reason why I came! Father, bring glory to your name."

Then a voice spoke from heaven, saying, "I have already brought it glory, and I will do it again." When the crowd heard the voice, some thought it was thunder, while others declared an angel had spoken to him.

Then Jesus told them, "The voice was for your benefit, not mine. The time of judgment for the world has come, when the prince of this world will be cast out. And when I am lifted up on the cross, I will draw everyone to myself." He said this to indicate how he was going to die.

"Die?" asked the crowd. "We understood from Scripture that the Messiah would live forever. Why are you saying the Son of Man will die? Who is this Son of Man you are talking about?"

Jesus replied, "My light will shine out for you just a little while longer. Walk in it while you can, so you will not stumble when the darkness falls. If you walk in the darkness, you cannot see where you are going. Believe in the light while there is still time; then you will become children of the light." After saying these things, Jesus went away and was hidden from them.

WHOM DO YOU SEEK?

The crowd could not believe what Jesus was saying about the Messiah. They were waving palm branches for a victorious leader who would set up a political, earthly kingdom that would never end. From their reading of certain Scriptures, they thought the Messiah would never die (Psalms 89:35-36; 110:4; Isaiah 9:7). Other passages, however, showed that he would (Isaiah 53:5-9). Jesus' words did not mesh with the crowd's concept of the Messiah! First he had to suffer and die—then he would one day set up his eternal Kingdom. What kind of Messiah, or Savior, are you seeking? Beware of trying to force Jesus into your own mold—he won't fit.

The ruler of this world is Satan, an angel who rebelled against God. Satan is real, not symbolic, and is constantly working against God and those who obey him. Satan has great power, but people can be delivered from his reign of spiritual darkness because of Christ's victory on the cross. Satan is powerful, but Jesus is much more powerful.

October 9

Most of the people do not believe in Jesus
John 12:37-43 *(Harmony 186)*

*B*ut despite all the miraculous signs he had done, most of the people did not believe in him. This is exactly what Isaiah the prophet had predicted: "Lord, who has believed our message? To whom will the Lord reveal his saving power?"

But the people couldn't believe, for as Isaiah also said, "The Lord has blinded their eyes and hardened their hearts—so their eyes cannot see, and their hearts cannot understand, and they cannot turn to me and let me heal them."

Isaiah was referring to Jesus when he made this prediction, because he was given a vision of the Messiah's glory. Many people, including some of the Jewish leaders, believed in him. But they wouldn't admit it to anyone because of their fear that the Pharisees would expel them from the synagogue. For they loved human praise more than the praise of God.

TEMPORARY PRAISE

Along with those who refused to believe, many believed but refused to admit it. This is just as bad, and Jesus had strong words for such people (see Matthew 10:32-33). People who will not take a stand for Jesus are afraid of rejection or ridicule. Many Jewish leaders wouldn't admit to faith in Jesus because they feared excommunication from the synagogue (which was their livelihood) and loss of their prestigious place in the community. But the praise of others is fickle and short-lived. We should be much more concerned about God's eternal acceptance than about the temporary approval of other people.

People in Jesus' time, like those in the time of Isaiah, would not believe despite the evidence (12:37). As a result, God hardened their hearts. Does that mean God intentionally prevented these people from believing in him? No, he simply confirmed their own choices. For such people, it is virtually impossible to come to God.

October 10

Jesus summarizes his message
John 12:44-50 *(Harmony 187)*

*J*esus shouted to the crowds, "If you trust me, you are really trusting God who sent me. For when you see me, you are seeing the one who sent me. I have come as a light to shine in this dark world, so that all who put their trust in me will no longer remain in the darkness. If anyone hears me and doesn't obey me, I am not his judge—for I have come to save the world and not to judge it. But all who reject me and my message will be judged at the day of judgment by the truth I have spoken. I don't speak on my own authority. The Father who sent me gave me his own instructions as to what I should say. And I know his instructions lead to eternal life; so I say whatever the Father tells me to say!"

The purpose of Jesus' first mission on earth was not to judge people but to show them the way to find salvation and eternal life. When he comes again, one of his main purposes will be to judge people for how they lived on earth. Christ's words that we would *not* accept and obey will condemn us. On the day of judgment, those who have accepted Jesus and have lived his way will be raised to eternal life (1 Corinthians 15:51-57; 1 Thessalonians 4:15-18; Revelation 21:1-7), and those who have rejected Jesus and have lived any way they pleased will face eternal punishment (Revelation 21:8). Decide now which side you'll be on, for the consequences of your decision last forever.

We often wonder what God is like. How can we know the Creator when he doesn't make himself visible? Jesus said plainly that those who see him see God because he is God. If you want to know what God is like, study the person and words of Jesus Christ.

October 11

Jesus says the disciples can pray for anything
Mark 11:20-25 (also in Matthew 21:18-22) *(Harmony 188)*

*T*he next morning as they passed by the fig tree he had cursed, the disciples noticed it was withered from the roots. Peter remembered what Jesus had said to the tree on the previous day and exclaimed, "Look, Teacher! The fig tree you cursed has withered!"

Then Jesus said to the disciples, "Have faith in God. I assure you that you can say to this mountain, 'May God lift you up and throw you into the sea,' and your command will be obeyed. All that's required is that you really believe and do not doubt in your heart. Listen to me! You can pray for anything, and if you believe, you will have it. But when you are praying, first forgive anyone you are holding a grudge against, so that your Father in heaven will forgive your sins, too."

Jesus' judgment on the fig tree occurred early in the spring fig season when the leaves usually would begin to bud. The figs normally grow as the leaves fill out, but this tree, though full of leaves, had no fruit. The tree looked promising but offered no figs. Jesus' harsh words to the fig tree could be applied to the nation of Israel. Fruitful in appearance only, Israel was spiritually barren.

THE PRAYER OF FAITH
The kind of prayer that moves mountains is prayer for the fruitfulness of God's Kingdom. It would seem impossible to move a mountain into the sea, so Jesus used that picture to say that God can do anything. God will answer your prayers, but not as a result of your positive mental attitude. Other condi-

tions must be met: (1) You must be a believer; (2) you must not hold a grudge against another person; (3) you must not pray with selfish motives; (4) your request must be for the good of God's Kingdom. To pray effectively, you need faith in *God,* not faith in the object of your request. If you focus only on your request, you will be left with nothing when your request is refused. Be a person of prayer, and watch God move mountains.

October 12

Religious leaders challenge Jesus' authority
Mark 11:27-33 (also in Matthew 21:23-27; Luke 20:1-8)
(Harmony 189)

*B*y this time they had arrived in Jerusalem again. As Jesus was walking through the Temple area, the leading priests, the teachers of religious law, and the other leaders came up to him. They demanded, "By whose authority did you drive out the merchants from the Temple? Who gave you such authority?"

"I'll tell who gave me authority to do these things if you answer one question," Jesus replied. "Did John's baptism come from heaven or was it merely human? Answer me!"

They talked it over among themselves. "If we say it was from heaven, he will ask why we didn't believe him. But do we dare say it was merely human?" For they were afraid that the people would start a riot, since everyone thought that John was a prophet. So they finally replied, "We don't know."

And Jesus responded, "Then I won't answer your question either."

TRUE MOTIVES
The religious leaders asked Jesus who had given him the authority to chase away the merchants and money changers. Their question was a trap. If Jesus said his authority was from God, they would accuse him of blasphemy; if he said his authority was his own, they would dismiss him as a fanatic. To expose their real motives, Jesus countered their question with a question about John the Baptist. The leaders' silence proved that they were not interested in the truth. They simply wanted to get rid of Jesus because he was undermining their authority. Sometimes people will ask questions about your faith to try to trip you up or make fun of you. Others will ask questions, sincerely looking for answers. Spend your time with those who really want answers.

Jesus took the Jewish leaders' trap and turned it back on them. How exasperated they must have been that they were unable to get Jesus to say anything that they could use against him!

October 13

Jesus tells the parable of the two sons
Matthew 21:28-32 *(Harmony 190)*

*B*ut what do you think about this? A man with two sons told the older boy, 'Son, go out and work in the vineyard today.' The son answered, 'No, I won't go,' but later he changed his mind and went anyway. Then the father told the other son, 'You go,' and he said, 'Yes, sir, I will.' But he didn't go. Which of the two was obeying his father?"

They replied, "The first, of course."

Then Jesus explained his meaning: "I assure you, corrupt tax collectors and prostitutes will get into the Kingdom of God before you do. For John the Baptist came and showed you the way to life, and you didn't believe him, while tax collectors and prostitutes did. And even when you saw this happening, you refused to turn from your sins and believe him."

PHONIES
The son who said he would obey and then didn't represented the nation of Israel in Jesus' day. The people said they wanted to do God's will, but they constantly disobeyed. They were phony, just going through the motions. It is dangerous to pretend to obey God when our hearts are far from him because God knows our true intentions. Our actions must match our words. *Knowing* God's will is not the same as *doing* it. Don't just go through the motions.

This indictment surely made the Jewish leaders furious. That such people as evil men and prostitutes could be in heaven and not the pious leaders was absurd. But Jesus turns the world's values upside down.

October 14

Jesus tells the parable of the wicked farmers
Matthew 21:33-46 (also in Mark 12:1-12; Luke 20:9-19)
(Harmony 191)

*N*ow listen to this story. A certain landowner planted a vineyard, built a wall around it, dug a pit for pressing out the grape juice, and built a lookout tower. Then he leased the vineyard to tenant farmers and moved to another country. At the time of the grape harvest he sent his servants to collect his share of the crop. But the farmers grabbed his servants, beat one, killed one, and stoned another. So the landowner sent a larger group of his servants to collect for him, but the results were the same.

"Finally, the owner sent his son, thinking, 'Surely they will respect my son.'

"But when the farmers saw his son coming, they said to one another, 'Here comes the heir to this estate. Come on, let's kill him and get the estate for ourselves!' So they grabbed him, took him out of the vineyard, and murdered him.

"When the owner of the vineyard returns," Jesus asked, "what do you think he will do to those farmers?"

The religious leaders replied, "He will put the wicked men to a horrible death and lease the vineyard to others who will give him his share of the crop after each harvest."

Then Jesus asked them, "Didn't you ever read this in the Scriptures? 'The stone rejected by the builders has now become the cornerstone. This is the Lord's doing, and it is marvelous to see.'

What I mean is that the Kingdom of God will be taken away from you and given to a nation that will produce the proper fruit. Anyone who stumbles over that stone will be broken to pieces, and it will crush anyone on whom it falls."

When the leading priests and Pharisees heard Jesus, they realized he was pointing at them—that they were the farmers in his story. They wanted to arrest him, but they were afraid to try because the crowds considered Jesus to be a prophet.

STUMBLING STONE

The characters in this story are easily identified. Even the religious leaders got the point. The owner of the vineyard is God; the vineyard is Israel; the vinedressers are the religious leaders; the servants are the prophets and priests God sent to Israel; the son is the Messiah, Jesus; and the others are the Gentiles. Jesus' parable indirectly answered the religious leaders' question about his authority; it also showed them that he knew about their plan to kill him. There is no difference between those who ignore Christ and those who refuse to believe. All who stumble over Jesus, the Cornerstone, will be judged in the end. When sharing your faith, keep the focus on Christ. He's the only one who really matters.

Jesus referred to himself as the stone rejected by the builders. Although he would be rejected by most of the Jewish leaders, he would become the cornerstone of a new "building," the church (Acts 4:11-12). Likewise, Jesus' life and teaching would be the church's foundation.

Jesus tells the parable of the wedding feast
Matthew 22:1-14 *(Harmony 192)*

*J*esus told them several other stories to illustrate the Kingdom. He said, "The Kingdom of Heaven can be illustrated by the story of a king who prepared a great wedding feast for his son. Many guests were invited, and when the banquet was ready, he sent his servants to notify everyone that it was time to come. But they all refused! So he sent other servants to tell them, 'The feast has been prepared, and choice meats have been cooked. Everything is ready. Hurry!' But the guests he had invited ignored them and went about their business, one to his farm, another to his store. Others seized his messengers and treated them shamefully, even killing some of them.

"Then the king became furious. He sent out his army to destroy the murderers and burn their city. And he said to his servants, 'The wedding feast is ready, and the guests I invited aren't worthy of the honor. Now go out to the street corners and invite everyone you see.'

"So the servants brought in everyone they could find, good and bad alike, and the banquet hall was filled with guests. But when the king came in to meet the guests, he noticed a man who wasn't wearing the proper clothes for a wedding. 'Friend,' he asked, 'how is it that you are here without wedding clothes?' And the man had no reply. Then the king said to his aides, 'Bind him hand and foot and throw him out into the outer darkness, where there is weeping and gnashing of teeth.' For many are called, but few are chosen."

R.S.V.P.
In this culture, two invitations were expected when wedding dinners were given. The first invitation asked the guests to attend; the second one announced that all was ready. In this story the king invited his guests three times, and each time they rejected his invitation. God wants us to join him at his banquet, which will last for eternity. That's why he sends us invitations again and again. What should you do to accept his invitation?

It was customary for wedding guests to be given special clothes to wear to the dinner. It was unthinkable to refuse to wear them. That would insult the host, who could only assume that the guest was arrogant and thought he didn't need them, or he didn't want to take part in the wedding celebration. The wedding clothes picture the righteousness needed to enter God's Kingdom.

October 16

Religious leaders question Jesus about taxes
Mark 12:13-17 (also in Matthew 22:15-22; Luke 20:20-26)
(Harmony 193)

*T*he leaders sent some Pharisees and supporters of Herod to try to trap Jesus into saying something for which he could be arrested. "Teacher," these men said, "we know how honest you are. You are impartial and don't play favorites. You sincerely teach the ways of God. Now tell us—is it right to pay taxes to the Roman government or not? Should we pay them, or should we not?"

Jesus saw through their hypocrisy and said, "Whom are you trying to fool with your trick questions? Show me a Roman coin, and I'll tell you." When they handed it to him, he asked, "Whose picture and title are stamped on it?"

"Caesar's," they replied.

"Well, then," Jesus said, "give to Caesar what belongs to him. But everything that belongs to God must be given to God." This reply completely amazed them.

WHOSE IMAGE?
Anyone who avoided paying taxes faced harsh penalties. The Jews hated to pay taxes to Rome because the money supported their oppressors and symbolized their subjection. Much of the tax money also went to maintain the heathen Temples and luxurious lifestyles of Rome's upper class. The Pharisees and Herodians hoped to trap Jesus with this tax question. A yes would mean that he supported Rome—this would turn the people against him. A no would bring accusations of treason and rebellion against Rome and could lead to civil penalties. But Jesus answered wisely, saying that the coin bearing the emperor's image should be given to the emperor. But human lives, which bear God's image, belong to God. Are you giving God all that is rightfully his? Give your life to God—you bear his image.

The Pharisees were primarily a religious group concerned for ritual purity; the Herodians were a Jewish political group that approved of Herod's compromises with Rome. Normally the two groups totally avoided each other.

October 17

Religious leaders question Jesus about the resurrection
Mark 12:18-27 (also in Matthew 22:23-32; Luke 20:27-40)
(Harmony 194)

*T*hen the Sadducees stepped forward—a group of Jews who say there is no resurrection after death. They posed this question: "Teacher, Moses gave us a law that if a man dies, leaving a wife without children, his brother should marry the widow and have a child who will be the brother's heir. Well, there were seven brothers. The oldest of them married and then died without children. So the second brother married the widow, but soon he too died and left no children. Then the next brother married her and died without children. This continued until all the brothers had married her and died, and still there were no children. Last of all, the woman died, too. So tell us, whose wife will she be in the resurrection? For all seven were married to her."

Jesus replied, "Your problem is that you don't know the Scriptures, and you don't know the power of God. For when the dead rise, they won't be married. They will be like the angels in heaven. But now, as to whether the dead will be raised—haven't you ever read about this in the writings of Moses, in the story of the burning bush? Long after Abraham, Isaac, and Jacob had died, God said to Moses, 'I am the God of Abraham, the God of Isaac, and the God of Jacob.' So he is the God of the living, not the dead. You have made a serious error."

FUTURE LIFE
What life will be like after the resurrection is far beyond our ability to understand or imagine (Isaiah 64:4; 1 Corinthians 2:9). We need not be afraid of eternal life because of the unknowns, however. Jesus' statement does not mean that people won't recognize their partners in the coming Kingdom. It simply means that God's new order will not be an extension of this life and that the same physical and natural rules won't apply. Instead of wondering what God's coming Kingdom will be like, we should concentrate on our relationship with Christ right now, because in the new Kingdom we will be with him. If we learn to love and trust Christ *now*, we will not be afraid of what he has in store for us then.

The Sadducees' real question was not about marriage but about the doctrine of resurrection. Because the Sadducees followed only the Pentateuch (Genesis through Deuteronomy), Jesus quoted from Exodus 3:6 to prove that there is life after death. God spoke of Abraham, Isaac, and Jacob years after their deaths as if they still lived. God's covenant with all people exists beyond death.

October 18

Religious leaders question Jesus about the greatest commandment
Mark 12:28-34 (also in Matthew 22:33-40) *(Harmony 195)*

*O*ne of the teachers of religious law was standing there listening to the discussion. He realized that Jesus had answered well, so he asked, "Of all the commandments, which is the most important?"

Jesus replied, "The most important commandment is this: 'Hear, O Israel! The Lord our God is the one and only Lord. And you must love the Lord your God with all your heart, all your soul, all your mind, and all your strength.' The second is equally important: 'Love your neighbor as yourself.' No other commandment is greater than these."

The teacher of religious law replied, "Well said, Teacher. You have spoken the truth by saying that there is only one God and no other. And I know it is important to love him with all my heart and all my understanding and all my strength, and to love my neighbors as myself. This is more important than to offer all of the burnt offerings and sacrifices required in the law."

Realizing this man's understanding, Jesus said to him, "You are not far from the Kingdom of God." And after that, no one dared to ask him any more questions.

LAW OF LOVE
God's laws are not burdensome. They can be reduced to two simple principles: (1) Love God and (2) love others. These commands are from the Old Testament (Deuteronomy 6:5; Leviticus 19:18). When you love God completely and care for others as you care for yourself, then you have fulfilled the intent of the Ten Commandments and the other Old Testament laws. According to Jesus, these two commandments summarize all God's laws. Let them rule your thoughts, decisions, and actions. When you are uncertain about what to do, ask yourself which course of action best demonstrates love for God and love for others.

The Pharisees, who had classified over six hundred laws, often tried to distinguish the more important from the less important. But they failed to see that all the commands in the Old Testament lead to Christ.

October 19

Religious leaders cannot answer Jesus' question
Matthew 22:41-46 (also in Mark 12:35-37; Luke 20:41-44)
(Harmony 196)

*T*hen, surrounded by the Pharisees, Jesus asked them a question: "What do you think about the Messiah? Whose son is he?"

They replied, "He is the son of David."

Jesus responded, "Then why does David, speaking under the inspiration of the Holy Spirit, call him Lord? For David said, 'The Lord said to my Lord, Sit in honor at my right hand until I humble your enemies beneath your feet.'

Since David called him Lord, how can he be his son at the same time?"

No one could answer him. And after that, no one dared to ask him any more questions.

THE MOST IMPORTANT QUESTION
The Pharisees and Sadducees had asked their questions. Then Jesus turned the tables and asked them a question that went right to the heart of the matter—what they thought about the Messiah's identity. The Pharisees knew that the Messiah would be a descendant of David, but they did not understand that he would be more than a human descendant—he would be God in the flesh. Jesus quoted from Psalm 110:1 to show that David had known that the Messiah would be both human and divine. The Pharisees expected only a human ruler to restore Israel's greatness as in the days of David and Solomon.

The Jewish religious leaders should have been the first to recognize Jesus as the promised Messiah, rejoice over his arrival, and lead the nation to follow him. Instead, they refused to believe.

The central issue of life is what we believe about Jesus. Other spiritual questions are irrelevant unless we first believe that Jesus is who he said.

October 20

Jesus warns against the religious leaders
Matthew 23:1-12 (also in Mark 12:38-40; Luke 20:45-47)
(Harmony 197)

*T*hen Jesus said to the crowds and to his disciples, "The teachers of religious law and the Pharisees are the official interpreters of the Scriptures. So practice and obey whatever they say to you, but don't follow their example. For they don't practice what they teach. They crush you with impossible religious demands and never lift a finger to help ease the burden.

"Everything they do is for show. On their arms they wear extra wide prayer boxes with Scripture verses inside, and they wear extra long tassels on their robes. And how they love to sit at the head table at banquets and in the most prominent seats in the synagogue! They enjoy the attention they get on the streets, and they enjoy being called 'Rabbi.' Don't ever let anyone call you 'Rabbi,' for you have only one teacher, and all of you are on the same level as brothers and sisters. And don't address anyone here on earth as 'Father,' for only God in heaven is your spiritual Father. And don't let anyone call you 'Master,' for there is only one master, the Messiah. The greatest among you must be a servant. But those who exalt themselves will be humbled, and those who humble themselves will be exalted."

MAKE SURE THEY MATCH

Jesus again exposed the hypocritical attitudes of the religious leaders who knew the Scriptures but did not live by them. The Pharisees' traditions and their interpretations and applications of the laws had become as important to them as God's law itself. Their laws were not all bad—some were beneficial. Usually Jesus did not condemn what the Pharisees taught but what they *were*—hypocrites. They didn't care about *being* holy but about just *looking* holy in order to receive the people's admiration and praise. Today many people, like the Pharisees, know the Bible but do not let it change their lives. They say they follow Jesus, but they don't live by his standards of love. Make sure that your actions match your beliefs.

The little prayer boxes, called phylacteries, contained Scripture verses. Very religious people wore these boxes on their forehead and arms in order to obey Deuteronomy 6:8 and Exodus 13:9, 16. But the prayer boxes had become more important for the status they gave than for the truth they contained.

October 21

Jesus condemns the religious leaders
Matthew 23:13-36 *(Harmony 198)*

*H*ow terrible it will be for you teachers of religious law and you Pharisees. Hypocrites! For you won't let others enter the Kingdom of Heaven, and you won't go in yourselves. Yes, how terrible it will be for you teachers of religious law and you Pharisees. For you cross land and sea to make one convert, and then you turn him into twice the son of hell as you yourselves are.

"Blind guides! How terrible it will be for you! For you say that it means nothing to swear 'by God's Temple'—you can break that oath. But then you say that it is binding to swear 'by the gold in the Temple.' Blind fools! Which is greater, the gold, or the Temple that makes the gold sacred? And you say that to take an oath 'by the altar' can be broken, but to swear 'by the gifts on the altar' is binding! How blind! For which is greater, the gift on the altar, , or the altar that makes the gift sacred? When you swear 'by the altar,' you are swearing by it and by everything on it. And when you swear 'by the Temple,' you are swearing by it and by God, who lives in it. And when you swear 'by heaven,' you are swearing by the throne of God and by God, who sits on the throne.

"How terrible it will be for you teachers of religious law and you Pharisees. Hypocrites! For you are careful to tithe even the tiniest part of your income, but you ignore the important things of the law—justice, mercy, and faith. You should tithe, yes, but you should not leave undone the more important things. Blind guides! You strain your water so you won't accidentally swallow a gnat; then you swallow a camel!

"How terrible it will be for you teachers of religious law and you Pharisees. Hypocrites! You are so careful to clean the outside of the cup and the dish, but inside you are filthy—full of greed and self-indulgence! Blind Pharisees! First wash the inside of the cup, and then the outside will become clean, too.

"How terrible it will be for you teachers of religious law and you Pharisees. Hypocrites! You are like whitewashed tombs—beautiful on the outside but filled on the inside with dead people's bones and all sorts of impurity. You try to look like upright people outwardly, but inside your hearts are filled with hypocrisy and lawlessness.

"How terrible it will be for you teachers of religious law and you Pharisees. Hypocrites! For you build tombs for the prophets your ancestors killed and decorate the graves of the godly people your ancestors destroyed. Then you say, 'We never would have joined them in killing the prophets.'

"In saying that, you are accusing yourselves of being the descendants of those who murdered the prophets. Go ahead. Finish what they started. Snakes! Sons of vipers! How will you escape the judgment of hell? I will send you prophets and wise men and teachers of religious law. You will kill some by crucifixion and whip others in your synagogues, chasing them from city to city. As a result, you will become guilty of murdering all the godly people from righteous Abel to Zechariah son of Barachiah, whom you murdered in the Temple between the altar and the sanctuary. I assure you, all the accumulated judgment of the centuries will break upon the heads of this very generation."

DON'T SWALLOW A CAMEL!

The Pharisees strained their water so they wouldn't accidentally swallow a gnat—an unclean insect according to the law. Meticulous about the details of ceremonial cleanliness, they nevertheless had lost their perspective on inner purity. Ceremonially clean on the outside, they had corrupt hearts. It's possible to obey the details of the law but still be disobedient in our general behavior. Jesus condemned the Pharisees and religious leaders for outwardly appearing saintly and holy but inwardly remaining full of corruption and greed. Living our Christianity merely as a show for others is like washing a cup on the outside only. When we are clean on the inside, our cleanliness on the outside won't be a sham.

Being a religious leader in Jerusalem was very different from being a pastor in a secular society today. Israel's history, culture, and daily life centered around its relationship with God. The religious leaders were the best known, most powerful, and most respected of all leaders. Jesus made these stinging accusations because the leaders' hunger for more power, money, and status had made them lose sight of God, and their blindness was spreading to the whole nation.

October 22

Jesus grieves over Jerusalem again
Matthew 23:37-39 (Harmony 199)

O Jerusalem, Jerusalem, the city that kills the prophets and stones God's messengers! How often I have wanted to gather your children together as a hen protects her chicks beneath her wings, but you wouldn't let me. And now look, your house is left to you, empty and desolate. For I tell you this, you will never see me again until you say, 'Bless the one who comes in the name of the Lord!' "

PROTECTION

Here we see the depth of Jesus' feelings for lost people and for his beloved city, which would soon be destroyed. Jesus wanted to gather his people together as a hen protects her chicks under her wings, but they wouldn't let him. Jesus also wants to protect us if we will just come to him. Many times we hurt and don't know where to turn. We reject Christ's help because we don't think he can give us what we need. But who knows our needs better than our Creator? Those who turn to Jesus will find that he helps and comforts as no one else can.

Jerusalem was the capital city of God's chosen people, the home of David, Israel's greatest king, and the location of the Temple, the earthly dwelling place of God. It was intended to be the center of worship of the true God and a symbol of justice to all people. But Jerusalem had become blind to God and insensitive to human need.

October 23

A poor widow gives all she has
Mark 12:41-44 (also in Luke 21:1-4) *(Harmony 200)*

*J*esus went over to the collection box in the Temple and sat and watched as the crowds dropped in their money. Many rich people put in large amounts. Then a poor widow came and dropped in two pennies. He called his disciples to him and said, "I assure you, this poor widow has given more than all the others have given. For they gave a tiny part of their surplus, but she, poor as she is, has given everything she has."

GIFTS THAT COUNT
In the Lord's eyes, this poor widow had given more than all the others put together, although her gift was by far the smallest. She had given all she had to live on, in contrast to the way most of us handle our money. When we consider giving a certain percentage of our income a great accomplishment, we resemble those who had given "what they didn't need." Here, Jesus was extolling generous and sacrificial giving. Not only was she poor, but as a widow she had few resources for making money. Her small gift was a sacrifice, but she gave it willingly. As believers, we should consider increasing our giving—whether of money, time, or talents—to a point beyond convenience or safety.

Jesus was in the area of the Temple called the Court of Women. The treasury was located there or in an adjoining walkway. In this area were seven boxes in which worshipers could deposit their Temple tax and six boxes for freewill offerings like the one given by this woman.

October 24

Jesus tells about the future
Mark 13:1-4 (also in Matthew 24:1-3; Luke 21:5-7) *(Harmony 201a)*

*A*s Jesus was leaving the Temple that day, one of his disciples said, "Teacher, look at these tremendous buildings! Look at the massive stones in the walls!"

Jesus replied, "These magnificent buildings will be so completely demolished that not one stone will be left on top of another."

Later, Jesus sat on the slopes of the Mount of Olives across the valley from the Temple. Peter, James, John, and Andrew came to him privately and asked him, "When will all this take place? And will there be any sign ahead of time to show us when all this will be fulfilled?"

BE READY

The disciples wanted to know when the Temple would be destroyed. Jesus gave them a prophetic picture of that time, including events leading up to it. He also talked about future events connected with his return to earth to judge all people. Jesus predicted both near and distant events without putting them in chronological order. Some of the disciples lived to see the destruction of Jerusalem in A.D. 70. This event would assure them that everything else Jesus predicted would also happen.

The Mount of Olives rises above Jerusalem to the east. From its slopes a person can look down into the city and see the Temple. Zechariah 14:1-4 predicts that the Messiah will stand on this very mountain when he returns to set up his eternal Kingdom.

Jesus warned his followers about the future so that they could learn how to live in the present. Many predictions Jesus made in this passage have not yet been fulfilled. He did not make them so that we would guess when they might be fulfilled, but to help us remain spiritually alert and prepared at all times as we wait for his return. What changes would you make if you knew that Jesus would return one of these days? Be ready for his second coming.

October 25

Jesus tells about the future
Mark 13:5 13 (also in Matthew 24:4-14, Luke 21:8-19)
(Harmony 201b)

*J*esus replied, "Don't let anyone mislead you, because many will come in my name, claiming to be the Messiah. They will lead many astray. And wars will break out near and far, but don't panic. Yes, these things must come, but the end won't follow immediately. Nations and kingdoms will proclaim war against each other, and there will be earthquakes in many parts of the world, and famines. But all this will be only the beginning of the horrors to come. But when these things begin to happen, watch out! You will be handed over to the courts and beaten in the synagogues. You will be accused before governors and kings of being my followers. This will be your opportunity to tell them about me. And the Good News must first be preached to every nation. But when you are arrested and stand trial, don't worry about what to say in your defense. Just say what God tells you to. Then it is not you who will be speaking, but the Holy Spirit.

"Brother will betray brother to death, fathers will betray their own children, and children will rise against their parents and cause them to be killed. And everyone will hate you because of your allegiance to me. But those who endure to the end will be saved."

END SIGNS

What are the signs of the end times? There have been people in every generation since Christ's resurrection claiming to know exactly when Jesus will return. No one has been right yet, however, because Christ will return on God's timetable, not ours. Jesus predicted that before his return, many believers would be misled by false teachers claiming to have revelations from God.

Jesus predicted that his followers would be severely persecuted by those who hated what he stood for. In the midst of terrible persecution, however, they could have hope, knowing that salvation was theirs.

According to Scripture, the one clear sign of Christ's return will be his unmistakable appearance in the clouds which will be seen by all people (13:26; Revelation 1:7). In other words, you do not have to wonder whether a certain person is the Messiah or whether these are the "end times." When Jesus returns, *you will know* beyond a doubt because it will be evident to all true believers. Beware of groups who claim special knowledge of the last days, because no one knows when that time will be (13:32). Be cautious about saying, "This is it!" but be bold in your total commitment to have your heart and life ready for Christ's return.

October 26

Jesus tells about the future
Matthew 24:15-22 (also in Mark 13:14-20; Luke 21:20-24)
(Harmony 201c)

The time will come when you will see what Daniel the prophet spoke about: the sacrilegious object that causes desecration standing in the Holy Place"—reader, pay attention! "Then those in Judea must flee to the hills. A person outside the house must not go inside to pack. A person in the field must not return even to get a coat. How terrible it will be for pregnant women and for mothers nursing their babies in those days. And pray that your flight will not be in winter or on the Sabbath. For that will be a time of greater horror than anything the world has ever seen or will ever see again. In fact, unless that time of calamity is shortened, the entire human race will be destroyed. But it will be shortened for the sake of God's chosen ones."

NEEDED KNOWLEDGE
Jesus was talking about the desecration of the Temple by God's enemies. This has happened repeatedly in Israel's history: in 597 B.C. when Nebuchadnezzar looted the Temple and took Judean captives to Babylon (2 Chronicles 36); in

168 B.C. when Antiochus Epiphanes sacrificed a pig to Zeus on the sacred Temple altar (Daniel 9:27; 11:30-31); in A.D. 70 when the Roman general Titus placed an idol on the site of the burned-out Temple after the destruction of Jerusalem. Just a few years after Jesus gave this warning the emperor Caligula made plans to put a statue of himself in the Temple, but he died before this could be carried out. Talking about the end times, Jesus telescoped near future and far future events, as did the Old Testament prophets. Many of these persecutions have already occurred; more are yet to come. But God is in control of even the length of each persecution. He will not forget his people. This is all we need to know about the future to motivate us to live rightly now.

While this desecration of the Temple has specific applications in history, it also can be seen as any deliberate attempt to mock and deny the reality of God's presence.

October 27

Jesus tells about his return
Matthew 24:23-28 (also in Mark 13:21-23) *(Harmony 202a)*

*T*hen if anyone tells you, 'Look, here is the Messiah,' or 'There he is,' don't pay any attention. For false messiahs and false prophets will rise up and perform great miraculous signs and wonders so as to deceive, if possible, even God's chosen ones. See, I have warned you.

"So if someone tells you, 'Look, the Messiah is out in the desert,' don't bother to go and look. Or, 'Look, he is hiding here,' don't believe it! For as the lightning lights up the entire sky, so it will be when the Son of Man comes. Just as the gathering of vultures shows there is a carcass nearby, so these signs indicate that the end is near."

DECEPTIONS
Is it possible for Christians to be deceived? Yes. So convincing will be the arguments and proofs from deceivers in the end times that it will be difficult *not* to fall away from Christ. If we are prepared, Jesus says, we can remain faithful. But if we are not prepared, we will turn away. To penetrate the disguises of false teachers we can ask: (1) Have their predictions come true, or do they have to revise them to fit what's already happened? (2) Does any teaching utilize a small section of the Bible to the neglect of the whole? (3) Does the teaching contradict what the

Jesus' warnings about false teachers still hold true. Upon close examination we can see that many nice-sounding messages don't agree with God's message in the Bible. Only a solid foundation in God's Word can equip believers to perceive the errors and distortions in false teaching.

Bible says about God? (4) Are the practices meant to glorify the teacher or Christ? (5) Do the teachings promote hostility toward other Christians?

October 28

Jesus tells about his return
Matthew 24:29-35 (also in Mark 13:24-31; Luke 21:25-33) (Harmony 202b)

*I*mmediately after those horrible days end, the sun will be darkened, the moon will not give light, the stars will fall from the sky, and the powers of heaven will be shaken.

And then at last, the sign of the coming of the Son of Man will appear in the heavens, and there will be deep mourning among all the nations of the earth. And they will see the Son of Man arrive on the clouds of heaven with power and great glory. And he will send forth his angels with the sound of a mighty trumpet blast, and they will gather together his chosen ones from the farthest ends of the earth and heaven.

"Now learn a lesson from the fig tree. When its buds become tender and its leaves begin to sprout, you know without being told that summer is near. Just so, when you see the events I've described beginning to happen, you can know his return is very near, right at the door. I assure you, this generation will not pass from the scene before all these things take place. Heaven and earth will disappear, but my words will remain forever."

ETERNAL TRUTH

In Jesus' day the world seemed concrete, dependable, and permanent. These days many people fear its destruction by nuclear war. Jesus tells us, however, that even if the earth should pass away, the truth of his words will never be changed or abolished. God and his Word provide the only stability in our unstable world. How shortsighted people are who spend their time learning about this temporary world and accumulating its possessions while neglecting the Bible and its eternal truths!

The nations of the earth will mourn because unbelievers will suddenly realize that they have chosen the wrong side. Everything they have mocked will be happening, and it will be too late for them.

Jesus tells about remaining watchful

Matthew 24:36-51 (also in Mark 13:32-37; Luke 21:34-38)
(Harmony 203)

*H*owever, no one knows the day or the hour when these things will happen, not even the angels in heaven or the Son himself. Only the Father knows.

"When the Son of Man returns, it will be like it was in Noah's day. In those days before the Flood, the people were enjoying banquets and parties and weddings right up to the time Noah entered his boat. People didn't realize what was going to happen until the Flood came and swept them all away. That is the way it will be when the Son of Man comes.

"Two men will be working together in the field; one will be taken, the other left. Two women will be grinding flour at the mill; one will be taken, the other left. So be prepared, because you don't know what day your Lord is coming.

"Know this: A homeowner who knew exactly when a burglar was coming would stay alert and not permit the house to be broken into. You also must be ready all the time. For the Son of Man will come when least expected.

"Who is a faithful, sensible servant, to whom the master can give the responsibility of managing his household and feeding his family? If the master returns and finds that the servant has done a good job, there will be a reward. I assure you, the master will put that servant in charge of all he owns. But if the servant is evil and thinks, 'My master won't be back for a while,' and begins oppressing the other servants, partying, and getting drunk—well, the master will return unannounced and unexpected. He will tear the servant apart and banish him with the hypocrites. In that place there will be weeping and gnashing of teeth."

WHILE WAITING . . .

Jesus' words here tell us how to live while we wait for his return: (1) We are not to be misled by confusing claims or speculative interpretations of what will happen. (2) We should not be afraid to tell people about Christ, despite what they might say or do to us. (3) We must stand firm by faith and not be surprised by persecution. (4) We must be morally alert, obedient to the commands for living found in God's Word. Jesus didn't

When Jesus said that even he did not know the time of the end, he was affirming his humanity. Of course God the Father knows the time, and Jesus and the Father are one. But when Jesus became a man, he voluntarily gave up the unlimited use of his divine attributes. The emphasis of this verse is not on Jesus' lack of knowledge but rather on the fact that no one knows. It is God the Father's secret to be revealed when he wills.

want to promote discussions on prophetic timetables. We're not supposed to "figure out" when he's coming back. Instead, it is good that we *don't* know exactly when Christ will return. If we knew the precise date, we might be tempted to be lazy in our work for Christ. Worse yet, we might plan to keep sinning and then turn to God right at the end. Heaven is not our only goal; we have work to do here. And we must keep on doing it until death or until we see the unmistakable return of our Savior.

October 30

Jesus tells the parable of the ten bridesmaids
Matthew 25:1-13 *(Harmony 204)*

*T*he Kingdom of Heaven can be illustrated by the story of ten bridesmaids who took their lamps and went to meet the bridegroom. Five of them were foolish, and five were wise. The five who were foolish took no oil for their lamps, but the other five were wise enough to take along extra oil. When the bridegroom was delayed, they all lay down and slept. At midnight they were roused by the shout, 'Look, the bridegroom is coming! Come out and welcome him!'

"All the bridesmaids got up and prepared their lamps. Then the five foolish ones asked the others, 'Please give us some of your oil because our lamps are going out.' But the others replied, 'We don't have enough for all of us. Go to a shop and buy some for yourselves.'

"But while they were gone to buy oil, the bridegroom came, and those who were ready went in with him to the marriage feast, and the door was locked. Later, when the other five bridesmaids returned, they stood outside, calling, 'Sir, open the door for us!' But he called back, 'I don't know you!'

"So stay awake and be prepared, because you do not know the day or hour of my return."

DON'T BE OUT SHOPPING

These ten virgins were waiting to join the bride and groom in their wedding procession, and they hoped to take part in the wedding banquet. But when the groom didn't come at the expected time, five of them were out of lamp oil. By the time they had purchased extra oil, it was too late to join the feast. When Jesus returns to take his people to heaven, we must be ready. Spiritual preparation cannot be bought or borrowed at the last minute. Our relationship with God must be our own. Christ's

This parable is about a wedding. On the wedding day the bridegroom went to the bride's house for the ceremony; then the bride and groom, along with a great procession, would return to the groom's house for a great feast, often lasting a week.

second coming will be swift and sudden. There will be no opportunity for last-minute repentance or bargaining. The choice we have already made will determine our eternal destiny.

October 31

Jesus tells the parable of the loaned money
Matthew 25:14-30 *(Harmony 205)*

*A*gain, the Kingdom of Heaven can be illustrated by the story of a man going on a trip. He called together his servants and gave them money to invest for him while he was gone. He gave five bags of gold to one, two bags of gold to another, and one bag of gold to the last—dividing it in proportion to their abilities—and then left on his trip. The servant who received the five bags of gold began immediately to invest the money and soon doubled it. The servant with two bags of gold also went right to work and doubled the money. But the servant who received the one bag of gold dug a hole in the ground and hid the master's money for safekeeping.

"After a long time their master returned from his trip and called them to give an account of how they had used his money. The servant to whom he had entrusted the five bags of gold said, 'Sir, you gave me five bags of gold to invest, and I have doubled the amount.' The master was full of praise. 'Well done, my good and faithful servant. You have been faithful in handling this small amount, so now I will give you many more responsibilities. Let's celebrate together!'

"Next came the servant who had received the two bags of gold, with the report, 'Sir, you gave me two bags of gold to invest, and I have doubled the amount.' The master said, 'Well done, my good and faithful servant. You have been faithful in handling this small amount, so now I will give you many more responsibilities. Let's celebrate together!'

"Then the servant with the one bag of gold came and said, 'Sir, I know you are a hard man, harvesting crops you didn't plant and gathering crops you didn't cultivate. I was afraid I would lose your money, so I hid it in the earth and here it is.'"

"But the master replied, 'You wicked and lazy servant! You think I'm a hard man, do you, harvesting crops I didn't plant and gathering crops I didn't cultivate? Well, you should at least have put my money into the bank so I could have some interest. Take the money from this servant and give it to the one with the ten bags of gold. To those who use well what they are given, even more will be given, and they will have an abundance. But from those who are unfaithful, even what little they have will be taken away. Now throw this useless servant into outer darkness, where there will be weeping and gnashing of teeth.'"

A GOOD INVESTMENT

The master divided the money among his servants according to their abilities. No one received more or less than he could handle. If he failed in his assignment, his excuse could not be that he was overwhelmed. Failure could come only from laziness or hatred toward the master. The talents represent any kind of resource we are given. God gives us time, gifts, and other resources according to our abilities, and he expects us to invest them wisely until he returns. Our time, abilities, and money aren't ours in the first place—we are caretakers, not owners. We are responsible to use well what God has given us. The issue is not how much we have but how well we use what we have.

This last man was thinking only of himself. He hoped to play it safe and protect himself from his hard master; thus, he was judged for his self-centeredness. We must not make excuses to avoid doing what God calls us to do.

November 1

Jesus tells about the final judgment
Matthew 25:31-46 *(Harmony 206)*

*B*ut when the Son of Man comes in his glory, and all the angels with him, then he will sit upon his glorious throne. All the nations will be gathered in his presence, and he will separate them as a shepherd separates the sheep from the goats. He will place the sheep at his right hand and the goats at his left. Then the King will say to those on the right, 'Come, you who are blessed by my Father, inherit the Kingdom prepared for you from the foundation of the world. For I was hungry, and you fed me. I was thirsty, and you gave me a drink. I was a stranger, and you invited me into your home. I was naked, and you gave me clothing. I was sick, and you cared for me. I was in prison, and you visited me.'

"Then these righteous ones will reply, 'Lord, when did we ever see you hungry and feed you? Or thirsty and give you something to drink? Or a stranger and show you hospitality? Or naked and give you clothing? When did we ever see you sick or in prison, and visit you?' And the King will tell them, 'I assure you, when you did it to one of the least of these my brothers and sisters, you were doing it to me!'

"Then the King will turn to those on the left and say, 'Away with you, you cursed ones, into the eternal fire prepared for the Devil and his demons! For I was hungry, and you didn't feed me. I was thirsty, and you didn't give me anything to drink. I was a stranger, and you didn't invite me into your home. I was naked, and you gave me no clothing. I was sick and in prison, and you didn't visit me.'

"Then they will reply, 'Lord, when did we ever see you hungry or thirsty or a stranger or naked or sick or in prison, and not help you?' And he will answer, 'I assure you, when you refused to help the least of these my brothers and sisters, you were refusing to help me.' And they will go away into eternal punishment, but the righteous will go into eternal life."

THE GREAT PRETENDERS
God will separate his obedient followers from pretenders and unbelievers. The real evidence of our belief is the way we act. To treat all persons we encounter as if they were Jesus is no easy task. What we do for others demonstrates what we really think about Jesus' words to us—feed the hungry, give the homeless a place to stay, look after the sick. These acts do not depend on wealth, ability, or intelligence; they are simple acts

freely given and freely received. We have no excuse to neglect those who have deep needs, and we cannot hand over this responsibility to the church or government. Jesus demands our personal involvement in caring for others' needs (Isaiah 58:7). How well do your actions separate you from pretenders and unbelievers?

Jesus used sheep and goats to picture the division between believers and unbelievers. Sheep and goats often grazed together but were separated when it came time to shear the sheep. Ezekiel 34:17-24 also refers to the separation of sheep and goats.

November 2

Religious leaders plot to kill Jesus
Matthew 26:1-5 (also in Mark 14:1-2; Luke 22:1-2) *(Harmony 207)*

When Jesus had finished saying these things, he said to his disciples, "As you know, the Passover celebration begins in two days, and I, the Son of Man, will be betrayed and crucified."

At that same time the leading priests and other leaders were meeting at the residence of Caiaphas, the high priest, to discuss how to capture Jesus secretly and put him to death. "But not during the Passover," they agreed, "or there will be a riot."

EASY TO JUSTIFY
Caiaphas was the ruling high priest during Jesus' ministry. He was the son-in-law of Annas, the previous high priest. The Roman government had taken over the process of appointing all political and religious leaders. Caiaphas served for eighteen years, longer than most high priests, suggesting that he was gifted at cooperating with the Romans. He was the first to recommend Jesus' death in order to "save" the nation (John 11:49-50). This was a deliberate plot to kill Jesus. With-

All Jewish males over the age of twelve were required to go to Jerusalem for the Passover feast, followed by a seven-day festival called the Festival of Unleavened Bread. For these feasts, Jews from all over the Roman Empire converged on Jerusalem to celebrate one of the most important events in their history.

out this plot there would have been no groundswell of popular opinion against him. In fact, because of Jesus' popularity, the religious leaders were afraid to arrest him during the Passover; they did not want their actions to incite a riot. So these religious leaders, so pious in their self-righteousness and law keeping, were at the high priest's house planning murder. We can criticize these leaders (and rightfully so), but we should admit that it is easy to justify our sinful actions! Be honest about sin—don't rationalize.

November 3

Judas agrees to betray Jesus
Luke 22:3-6 (also in Matthew 26:14-16; Mark 14:10-11)
(Harmony 208)

T hen Satan entered into Judas Iscariot, who was one of the twelve disciples, and he went over to the leading priests and captains of the Temple guard to discuss the best way to betray Jesus to them. They were delighted that he was ready to help them, and they promised him a reward. So he began looking for an opportunity to betray Jesus so they could arrest him quietly when the crowds weren't around.

WEAK SPOTS
Why would Judas want to betray Jesus? Judas, like the other disciples, expected Jesus to start a political rebellion and overthrow Rome. As treasurer, Judas certainly assumed that he would be given an important position in Jesus' new government. However, Judas soon realized that Jesus' Kingdom was not physical or political but spiritual. Judas's greedy desire for money and status could not be realized if he followed Jesus, so he betrayed Jesus in exchange for money and favor from the religious leaders. Judas allowed his desires to put him in a position where Satan could manipulate him. Satan is good at finding our weak spots and trying to use them for his purposes. That's why it's so important to yield every part of your life to Christ. Recognize your weak spots and yield them to Jesus' power.

Satan's part in the betrayal of Jesus does not remove any of the responsibility from Judas. Disillusioned because Jesus had been talking about dying rather than about setting up his Kingdom, Judas may have been trying to force Jesus' hand and make him use his power to prove he was the Messiah.

November 4

Disciples prepare for the Passover
Luke 22:7-13 (also in Matthew 26:17-19; Mark 14:12-16)
(Harmony 209)

N ow the Festival of Unleavened Bread arrived, when the Passover lambs were sacrificed. Jesus sent Peter and John ahead and said, "Go and prepare the Passover meal, so we can eat it together." "Where do you want us to go?" they asked him.
He replied, "As soon as you enter Jerusalem, a man carrying a pitcher of

water will meet you. Follow him. At the house he enters, say to the owner, 'The Teacher asks, Where is the guest room where I can eat the Passover meal with my disciples?' He will take you upstairs to a large room that is already set up. That is the place. Go ahead and prepare our supper there." They went off to the city and found everything just as Jesus had said, and they prepared the Passover supper there.

REMEMBERING

Passover became an annual remembrance of how God delivered the Hebrews from Egypt. Each year the people would pause to remember the day when the destroyer (God's angel of death) had passed over their homes. They would give thanks to God for saving them from death and bringing them out of a land of slavery and sin. Believers today have experienced a day of deliverance as well—the day we were delivered from spiritual death and slavery to sin. The Lord's Supper is our Passover remembrance of our new life and freedom from sin. The next time struggles and trials come, remember how God has delivered you in the past and focus on his promise of new life with him.

The Passover meal included the sacrifice of a lamb because of the association with the exodus from Egypt. When the Jews were getting ready to leave, God told them to kill a lamb and paint its blood on the doorposts of their houses. They then were to prepare the meat for food. Peter and John had to buy and prepare the lamb as well as the unleavened bread, herbs, wine, and other ceremonial food.

November 5

Jesus washes the disciples' feet
John 13:1-11 *(Harmony 210a)*

*B*efore the Passover celebration, Jesus knew that his hour had come to leave this world and return to his Father. He now showed the disciples the full extent of his love. It was time for supper, and the Devil had already enticed Judas, son of Simon Iscariot, to carry out his plan to betray Jesus. Jesus knew that the Father had given him authority over everything and that he had come from God and would return to God. So he got up from the table, took off his robe, wrapped a towel around his waist, and poured water into a basin. Then he began to wash the disciples' feet and to wipe them with the towel he had around him.

When he came to Simon Peter, Peter said to him, "Lord, why are you going to wash my feet?"

Jesus replied, "You don't understand now why I am doing it; someday you will."

"No," Peter protested, "you will never wash my feet!"

Jesus replied, "But if I don't wash you, you won't belong to me."

Simon Peter exclaimed, "Then wash my hands and head as well, Lord, not just my feet!"

Jesus replied, "A person who has bathed all over does not need to wash, except for the feet, to be entirely clean. And you are clean, but that isn't true of everyone here." For Jesus knew who would betray him. That is what he meant when he said, "Not all of you are clean."

TRUE LEADERS

John 13–17 tells us what Jesus said to his disciples on the night before his death. These words were all spoken in one evening. With only the disciples as his audience, Jesus gave final instructions to prepare them for his death and resurrection, events that would change their lives forever.

Imagine being Peter and watching Jesus wash the others' feet, all the while moving closer to you. Seeing his Master behave like a slave must have confused Peter. He still did not understand Jesus' teaching that to be a leader, a person must be a servant. This is not a comfortable passage for leaders who find it difficult to serve those beneath them. The world's system of leadership is very different from leadership in God's Kingdom. Worldly leaders are often selfish and arrogant as they claw their way to the top. (Some kings in the ancient world gave themselves the title "Benefactor.") But among Christians, the leader is to be the one who serves best. There are different styles of leadership—some lead through public speaking, some through administering, some through relationships—but every Christian leader needs a servant's heart. How do you treat those who work under you (whether children, employees, or volunteers)? Ask the people you lead how you can serve them better.

November 6

Jesus washes the disciples' feet
John 13:12-20 *(Harmony 210b)*

*A*fter washing their feet, he put on his robe again and sat down and asked, "Do you understand what I was doing? You call me 'Teacher' and 'Lord,' and you are right, because it is true. And since I, the Lord and Teacher, have washed your feet, you ought to wash each other's feet. I have given you an example to follow. Do as I have done to you. How true it is that a servant is not greater than the master. Nor are messengers more important than the one who sends them. You know these things—now do them! That is the path of blessing.

"I am not saying these things to all of you; I know so well each one of you I chose. The Scriptures declare, 'The one who shares my food has turned against me,' and this will soon come true. I tell you this now, so that when it happens you will believe I am the Messiah. Truly, anyone who welcomes my messenger is welcoming me, and anyone who welcomes me is welcoming the Father who sent me."

FOLLOW THROUGH

Jesus was the model servant, and he showed his servant attitude to his disciples. Washing guests' feet was a job for a household servant to carry out when guests arrived. But Jesus wrapped a towel around his waist, as the lowliest slave would do, and washed and dried his disciples' feet. If even he, God in the flesh, is willing to serve, we his followers must also be servants, willing to serve in any way that glorifies God. Are you willing to follow Christ's example of serving? Whom can you serve today? There is a special blessing for those who not only agree that humble service is Christ's way but who also follow through and do it (13:17).

Jesus did not wash his disciples' feet just to get them to be nice to each other. His far greater goal for them was to extend his mission on earth after he had left them. These men were to move into the world, serving God, each other, and all people to whom they took the message of salvation.

November 7

Jesus and his disciples have the Last Supper

John 13:21-30 (also in Matthew 26:20-29; Mark 14:17-25; Luke 22:14-30 *(Harmony 211)*

*N*ow Jesus was in great anguish of spirit, and he exclaimed, "The truth is, one of you will betray me!"

The disciples looked at each other, wondering whom he could mean. One of Jesus' disciples, the one Jesus loved, was sitting next to Jesus at the table. Simon Peter motioned to him to ask who would do this terrible thing. Leaning toward Jesus, he asked, "Lord, who is it?"

Jesus said, "It is the one to whom I give the bread dipped in the sauce." And when he had dipped it, he gave it to Judas, son of Simon Iscariot. As soon as Judas had eaten the bread, Satan entered into him. Then Jesus told him, "Hurry. Do it now." None of the others at the table knew what Jesus meant. Since Judas was their treasurer, some thought Jesus was telling him to go and pay for the food or to give some money to the poor. So Judas left at once, going out into the night.

MATCHING WORDS AND ACTIONS

Judas, the very man who would betray Jesus, was at the table with the others. Judas had already determined to betray Jesus, but in cold-blooded hypocrisy he shared the fellow-

The honored guest at a meal would be singled out by the host by giving him or her a piece of bread dipped in sauce.

ship of this meal. It is easy to become enraged or shocked by what Judas did; yet professing commitment to Christ and then denying him with one's life is also betraying him. It is denying Christ's love to disobey him; it is denying his truth to distrust him; it is denying his deity to reject his authority. Do your words and actions match? If not, consider a change of mind and heart that will protect you from making a terrible mistake.

November 8

Jesus predicts Peter's denial
John 13:31-38 (also in Luke 22:31-38) *(Harmony 212)*

*A*s soon as Judas left the room, Jesus said, "The time has come for me, the Son of Man, to enter into my glory, and God will receive glory because of all that happens to me. And God will bring me into my glory very soon. Dear children, how brief are these moments before I must go away and leave you! Then, though you search for me, you cannot come to me—just as I told the Jewish leaders. So now I am giving you a new command-ment: Love each other. Just as I have loved you, you should love each other. Your love for one another will prove to the world that you are my disciples."

Simon Peter said, "Lord, where are you going?"

And Jesus replied, "You can't go with me now, but you will follow me later."

"But why can't I come now, Lord?" he asked. "I am ready to die for you."

Jesus answered, "Die for me? No, before the rooster crows tomorrow morning, you will deny three times that you even know me."

LOVING AS CHRIST LOVED

Love is more than simply warm feelings; it is an attitude that reveals itself in action. To love others was not a new commandment (see Leviticus 19:18), but to love others as much as Christ loved others was revolution-ary. Now we are to love others based on Jesus' sacrificial love for us. Such love will not

Peter proudly told Jesus that he was ready to die for him. But Jesus corrected him. Jesus knew Peter would deny that he knew Jesus that very night to protect himself (18:25-27).

only bring unbelievers to Christ; it will also keep believers strong and united in a world hostile to God. Jesus was a living example of God's love as we are to be living examples of Jesus' love. How can we love others as Jesus loves us? By helping when it's not convenient, by giving when it hurts, by devoting energy to others' welfare rather than our own, by absorbing hurts from others without complaining or fighting back. This kind of loving is difficult to do. That is why people notice when you do it and know you are empowered by a supernatural source.

November 9

Jesus is the way to the Father
John 14:1-7 *(Harmony 213a)*

*D*on't be troubled. You trust God, now trust in me. There are many rooms in my Father's home, and I am going to prepare a place for you. If this were not so, I would tell you plainly. When everything is ready, I will come and get you, so that you will always be with me where I am. And you know where I am going and how to get there."

"No, we don't know, Lord," Thomas said. "We haven't any idea where you are going, so how can we know the way?"

Jesus told him, "I am the way, the truth, and the life. No one can come to the Father except through me. If you had known who I am, then you would have known who my Father is. From now on you know him and have seen him!"

ONE WAY

Jesus says he is the *only* way to God the Father. This is one of the most basic and important passages in Scripture. How can we know the way to God? Only through Jesus. Some people may argue that this way is too narrow. In reality, it is wide enough for the whole world, if the world chooses to accept it. Instead of worrying about how limited it sounds to have only one way, we should be saying, "Thank you, God, for providing a sure way to get to you!" Jesus is the way because he is both God and man. By uniting our lives with his, we are united with God. Trust Jesus to take you to the Father, and all the benefits of being God's child will be yours.

As the way, Jesus is our path to the Father. As the truth, he is the reality of all God's promises. As the life, he joins his divine life to ours, both now and eternally.

Jesus is the way to the Father
John 14:8-14 *(Harmony 213b)*

*P*hilip said, "Lord, show us the Father and we will be satisfied."
Jesus replied, "Philip, don't you even yet know who I am, even after all the time I have been with you? Anyone who has seen me has seen the Father! So why are you asking to see him? Don't you believe that I am in the Father and the Father is in me? The words I say are not my own, but my Father who lives in me does his work through me. Just believe that I am in the Father and the Father is in me. Or at least believe because of what you have seen me do.

"The truth is, anyone who believes in me will do the same works I have done, and even greater works, because I am going to be with the Father. You can ask for anything in my name, and I will do it, because the work of the Son brings glory to the Father. Yes, ask anything in my name, and I will do it!"

ASKING IN FAITH

When Jesus says we can ask for anything, we must remember that our asking must be in his name—that is, according to God's character and will. God will not grant requests contrary to his nature or his will, and we cannot use his name as a magic formula to fulfill our selfish desires. If we are sincerely following God and seeking to do his will, then our requests will be in line with what he wants, and he will grant them.

Jesus is the visible, tangible image of the invisible God. He is the complete revelation of what God is like. Jesus explained to Philip, who wanted to see the Father, that to know Jesus is to know God. The search for God, for truth and reality, ends in Christ.

Jesus promises the Holy Spirit
John 14:15-21 *(Harmony 214a)*

*I*f you love me, obey my commandments. And I will ask the Father, and he will give you another Counselor, who will never leave you. He is the Holy Spirit, who leads into all truth. The world at large cannot receive him, because it isn't looking for him and doesn't recognize him. But you do, because he lives with you now and later will be in you. No, I will not abandon you as orphans—I will come to you. In just a little while the world will not see me again, but you will. For I will live again, and you will, too. When I am raised to life again, you will know that I am in my Father, and you are in me, and I am in you. Those who obey my commandments are the ones who love me. And because they love me, my Father will love them, and I will love them. And I will reveal myself to each one of them."

GOD KNOWS THE FUTURE

Sometimes people wish they knew the future so they could prepare for it. God has chosen not to give us this knowledge. He alone knows what will happen, but he tells us all we need to know to *prepare* for the future. When we live by his standards, he will not leave us; he will come to us, he will be in us, and he will show himself to us. God knows what will happen, and, because he will be with us through it all, we need not fear. We don't have to know the future to have faith in God; we have to have faith in God to be secure about the future.

Jesus was soon going to leave the disciples, but he would remain with them. How could this be? The Helper—the Spirit of God himself—would come after Jesus was gone to care for and guide the disciples. The Holy Spirit is the very presence of God within us and all believers, helping us live as God wants and building Christ's church on earth.

November 12

Jesus promises the Holy Spirit
John 14:22-26 *(Harmony 214b)*

*J*udas (not Judas Iscariot, but the other disciple with that name) said to him, "Lord, why are you going to reveal yourself only to us and not to the world at large?"

Jesus replied, "All those who love me will do what I say. My Father will love them, and we will come to them and live with them. Anyone who doesn't love me will not do what I say. And remember, my words are not my own. This message is from the Father who sent me. I am telling you these things now while I am still with you. But when the Father sends the Counselor as my representative—and by the Counselor I mean the Holy Spirit—he will teach you everything and will remind you of everything I myself have told you."

CONFIDENT IN THE WORD

Jesus promised the disciples that the Holy Spirit would help them remember what he had been teaching them. This promise ensures the validity of the New Testament. The disciples were eyewitnesses of Jesus' life and teachings, and the Holy Spirit helped them remember what they had seen and heard without taking away their individual perspectives. We can be confident that the Gospels are accurate records of what Jesus taught and did (see 1 Corinthians 2:10-14). The Holy Spirit can also help us. As we study the Bible, we can trust him to plant truth in our mind, convince us of God's will, and remind us when we stray from it.

Because the disciples were still expecting Jesus to establish an earthly kingdom and overthrow Rome, they found it hard to understand why he did not tell the world at large that he was the Messiah. Ever since Pentecost, the gospel of the Kingdom has been proclaimed in the whole world.

November 13

Jesus promises the Holy Spirit
John 14:27-31 *(Harmony 214c)*

I am leaving you with a gift—peace of mind and heart. And the peace I give isn't like the peace the world gives. So don't be troubled or afraid. Remember what I told you: I am going away, but I will come back to you again. If you really love me, you will be very happy for me, because now I can go to the Father, who is greater than I am. I have told you these things before they happen so that you will believe when they do happen.

"I don't have much more time to talk to you, because the prince of this world approaches. He has no power over me, but I will do what the Father requires of me, so that the world will know that I love the Father. Come, let's be going."

THE PEACE OF GOD
Sin, fear, uncertainty, doubt, and numerous other forces are at war within us. The peace of God comes into our heart, helping to restrain these hostile forces and offering comfort in place of conflict. Jesus says he will give us that peace if we are willing to accept it from him.

As God the Son, Jesus willingly submits to God the Father. On earth, Jesus also submitted to many of the physical limitations of his humanity (Philippians 2:6-7). (See verse 31)

The end result of the Holy Spirit's work in our lives is deep and lasting peace. Unlike worldly peace, which is usually defined as the absence of conflict, this peace is confident assurance in any circumstance; with Christ's peace, we have no need to fear the present or the future. If your life is full of stress, allow the Holy Spirit to fill you with Christ's peace.

November 14

Jesus teaches about the vine and the branches
John 15:1-4 *(Harmony 215a)*

I am the true vine, and my Father is the gardener. He cuts off every branch that doesn't produce fruit, and he prunes the branches that do bear fruit so they will produce even more. You have already been pruned for greater fruitfulness by the message I have given you. Remain in me, and I will remain in you. For a branch cannot produce fruit if it is severed from the vine, and you cannot be fruitful apart from me."

VINE AND BRANCHES
Christ is the vine, and God is the gardener who cares for the branches to make them fruitful. The branches are all those who claim to be followers of Christ. The fruitful branches are true believers who by their living union with Christ produce much fruit. But those who become unproductive—those who turn back from following Christ after making a superficial commitment—will be separated from the vine. Unproductive followers are as good as dead and will be cut off and tossed aside. Those who won't bear fruit for God or who try to block the efforts of God's followers will be cut off from the divine flow of life. Keep your focus on Christ, the vine—that is your only source of strength and life.

The grapevine is a prolific plant; a single vine bears many grapes. In the Old Testament, grapes symbolized Israel's fruitfulness in doing God's work on the earth (Psalm 80:8; Isaiah 5:1-7; Ezekiel 19:10-14). In the Passover meal, the fruit of the vine symbolized God's goodness to his people.

November 15

Jesus teaches about the vine and the branches
John 15:5-8 *(Harmony 215b)*

Y es, I am the vine; you are the branches. Those who remain in me, and I in them, will produce much fruit. For apart from me you can do nothing. Anyone who parts from me is thrown away like a useless branch and withers. Such branches are gathered into a pile to be burned. But if you stay joined to me and my words remain in you, you may ask any request you like, and it will be granted! My true disciples produce much fruit. This brings great glory to my Father."

LIFE IN CHRIST

Many people try to be good, honest people who do what is right. But Jesus says that the only way to live a truly good life is to stay close to him, like a branch attached to the vine. Apart from Christ our efforts are unfruitful. Living in Christ means (1) believing that he is God's Son (1 John 4:15), (2) receiving him as Savior and Lord (1:12), (3) doing what God says (1 John 3:24), (4) continuing to believe the gospel (1 John 2:24), and (5) relating in love to the community of believers, Christ's body (15:12). Are you receiving the nourishment and life offered by Christ, the vine? If not, you are missing a special gift he has for you.

Fruit is not limited to soul winning. In this chapter, answered prayer, joy, and love are mentioned as fruit (15:7, 11-12). Galatians 5:22-24 and 2 Peter 1:5-8 describe additional fruit: qualities of Christian character.

November 16

Jesus teaches about the vine and the branches
John 15:9-16 *(Harmony 215c)*

I have loved you even as the Father has loved me. Remain in my love. When you obey me, you remain in my love, just as I obey my Father and remain in his love. I have told you this so that you will be filled with my joy. Yes, your joy will overflow! I command you to love each other in the same way that I love you. And here is how to measure it—the greatest love is shown when people lay down their lives for their friends. You are my friends if you obey me. I no longer call you servants, because a master doesn't confide in his servants. Now you are my friends, since I have told you everything the Father told me. You didn't choose me. I chose you. I appointed you to go and produce fruit that will last, so that the Father will give you whatever you ask for, using my name."

HIGHS AND LOWS

When things are going well, we feel elated. When hardships come, we can sink into depression. But true joy transcends the rolling waves of circumstance. Joy comes from a consistent relationship with Jesus Christ. When our lives are intertwined with his, he will help us to walk through adversity without sinking into debilitating lows and to manage prosperity without moving into deceptive highs. The joy of living with Jesus Christ daily will keep us levelheaded, no matter how high or low our circumstances.

Jesus made the first choice—to live and to die for us, to invite us to live with him forever. We make the next choice—to accept or reject his offer. Without his choice, we would have no choice to make.

November 17

Jesus warns about the world's hatred
John 15:17-25 *(Harmony 216a)*

I command you to love each other.

"When the world hates you, remember it hated me before it hated you. The world would love you if you belonged to it, but you don't. I chose you to come out of the world, and so it hates you. Do you remember what I told you? 'A servant is not greater than the master.' Since they persecuted me, naturally they will persecute you. And if they had listened to me, they would listen to you! The people of the world will hate you because you belong to me, for they don't know God who sent me. They would not be guilty if I had not come and spoken to them. But now they have no excuse for their sin. Anyone who hates me hates my Father, too. If I hadn't done such miraculous signs among them that no one else could do, they would not be counted guilty. But as it is, they saw all that I did and yet hated both of us—me and my Father. This has fulfilled what the Scriptures said: 'They hated me without cause.' "

COMMANDED TO LOVE

Jesus offers hope. The Holy Spirit gives strength to endure the unreasonable hatred and evil in our world and the hostility many have toward Christ. This is especially comforting for those facing persecution. But all Christians should expect to get plenty of hatred from the world. Thus, it's important to give one another love and support. Do you allow small problems to get in the way of loving other believers? Jesus commands that you love them, and he will give you the strength to do it.

Because Jesus Christ is Lord and Master, he should call us servants; instead, he calls us friends. How comforting and reassuring to be chosen as Christ's friends. Because he is Lord and Master, we owe him our unqualified obedience. But most important, Jesus asks us to obey him because we love him.

November 18

Jesus warns about the world's hatred
John 15:26–16:4 *(Harmony 216b)*

 B ut I will send you the Counselor—the Spirit of truth. He will come to you from the Father and will tell you all about me. And you must also tell others about me because you have been with me from the beginning.

"I have told you these things so that you won't fall away. For you will be expelled from the synagogues, and the time is coming when those who kill you will think they are doing God a service. This is because they have never known the Father or me. Yes, I'm telling you these things now, so that when they happen, you will remember I warned you. I didn't tell you earlier because I was going to be with you for a while longer."

NEVER ALONE

In his last moments with his disciples, Jesus (1) warned them about further persecution, (2) told them where, when, and why he was going, and (3) assured them that they would not be left alone but that the Spirit would come. Jesus knew what lay ahead, and he did not want the disciples' faith shaken or destroyed. God wants you to know that you are not alone. You have the Holy Spirit to comfort you, teach you truth, and help you.

Jesus uses two names for the Holy Spirit—Counselor and the spirit of truth. The word Counselor conveys the helping, encouraging, and strengthening work of the Spirit. Spirit of truth points to the teaching, illuminating, and reminding work of the Spirit.

November 19

Jesus teaches about the Holy Spirit
John 16:5-11 *(Harmony 217a)*

*B*ut now I am going away to the one who sent me, and none of you has asked me where I am going. Instead, you are very sad. But it is actually best for you that I go away, because if I don't, the Counselor won't come. If I do go away, he will come because I will send him to you. And when he comes, he will convince the world of its sin, and of God's righteousness, and of the coming judgment. The world's sin is unbelief in me. Righteousness is available because I go to the Father, and you will see me no more. Judgment will come because the prince of this world has already been judged."

Three important tasks of the Holy Spirit are (1) convicting the world of its sin and calling it to repentance; (2) revealing the standard of God's righteousness to anyone who believes, because Christ would no longer be physically present on earth; and (3) demonstrating Christ's judgment over Satan.

THE SPIRIT

Unless Jesus had done what he had come to do, there would be no gospel. If he had not died, he could not have removed our sins; he could not have risen again and defeated death. If he had not gone back to the Father, the Holy Spirit would not have come. Christ's presence on earth was limited to one place at a time. His leaving meant that he could be present to the whole world through the Holy Spirit. God wants you to know you are not alone.

November 20

Jesus teaches about the Holy Spirit
John 16:12-16 *(Harmony 217b)*

*O*h, there is so much more I want to tell you, but you can't bear it now. When the Spirit of truth comes, he will guide you into all truth. He will not be presenting his own ideas; he will be telling you what he has heard. He will tell you about the future. He will bring me glory by revealing to you whatever he receives from me. All that the Father has is mine; this is what I mean when I say that the Spirit will reveal to you whatever he receives from me.

"In just a little while I will be gone, and you won't see me anymore. Then, just a little while after that, you will see me again."

THE PATHFINDER
The Holy Spirit is our guide, navigator, and pathfinder. Jesus also gave us a reliable map when he gave us his Word. These essential resources assist us to find our way as his disciples. The twelve disciples could not absorb all Jesus taught them. Jesus said the Holy Spirit would tell them "about the future"—the nature of their mission, the opposition they would face, and the final outcome of their efforts. They didn't fully understand these promises until the Holy Spirit had come after Jesus' death and resurrection. Some steps of discipleship cannot even be comprehended until we have taken steps of obedience. Our knowledge of the way and the future will always be limited. But as we trust Christ and read his Word, the Holy Spirit will guide and direct our steps.

When Jesus said he would be "gone" in just a little while, he was referring to his death, now only a few hours away. But they would see him again after his resurrection three days later.

Jesus teaches about using his name in prayer
John 16:17-28 *(Harmony 218a)*

*T*he disciples asked each other, "What does he mean when he says, 'You won't see me, and then you will see me'? And what does he mean when he says, 'I am going to the Father'? And what does he mean by 'a little while'? We don't understand."

Jesus realized they wanted to ask him, so he said, "Are you asking yourselves what I meant? I said in just a little while I will be gone, and you won't see me anymore. Then, just a little while after that, you will see me again. Truly, you will weep and mourn over what is going to happen to me, but the world will rejoice. You will grieve, but your grief will suddenly turn to wonderful joy when you see me again. It will be like a woman experiencing the pains of labor. When her child is born, her anguish gives place to joy because she has brought a new person into the world. You have sorrow now, but I will see you again; then you will rejoice, and no one can rob you of that joy. At that time you won't need to ask me for anything. The truth is, you can go directly to the Father and ask him, and he will grant your request because you use my name. You haven't done this before. Ask, using my name, and you will receive, and you will have abundant joy.

"I have spoken of these matters in parables, but the time will come when this will not be necessary, and I will tell you plainly all about the Father. Then you will ask in my name. I'm not saying I will ask the Father on your behalf, for the Father himself loves you dearly because you love me and believe that I came from God. Yes, I came from the Father into the world, and I will leave the world and return to the Father."

A NEW DAY

Jesus is talking about a new relationship between the believer and God. Previously, people had approached God through priests. After Jesus' resurrection, any believer could approach God directly. A new day has dawned and now all believers, as priests, can talk with God personally and directly (see Hebrews 10:19-23). We can now approach God, not because of our own merit, but because Jesus, our great High Priest, has made us acceptable to God.

What a contrast between the disciples and the world! The world rejoiced as the disciples wept, but the disciples would see him again (in three days) and rejoice. The world's values are often the opposite of God's values.

November 22

Jesus teaches about using his name in prayer
John 16:29-33 *(Harmony 218b)*

*T*hen his disciples said, "At last you are speaking plainly and not in parables. Now we understand that you know everything and don't need anyone to tell you anything. From this we believe that you came from God."

Jesus asked, "Do you finally believe? But the time is coming—in fact, it is already here—when you will be scattered, each one going his own way, leaving me alone. Yet I am not alone because the Father is with me. I have told you all this so that you may have peace in me. Here on earth you will have many trials and sorrows. But take heart, because I have overcome the world."

THE OVERCOMER
With these words, Jesus told his disciples to take courage. In spite of the inevitable struggles they would face, they could take courage that Jesus had "overcome the world." In the book of Revelation, Jesus is called "the Alpha and the Omega—the beginning and the end" (Revelation 1:8). Jesus is the eternal Lord and Ruler of the past, present, and future (see also Revelation 4:8; Isaiah 44:6; 48:12-15). Without him you have nothing that is eternal, nothing that can change your life, nothing that can save you from sin. Is the Lord your reason for living—the beginning and the end of your life? Honor the one who is the beginning and the end of all existence, wisdom, and power.

The disciples believed Jesus' words because they were convinced that he knew everything. But their belief was only a first step toward the great faith they would receive when the Holy Spirit would come to live in them.

November 23

Jesus prays for himself
John 17:1-5 *(Harmony 219)*

*W*hen Jesus had finished saying all these things, he looked up to heaven and said, "Father, the time has come. Glorify your Son so he can give glory back to you. For you have given him authority over everyone in all the earth. He gives eternal life to each one you have given him. And this is the way to have eternal life—to know you, the only true God, and Jesus Christ, the one you sent to earth. I brought glory to you here on earth by doing everything you told me to do. And now, Father, bring me into the glory we shared before the world began."

KNOWING GOD

Jesus explained knowing God as the essence of having eternal life. Eternal life is a gift we receive when we enter into a personal relationship with God in Jesus Christ. We cannot know God unless we have eternal life, and at the core of eternal life is intimate knowledge of God.

Eternal life gives us the capacity for intimacy with others who have eternal life. Jesus is the source of eternal life. Our first step toward eternal life includes realizing that we don't have it. That sense of separation, rebellion, lostness, or inadequacy before God is defined as "sin" in the Bible. When we admit our sin, turn away from it and then to Christ, Christ's love lives in us through the Holy Spirit. Eternal life is not just being around forever; for believers it means eternity with God, their loving Father.

Before Jesus came to earth, he was one with God. At this point, when his mission on earth was almost finished, Jesus was asking his Father to restore him to his original place of honor and authority. Jesus' resurrection and ascension—and Stephen's dying exclamation (Acts 7:56)—attest that Jesus did return to his exalted position at the right hand of God.

November 24

Jesus prays for his disciples
John 17:6-12 *(Harmony 220a)*

I have told these men about you. They were in the world, but then you gave them to me. Actually, they were always yours, and you gave them to me; and they have kept your word. Now they know that everything I have is a gift from you, for I have passed on to them the words you gave me; and they accepted them and know that I came from you, and they believe you sent me.

"My prayer is not for the world, but for those you have given me, because they belong to you. And all of them, since they are mine, belong to you; and you have given them back to me, so they are my glory! Now I am departing the world; I am leaving them behind and coming to you. Holy Father, keep them and care for them—all those you have given me—so that they will be united just as we are. During my time here, I have kept them safe. I guarded them so that not one was lost, except the one headed for destruction, as the Scriptures foretold."

IN THE WORLD

Like Jesus' original disciples, we still live in the world. "The world" is a system of values typified by Satan himself, centered on power, deceit, and self-will. While we're in the world,

Judas was "the one headed for destruction," who was lost because he betrayed Jesus (see Psalm 41:9).

Satan wants to neutralize or destroy us. As Jesus' disciples today, we are on a collision course with the world's values; therefore, we need God's protection. The fact that we are *in* the world does not grant us license to become *of* the world. We must not betray Jesus by loving the world. We must be sure that we allow Christ—not the media and the world around us—to define who we are.

November 25

Jesus prays for his disciples
John 17:13-19 *(Harmony 220b)*

*A*nd now I am coming to you. I have told them many things while I was with them so they would be filled with my joy. I have given them your word. And the world hates them because they do not belong to the world, just as I do not. I'm not asking you to take them out of the world, but to keep them safe from the evil one. They are not part of this world any more than I am. Make them pure and holy by teaching them your words of truth. As you sent me into the world, I am sending them into the world. And I give myself entirely to you so they also might be entirely yours."

SENT ONES

The world hates Christians because Christians' values differ from the world's. Because Christ's followers don't cooperate with the world by joining in its sin, they are living accusations against the world's immorality. The world follows Satan's agenda, and Satan is the avowed enemy of Jesus and his people. Yet Jesus asked God not to take believers *out* of the world but to use them *in* the world. Because Jesus sends us into the world, we should not try to escape from the world, nor should we avoid all relationships with non-

A follower of Christ becomes pure and holy through believing and obeying the Word of God (Hebrews 4:12). He or she has already accepted forgiveness through Christ's sacrificial death (Hebrews 7:26-27). But daily application of God's Word has a purifying effect on our mind and heart.

Christians. We are called to be salt and light (Matthew 5:13-16), and we are to do the work that God sent us to do.

November 26

Jesus prays for future believers
John 17:20-21 *(Harmony 221a)*

I am praying not only for these disciples but also for all who will ever believe in me because of their testimony. My prayer for all of them is that they will be one, just as you and I are one, Father—that just as you are in me and I am in you, so they will be in us, and the world will believe you sent me."

ON HIS MIND

When Jesus prayed for all who would believe through the apostles' testimony, he was praying for every future believer. In a sense, everyone who has become a Christian has done so through the apostles' message because they wrote the New Testament and were the founders of the Christian church.

The pattern of Jesus' prayer provides a helpful outline for us. He prayed for himself, for those close to him, and for those beyond his immediate sphere who would be affected by the ministry of his friends.

Jesus prayed for you and others you know, that you would have unity (17:11), protection from Satan (17:15), and holiness (17:17). Realizing that Jesus was praying for you should give you great comfort during times of discouragement and confidence as you work for his Kingdom. Jesus had you in mind as he prepared for the Cross.

November 27

Jesus prays for future believers
John 17:22-26 *(Harmony 221b)*

I have given them the glory you gave me, so that they may be one, as we are—I in them and you in me, all being perfected into one. Then the world will know that you sent me and will understand that you love them as much as you love me. Father, I want these whom you've given me to be with me, so they can see my glory. You gave me the glory because you loved me even before the world began!

"O righteous Father, the world doesn't know you, but I do; and these disciples know you sent me. And I have revealed you to them and will keep on revealing you. I will do this so that your love for me may be in them and I in them."

Jesus' great desire for his disciples was that they would become one. He wanted them unified as a powerful witness to the reality of God's love. Christian unity provides an environment for the gospel message to make its clearest impact; lack of unity among Christians frequently drives people away. Are you helping to unify the body of Christ, the church? You can pray for other Christians, avoid gossip, build others up, work together in humility, give your time and money, exalt Christ, and refuse to get sidetracked arguing over divisive matters.

Jesus asked that the Father's love would be in believers and that he himself (Jesus) would be in them. This expresses the Father's desire, and because it is his desire, he will make sure it is accomplished.

November 28

Jesus again predicts Peter's denial
Mark 14:26-31 (also in Matthew 26:30-35) *(Harmony 222)*

*T*hen they sang a hymn and went out to the Mount of Olives.

"All of you will desert me," Jesus told them. "For the Scriptures say, 'God will strike the Shepherd, and the sheep will be scattered.' But after I am raised from the dead, I will go ahead of you to Galilee and meet you there."

Peter said to him, "Even if everyone else deserts you, I never will."

"Peter," Jesus replied, "the truth is, this very night, before the rooster crows twice, you will deny me three times."

"No!" Peter insisted. "Not even if I have to die with you! I will never deny you!" And all the others vowed the same.

FAITH IN A CRUCIBLE
This was the second time that evening that Jesus predicted that his disciples would desert him (see Luke 22:31-34; John 13:31-38 for the first prediction). And for a second time, all the disciples declared that they would die before deserting Jesus. A few hours later, however, they all would scatter. Talk is cheap. It is easy to say we are devoted to Christ, but our claims are meaningful only when they are tested in the crucible of persecution. How strong is your faith? Is it strong enough to stand up under intense trial?

It's easy to think that Satan temporarily gained the upper hand in this drama about Jesus' death. But we see later that God was in control, even in the death of his Son. Satan gained no victory—everything occurred exactly as God had planned.

November 29

Jesus agonizes in the garden
Mark 14:32-42 (also in Matthew 26:36-46; Luke 22:39-46)
(Harmony 223)

*A*nd they came to an olive grove called Gethsemane, and Jesus said, "Sit here while I go and pray." He took Peter, James, and John with him, and he began to be filled with horror and deep distress. He told them, "My soul is crushed with grief to the point of death. Stay here and watch with me."

He went on a little farther and fell face down on the ground. He prayed that, if it were possible, the awful hour awaiting him might pass him by. "Abba, Father," he said, "everything is possible for you. Please take this cup of suffering away from me. Yet I want your will, not mine."

Then he returned and found the disciples asleep. "Simon!" he said to Peter. "Are you asleep? Couldn't you stay awake and watch with me even one hour? Keep alert and pray. Otherwise temptation will overpower you. For though the spirit is willing enough, the body is weak."

Then Jesus left them again and prayed, repeating his pleadings. Again he returned to them and found them sleeping, for they just couldn't keep their eyes open. And they didn't know what to say.

When he returned to them the third time, he said, "Still sleeping? Still resting? Enough! The time has come. I, the Son of Man, am betrayed into the hands of sinners. Up, let's be going. See, my betrayer is here!"

WANTING GOD'S WILL

Was Jesus trying to get out of his task? Jesus expressed his true feelings, but he did not deny or rebel against God's will. He reaffirmed his desire to do what God wanted. Jesus' prayer highlights the terrible suffering he had to endure—an agony so much more magnified because he had to take on the sins of the whole world. This "cup" was the agony of alienation from God, his Father, at the cross (Hebrews 5:7-9). The sinless Son of God took on our sins and was separated for a while from God so that we could be eternally saved. While praying, Jesus was aware of what doing the Father's will would cost him. He understood the suffering he was about to encounter, and he did not want to have to endure the horrible experience. But Jesus prayed, "I want your will, not mine." Anything worth having costs something. What does your commitment to God cost you? Be willing to pay the price to gain something worthwhile in the end.

Jesus was in great sorrow and distress over his approaching physical pain, separation from the Father, and death for the sins of the world. The divine course was set, but he, in his human nature, still struggled (Hebrews 5:7-9). Because of the anguish Jesus experienced, he can relate to our suffering.

November 30

Jesus is betrayed and arrested
John 18:1-9 (also in Matthew 26:47; Mark 14:43; Luke 22:47)
(Harmony 224a)

*A*fter saying these things, Jesus crossed the Kidron Valley with his disciples and entered a grove of olive trees. Judas, the betrayer, knew this place, because Jesus had gone there many times with his disciples. The leading priests and Pharisees had given Judas a battalion of Roman soldiers and Temple guards to accompany him. Now with blazing torches, lanterns, and weapons, they arrived at the olive grove.

Jesus fully realized all that was going to happen to him. Stepping forward to meet them, he asked, "Whom are you looking for?"

"Jesus of Nazareth," they replied.

"I am he," Jesus said. Judas was standing there with them when Jesus identified himself. And as he said, "I am he," they all fell backward to the ground! Once more he asked them, "Whom are you searching for?"

And again they replied, "Jesus of Nazareth."

"I told you that I am he," Jesus said. "And since I am the one you want, let these others go." He did this to fulfill his own statement: "I have not lost a single one of those you gave me."

DON'T RUN AWAY
John does not record Judas's kiss of greeting (Matthew 26:49; Mark 14:45; Luke 22:47-48), but Judas's kiss marked a turning point for the disciples. With Jesus' arrest, each one's life would be radically different. For the first time, Judas openly betrayed Jesus before the other disciples. For the first time, Jesus' loyal disciples ran away from him (Matthew 26:56). The band of disciples would undergo severe testing before they were transformed from hesitant followers to dynamic leaders. You may have made big mistakes in your life, committed sins you're ashamed to remember. Yet nothing is beyond Jesus' forgiveness. He can help you become the person he wants you to become, but you must allow him to forgive you and work in your life. He did it for these disciples—and they changed the world!

Judas was given a contingent of police and soldiers in order to seize Jesus and bring him before the religious court for trial. The religious leaders had issued the warrant for Jesus' arrest, and Judas was acting as Jesus' official accuser.

December 1

Jesus is betrayed and arrested
Matthew 26:48-56 (also in Mark 14:44-52; Luke 22:48-53; John 18:10-11) *(Harmony 224b)*

*J*udas had given them a prearranged signal: "You will know which one to arrest when I go over and give him the kiss of greeting." So Judas came straight to Jesus. "Greetings, Teacher!" he exclaimed and gave him the kiss.

Jesus said, "My friend, go ahead and do what you have come for." Then the others grabbed Jesus and arrested him. One of the men with Jesus pulled out a sword and slashed off an ear of the high priest's servant.

"Put away your sword," Jesus told him. "Those who use the sword will be killed by the sword. Don't you realize that I could ask my Father for thousands of angels to protect us, and he would send them instantly? But if I did, how would the Scriptures be fulfilled that describe what must happen now?"

Then Jesus said to the crowd, "Am I some dangerous criminal, that you have come armed with swords and clubs to arrest me? Why didn't you arrest me in the Temple? I was there teaching every day. But this is all happening to fulfill the words of the prophets as recorded in the Scriptures." At that point, all the disciples deserted him and fled.

FORCING THE ISSUE

The religious leaders had not arrested Jesus in the Temple for fear of a riot. Instead, they came secretly at night, under the influence of the prince of darkness, Satan himself. Although it had looked as though Satan were getting the upper hand, everything was proceeding according to God's plan. It was time for Jesus to die. Still not understanding this and wanting to protect Jesus, one of the disciples (Peter, see John 18:10) pulled out a sword and wounded the high priest's servant. But Jesus told Peter to put away his sword and allow God's plan to unfold. At times it is tempting to take matters into our own hands, to force the issue. Usually such moves lead to sin. Instead, we must trust God to work out his plan.

Judas had told the crowd to arrest the man he kissed. This was not an arrest by Roman soldiers under Roman law but an arrest by the religious leaders. Judas pointed Jesus out, not because Jesus was hard to recognize, but because Judas had agreed to be the formal accuser in case a trial was called.

December 2

Annas questions Jesus
John 18:12-24 *(Harmony 225)*

*S*o the soldiers, their commanding officer, and the Temple guards arrested Jesus and tied him up. First they took him to Annas, the father-in-law of Caiaphas, the high priest that year. Caiaphas was the one who had told the other Jewish leaders, "Better that one should die for all."

Simon Peter followed along behind, as did another of the disciples. That other disciple was acquainted with the high priest, so he was allowed to enter the courtyard with Jesus. Peter stood outside the gate. Then the other disciple spoke to the woman watching at the gate, and she let Peter in. The woman asked Peter, "Aren't you one of Jesus' disciples?"

"No," he said, "I am not."

The guards and the household servants were standing around a charcoal fire they had made because it was cold. And Peter stood there with them, warming himself.

Inside, the high priest began asking Jesus about his followers and what he had been teaching them. Jesus replied, "What I teach is widely known, because I have preached regularly in the synagogues and the Temple. I have been heard by people everywhere, and I teach nothing in private that I have not said in public. Why are you asking me this question? Ask those who heard me. They know what I said."

One of the Temple guards standing there struck Jesus on the face. "Is that the way to answer the high priest?" he demanded.

Jesus replied, "If I said anything wrong, you must give evidence for it. Should you hit a man for telling the truth?"

Then Annas bound Jesus and sent him to Caiaphas, the high priest.

POINTING FINGERS
We can easily get angry at the Jewish religious leaders for their injustice toward Jesus, but we must remember that Peter and the rest of the disciples also contributed to Jesus' pain by deserting and denying him (Matthew 26:56, 75). Only hours earlier, these disciples had vowed never to leave Jesus (Matthew 26:35). While most of us are

Both Annas and Caiaphas had been high priests. Annas was Israel's high priest from A.D. 6 to 15, when he was deposed by Roman rulers. Caiaphas, Annas's son-in-law, was appointed high priest from A.D. 18 to 36 or 37. According to Jewish law, the office of high priest was held for life. Many Jews, therefore, still considered Annas the high priest and continued to call him by that title. But although Annas retained much authority among the Jews, Caiaphas made the final decisions.

not like the religious leaders, we are all like the disciples, for all of us have been guilty of denying that Christ is Lord in vital areas of our life or of keeping secret our identity as believers in times of pressure. Don't excuse yourself by pointing at others whose sins seem worse than yours. Instead, admit your guilt and come to Jesus for forgiveness and healing.

December 3

Caiaphas questions Jesus
Mark 14:53-65 (also in Matthew 26:57-68) *(Harmony 226)*

*J*esus was led to the high priest's home where the leading priests, other leaders, and teachers of religious law had gathered. Meanwhile, Peter followed far behind and then slipped inside the gates of the high priest's courtyard. For a while he sat with the guards, warming himself by the fire.

Inside, the leading priests and the entire high council were trying to find witnesses who would testify against Jesus, so they could put him to death. But their efforts were in vain. Many false witnesses spoke against him, but they contradicted each other. Finally, some men stood up to testify against him with this lie: "We heard him say, 'I will destroy this Temple made with human hands, and in three days I will build another, made without human hands.'" But even then they didn't get their stories straight!

Then the high priest stood up before the others and asked Jesus, "Well, aren't you going to answer these charges? What do you have to say for yourself?" Jesus made no reply. Then the high priest asked him, "Are you the Messiah, the Son of the blessed God?"

Jesus said, "I am, and you will see me, the Son of Man, sitting at God's right hand in the place of power and coming back on the clouds of heaven."

Then the high priest tore his clothing to show his horror and said, "Why do we need other witnesses? You have all heard his blasphemy. What is your verdict?" And they all condemned him to death.

Then some of them began to spit at him, and they blindfolded him and hit his face with their fists. "Who hit you that time, you prophet?" they jeered. And even the guards were hitting him as they led him away.

YOU MUST DECIDE
Jesus made no reply to the first question because it was based on confusing and erroneous evidence. Not answering was wiser than trying to clarify the fabricated accusations. But if Jesus had refused to answer the second question,

it could have been taken as a denial of his mission. Jesus declared, in no uncertain terms, that he was the Messiah. The high priest accused Jesus of blasphemy—calling himself God. To the Jews, this was a great crime, punishable by death (Leviticus 24:16). The religious leaders refused even to consider that Jesus' words might be true. They had decided against Jesus and in so doing had sealed their own fate as well as his. Like the members of the council, you must decide whether Jesus' words are blasphemy or truth. Your decision has eternal implications.

The Romans controlled Israel, but the Jews were given some authority over religious and minor civil disputes. The Jewish ruling body, the Sanhedrin, was made up of seventy-one of Israel's religious leaders. This trial by the Sanhedrin (the Jewish council of religious leaders) had two phases. A small group met at night (John 18:12-24), and then the full Sanhedrin met at daybreak (Luke 22:66-71).

December 4

Peter denies knowing Jesus
Mark 14:66-72 (also in Matthew 26:69-75; Luke 22:54-65; John 18:25-27) *(Harmony 227)*

*M*eanwhile, Peter was below in the courtyard. One of the servant girls who worked for the high priest noticed Peter warming himself at the fire. She looked at him closely and then said, "You were one of those with Jesus, the Nazarene."

Peter denied it. "I don't know what you're talking about," he said, and he went out into the entryway. Just then, a rooster crowed.

The servant girl saw him standing there and began telling the others, "That man is definitely one of them!" Peter denied it again.

A little later some other bystanders began saying to Peter, "You must be one of them because you are from Galilee."

Peter said, "I swear by God, I don't know this man you're talking about." And immediately the rooster crowed the second time. Suddenly, Jesus' words flashed through Peter's mind: "Before the rooster crows twice, you will deny me three times." And he broke down and cried.

STAGES OF DENIAL
There were three stages to Peter's denial. First he acted confused and tried to divert attention from himself by changing the subject. Second, using an oath, he denied that he knew Jesus. Third, he began to curse and swear. Believers who deny Christ often begin doing so subtly by pretending not to know him. When opportunities to discuss religious issues come up, they walk away or pretend they don't know the answers. With only a little more pressure, they can

be induced to deny flatly their relationship with Christ. If you find yourself subtly diverting conversation so you don't have to talk about Christ, watch out. You may be on the road to denying him.

Peter's curse was more than just a common swear word. He was making the strongest denial he could think of by denying with an oath that he knew Jesus. He was saying, in effect, "May God strike me dead if I'm lying."

December 5

The council of religious leaders condemns Jesus
Luke 22:66-71 (also in Matthew 27:1-2; Mark 15:1) *(Harmony 228)*

*A*t daybreak all the leaders of the people assembled, including the leading priests and the teachers of religious law. Jesus was led before this high council, and they said, "Tell us if you are the Messiah."

But he replied, "If I tell you, you won't believe me. And if I ask you a question, you won't answer. But the time is soon coming when I, the Son of Man, will be sitting at God's right hand in the place of power."

They all shouted, "Then you claim you are the Son of God?"

And he replied, "You are right in saying that I am."

"What need do we have for other witnesses?" they shouted. "We ourselves heard him say it."

I AM

Jesus agreed with the high priest's words that Jesus was the Son of God by saying, in effect, "Yes, I am." Jesus identified himself with God by using a familiar title for God found in the Old Testament: "I AM" (Exodus 3:14). The high priest recognized Jesus' claim and accused him of blasphemy. For any other human this claim would have been blas-

These leaders tried Jesus for religious offenses, such as calling himself the Son of God, which, according to law, was blasphemy. The trial was fixed: These religious leaders had already decided to kill Jesus (Luke 22:2).

phemy, but in this case it was true. Blasphemy, the sin of claiming to be God or of attacking God's authority and majesty in any way, was punishable by death. The Jewish leaders had the evidence they wanted. The one man in all of history for whom they had been looking and waiting stood in their midst and told them who he was, and they chose to kill him. Jesus is standing with us today; he is the answer to what all humanity needs and desires. Unfortunately, many decide to crucify him rather than fall to their knees in worship. Have you taken Jesus at his word? Have you believed in him as your Messiah?

December 6

Judas kills himself
Matthew 27:3-10 *(Harmony 229)*

*W*hen Judas, who had betrayed him, realized that Jesus had been condemned to die, he was filled with remorse. So he took the thirty pieces of silver back to the leading priests and other leaders. "I have sinned," he declared, "for I have betrayed an innocent man."

"What do we care?" they retorted. "That's your problem." Then Judas threw the money onto the floor of the Temple and went out and hanged himself. The leading priests picked up the money. "We can't put it in the Temple treasury," they said, "since it's against the law to accept money paid for murder." After some discussion they finally decided to buy the potter's field, and they made it into a cemetery for foreigners. That is why the field is still called the Field of Blood. This fulfilled the prophecy of Jeremiah that says, "They took the thirty pieces of silver—the price at which he was valued by the people of Israel—and purchased the potter's field, as the Lord directed."

TOO LATE

Jesus' formal accuser wanted to drop his charges, but the religious leaders refused to halt the trial. When he betrayed Jesus, perhaps Judas was trying to force Jesus' hand to get him to lead a revolt against Rome. This did not work, of course. Whatever his reason, Judas changed his mind, but it was too late. Many of the plans we set into motion cannot be reversed. It is best to think of the potential consequences before we launch into an action we may later regret.

These chief priests felt no guilt in giving Judas money to betray an innocent man, but when Judas returned the money, the priests couldn't accept it because it was wrong to accept money paid for murder! Their hatred for Jesus had caused them to lose all sense of justice.

Jesus stands trial before Pilate
John 18:28-38 (also in Matthew 27:11-14; Mark 15:2-5; Luke 23:1-5) *(Harmony 230)*

*J*esus' trial before Caiaphas ended in the early hours of the morning. Then he was taken to the headquarters of the Roman governor. His accusers didn't go in themselves because it would defile them, and they wouldn't be allowed to celebrate the Passover feast. So Pilate, the governor, went out to them and asked, "What is your charge against this man?"

"We wouldn't have handed him over to you if he weren't a criminal!" they retorted.

"Then take him away and judge him by your own laws," Pilate told them.

"Only the Romans are permitted to execute someone," the Jewish leaders replied. This fulfilled Jesus' prediction about the way he would die.

Then Pilate went back inside and called for Jesus to be brought to him. "Are you the King of the Jews?" he asked him.

Jesus replied, "Is this your own question, or did others tell you about me?"

"Am I a Jew?" Pilate asked. "Your own people and their leading priests brought you here. Why? What have you done?"

Then Jesus answered, "I am not an earthly king. If I were, my followers would have fought when I was arrested by the Jewish leaders. But my Kingdom is not of this world."

Pilate replied, "You are a king then?"

"You say that I am a king, and you are right," Jesus said. "I was born for that purpose. And I came to bring truth to the world. All who love the truth recognize that what I say is true."

"What is truth?" Pilate asked. Then he went out again to the people and told them, "He is not guilty of any crime.

THE TRUTH
Some people today try to say that if only they could talk to Jesus, question him, and spend time with him personally, they would believe. Pilate had that chance. Pilate asked Jesus a straightforward question, and Jesus answered clearly. Jesus is a king, but one whose Kingdom is not of this world. There seems to have been no question in Pilate's mind that Jesus spoke the truth and was innocent of any crime. It also seems apparent that while recognizing the truth, Pilate

Pilate knew what was going on; he knew that the religious leaders hated Jesus, and he did not want to act as their executioner. They could not sentence Jesus to death themselves—permission had to come from a Roman leader. But Pilate initially refused to sentence Jesus without sufficient evidence.

chose to reject it. It is a tragedy when we fail to recognize the truth. It is a greater tragedy when we recognize the truth but fail to heed it.

December 8

Jesus stands trial before Herod
Luke 23:6-12 *(Harmony 231)*

*O*h, is he a Galilean?" Pilate asked. When they answered that he was, Pilate sent him to Herod Antipas, because Galilee was under Herod's jurisdiction, and Herod happened to be in Jerusalem at the time. Herod was delighted at the opportunity to see Jesus, because he had heard about him and had been hoping for a long time to see him perform a miracle. He asked Jesus question after question, but Jesus refused to answer. Meanwhile, the leading priests and the teachers of religious law stood there shouting their accusations. Now Herod and his soldiers began mocking and ridiculing Jesus. Then they put a royal robe on him and sent him back to Pilate. Herod and Pilate, who had been enemies before, became friends that day.

"NOT GUILTY"

Herod, also called Herod Antipas, was in Jerusalem that weekend for the Passover celebration. (This was the Herod who had killed John the Baptist.) Pilate hoped to pass Jesus off on Herod because he knew that Jesus had lived and worked in Galilee. Herod Antipas had two advantages over Pilate: He came from a hereditary, part-Jewish monarchy, and he had held his position much longer. But Pilate had two advantages over Herod: He was a Roman citizen and an envoy of the emperor, and his position had been created to replace Herod's ineffective half brother. It is not surprising that the two men were uneasy around each other. Jesus' trial, however, brought them together. Because Pilate had recognized Herod's authority over Galilee, Herod had stopped feeling threatened by the Roman politician. And because neither man knew what to do in this predicament, their common problem united them. When Herod sent Jesus back to Pilate, it was with the verdict of "not guilty." How unfortunate that these two leaders were unable to save an inno-

Herod was the part-Jewish ruler of Galilee and Perea. Pilate was the Roman governor of Judea and Samaria. Those four provinces had been united under Herod the Great. But when Herod died in 4 B.C., the kingdom was divided among his sons. Archelaus, the son who had received Judea and Samaria, was removed from office within ten years, and his provinces were then ruled by a succession of Roman governors, of whom Pilate was the fifth.

cent man! If you had been in their position, how would you have decided? When you face a tough decision, you can take the easy way out, or you can stand for what is right, regardless of the cost. If we know to do right and don't do it, it is sin (James 4:17).

December 9

Pilate hands Jesus over to be crucified
John 18:39–19:16 (also in Matthew 27:15-26; Mark 15:6-15; Luke 23:13-25) *(Harmony 232)*

*B*ut you have a custom of asking me to release someone from prison each year at Passover. So if you want me to, I'll release the King of the Jews."

But they shouted back, "No! Not this man, but Barabbas!" (Barabbas was a criminal.)

Then Pilate had Jesus flogged with a lead-tipped whip. The soldiers made a crown of long, sharp thorns and put it on his head, and they put a royal purple robe on him. "Hail! King of the Jews!" they mocked, and they hit him with their fists.

Pilate went outside again and said to the people, "I am going to bring him out to you now, but understand clearly that I find him not guilty." Then Jesus came out wearing the crown of thorns and the purple robe. And Pilate said, "Here is the man!"

When they saw him, the leading priests and Temple guards began shouting, "Crucify! Crucify!"

"You crucify him," Pilate said. "I find him not guilty."

The Jewish leaders replied, "By our laws he ought to die because he called himself the Son of God."

When Pilate heard this, he was more frightened than ever. He took Jesus back into the headquarters again and asked him, "Where are you from?" But Jesus gave no answer. "You won't talk to me?" Pilate demanded. "Don't you realize that I have the power to release you or to crucify you?"

Then Jesus said, "You would have no power over me at all unless it were given to you from above. So the one who brought me to you has the greater sin."

Then Pilate tried to release him, but the Jewish leaders told him, "If you release this man, you are not a friend of Caesar. Anyone who declares himself a king is a rebel against Caesar."

When they said this, Pilate brought Jesus out to them again. Then Pilate sat down on the judgment seat on the platform that is called the Stone Pavement (in Hebrew, *Gabbatha*). It was now about noon of the day of preparation for the Passover. And Pilate said to the people, "Here is your king!"

"Away with him," they yelled. "Away with him—crucify him!"

"What? Crucify your king?" Pilate asked.

"We have no king but Caesar," the leading priests shouted back.

Then Pilate gave Jesus to them to be crucified. So they took Jesus and led him away.

WHO'S IN CONTROL?

Throughout the trial we see that Jesus was in control, not Pilate or the religious leaders. Pilate vacillated, the Jewish leaders reacted out of hatred and anger, but Jesus remained composed. He knew the truth, he knew God's plan, and he knew the reason for his trial. Despite the pressure and persecution, Jesus remained unmoved. It was really Pilate and the religious leaders who were on trial, not Jesus. When you are questioned or ridiculed because of your faith, remember that while you may be on trial before your accusers, they are on trial before God.

Scourging could have killed Jesus. The usual procedure was to bare the upper half of the victim's body and tie his hands to a pillar before whipping him with a three-pronged whip. The number of lashes was determined by the severity of the crime; up to forty were permitted under Jewish law (Deuteronomy 25:3).

December 10

Roman soldiers mock Jesus
Mark 15:16-20 (also in Matthew 27:27-31) *(Harmony 233)*

*T*he soldiers took him into their headquarters and called out the entire battalion. They dressed him in a purple robe and made a crown of long, sharp thorns and put it on his head. Then they saluted, yelling, "Hail! King of the Jews!" And they beat him on the head with a stick, spit on him, and dropped to their knees in mock worship. When they were finally tired of mocking him, they took off the purple robe and put his own clothes on him again. Then they led him away to be crucified.

Crucifixion was the Roman penalty for rebellion. Only slaves or those who were not Roman citizens could be crucified. If Jesus died by crucifixion, he would die the death of a rebel and slave. Crucifixion also put the responsibility for killing Jesus on the Romans, and thus the crowds could not blame the religious leaders.

ALONE BUT UNAFRAID

These Roman soldiers were merciless in their torture of Jesus. Yet Jesus had already been deserted by all his disciples when they ran from the garden in terror. One of his closest friends, Peter, denied that he ever knew Jesus. Another disciple, Judas, betrayed him. The crowds who had followed Jesus stood by and did nothing. Two influential leaders, Pilate and Herod, refused to do anything. The religious leaders, who should have been the first to recognize the Messiah, actively promoted Jesus' death. Jesus took all of this for our sakes so that he could go to the cross and carry out the plan of salvation. When people don't understand your faith, or they make fun of it, remember what Jesus went through for you and remain strong.

December 11

Jesus is led away to be crucified
Luke 23:26-31 (also in Matthew 27:32-34; Mark 15:21-24; John 19:17) *(Harmony 234)*

*A*s they led Jesus away, Simon of Cyrene, who was coming in from the country just then, was forced to follow Jesus and carry his cross. Great crowds trailed along behind, including many grief-stricken women. But Jesus turned and said to them, "Daughters of Jerusalem, don't weep for me, but weep for yourselves and for your children. For the days are coming when they will say, 'Fortunate indeed are the women who are childless, the wombs that have not borne a child and the breasts that have never nursed.' People will beg the mountains to fall on them and the hills to bury them. For if these things are done when the tree is green, what will happen when it is dry?"

SIMON'S SERVICE

Colonies of Jews existed outside Judea. Simon had made a Passover pilgrimage to Jerusalem all the way from Cyrene in North Africa. Simon certainly never expected to carry a condemned man's cross to the execution site, yet the Roman soldiers forced him to do so. Simon alone is remembered for this particular act of service—carrying the crossbeam after Jesus, in his beaten humanity, was unable to do so. Small acts can have big effects. Simon could not have saved Jesus' life, but he did

Luke alone mentions the tears of the Jewish women while Jesus was being led through the streets to his execution. Jesus told them not to weep for him but weep for themselves. He knew that in only about forty years, Jerusalem and the Temple would be destroyed by the Romans.

help carry the cross. At some point, it seems that Simon also came to believe in this condemned man as his Savior, for the Bible records that his sons, Alexander and Rufus, became well known later in the early church (Romans 16:13). Never discount the long-reaching effects of small acts of help and service.

Jesus is placed on the cross
Matthew 27:35-44 (also in Mark 15:25-32; Luke 23:32-43; John 19:18-27) *(Harmony 235)*

*A*fter they had nailed him to the cross, the soldiers gambled for his clothes by throwing dice. Then they sat around and kept guard as he hung there. A signboard was fastened to the cross above Jesus' head, announcing the charge against him. It read: "This is Jesus, the King of the Jews."

Two criminals were crucified with him, their crosses on either side of his. And the people passing by shouted abuse, shaking their heads in mockery. "So! You can destroy the Temple and build it again in three days, can you? Well then, if you are the Son of God, save yourself and come down from the cross!"

The leading priests, the teachers of religious law, and the other leaders also mocked Jesus. "He saved others," they scoffed, "but he can't save himself! So he is the king of Israel, is he? Let him come down from the cross, and we will believe in him! He trusted God—let God show his approval by delivering him! For he said, 'I am the Son of God.' " And the criminals who were crucified with him also shouted the same insults at him.

THE WAY OF THE CROSS
When James and John asked Jesus for the places of honor next to him in his Kingdom, he told them they didn't know what they were asking (Mark 10:35-39). Here, as Jesus was preparing to inaugurate his Kingdom through his death, the places on his right and on his left were taken by dying men—criminals. As Jesus explained to his two position-conscious disciples, a person who wants to be close to Jesus must be prepared to suffer and die. The way to the Kingdom is the way of the cross. Taking a stand for Christ may invite suffering and pain, but Jesus will be there with you, through it all.

Jesus was the Son of God, but the people who mocked him didn't believe it—they assumed that the Son of God would save himself. They didn't understand that Jesus' purpose was not to save himself but to save others.

December 13

Jesus dies on the cross
Matthew 27:45-50 (also in Mark 15:33-37; Luke 23:44-46; John 19:28-30) *(Harmony 236a)*

*A*t noon, darkness fell across the whole land until three o'clock. At about three o'clock, Jesus called out with a loud voice, "Eli, Eli, lema sabachthani?" which means, "My God, my God, why have you forsaken me?"

Some of the bystanders misunderstood and thought he was calling for the prophet Elijah. One of them ran and filled a sponge with sour wine, holding it up to him on a stick so he could drink. But the rest said, "Leave him alone. Let's see whether Elijah will come and save him."

Then Jesus shouted out again, and he gave up his spirit.

THE CUP
Jesus was not questioning God; he was quoting the first line of Psalm 22—a deep expression of the anguish he was feeling as he was taking on the sins of the world, which caused him to be separated from his Father. *This was* what Jesus had dreaded as he had prayed to God in the garden to take the cup from him (26:39). The physical agony was horrible; even worse was the period of spiritual separation from his Father. Jesus suffered this double death so that we would never have to experience eternal separation from God. Jesus has gone through so much for you. What can you do for him?

We do not know how this darkness occurred, but it is clear that God caused it. Nature testified to the gravity of Jesus' death, while Jesus' friends and enemies alike fell silent in the encircling gloom. The darkness on that Friday afternoon was both physical and spiritual.

December 14

Jesus dies on the cross
Matthew 27:51-56 (also in Mark 15:38-41; Luke 23:47-49; John 19:31-37) *(Harmony 236b)*

*A*t that moment the curtain in the Temple was torn in two, from top to bottom. The earth shook, rocks split apart, and tombs opened. The bodies of many godly men and women who had died were raised from the dead after Jesus' resurrection. They left the cemetery, went into the holy city of Jerusalem, and appeared to many people.

The Roman officer and the other soldiers at the crucifixion were terrified by the earthquake and all that had happened. They said, "Truly, this was the Son of God!"

And many women who had come from Galilee with Jesus to care for him were watching from a distance. Among them were Mary Magdalene, Mary (the mother of James and Joseph), and Zebedee's wife, the mother of James and John.

DIRECT ACCESS

The tearing of the Temple curtain symbolized Christ's work on the cross. The Temple had three parts: the courts for all the people; the Holy Place, where only priests could enter; and the Most Holy Place, where the high priest alone could enter once a year to atone for the sins of the people. It was in the Most Holy Place that the Ark of the Covenant, and God's presence with it, rested. The curtain that was torn had closed off the Most Holy Place from view. At Christ's death, the barrier between God and man was split in two. Now all people can approach God directly through Christ (Hebrews 9:1-14; 10:19-22). Because of Christ's ultimate sacrifice, we have direct access to God. You can talk to God about anything, at any time. Stay close to him.

Christ's death was accompanied by at least four miraculous events: darkness, the tearing in two of the veil in the Temple, an earthquake, and dead people rising from their tombs. Jesus' death, therefore, could not have gone unnoticed. Everyone knew something significant had happened.

December 15

Jesus is laid in the tomb
John 19:38-42 (also in Matthew 27:57-61; Mark 15:42-47; Luke 23:50-56) *(Harmony 237)*

*A*fterward Joseph of Arimathea, who had been a secret disciple of Jesus (because he feared the Jewish leaders), asked Pilate for permission to take Jesus' body down. When Pilate gave him permission, he came and took the body away. Nicodemus, the man who had come to Jesus at night, also came, bringing about seventy-five pounds of embalming ointment made from myrrh and aloes. Together they wrapped Jesus' body in a long linen cloth with the spices, as is the Jewish custom of burial. The place of crucifixion was near a garden, where there was a new tomb, never used before. And so, because it was the day of preparation before the Passover and since the tomb was close at hand, they laid Jesus there.

CHANGED LIVES

The Gospel writers described four particular people who were changed in the process of Jesus' death. The criminal, dying on the cross beside Jesus, asked Jesus to include him in his Kingdom (Luke 23:39-43). The Roman centurion proclaimed that surely Jesus was the Son of God (Mark 15:39). Joseph and Nicodemus, members of the council and secret followers of Jesus (7:50-52), came out of hiding. These men were changed more by Jesus' death than by his life. They realized who Jesus was, and that realization brought out their belief, proclamation, and action. When confronted with Jesus and his death, we should be changed—to believe, proclaim, and act.

Joseph of Arimathea and Nicodemus were secret followers of Jesus. Joseph was a leader and honored member of the Jewish council (the Sanhedrin). Nicodemus, also a member of the council, had come to Jesus by night (3:1) and later tried to defend him before the other religious leaders (7:50-52). They risked their reputations to provide for Jesus' burial.

December 16

Guards are posted at the tomb
Matthew 27:62-66 (Harmony 238)

*T*he next day—on the first day of the Passover ceremonies—the leading priests and Pharisees went to see Pilate. They told him, "Sir, we remember what that deceiver once said while he was still alive: 'After three days I will be raised from the dead.' So we request that you seal the tomb until the third day. This will prevent his disciples from coming and stealing his body and then telling everyone he came back to life! If that happens, we'll be worse off than we were at first."

Pilate replied, "Take guards and secure it the best you can." So they sealed the tomb and posted guards to protect it.

NOTHING CAN STOP IT

The religious leaders took Jesus' resurrection claims more seriously than the disciples did. The disciples didn't remember Jesus' teaching about his resurrection (20:17-19), but the religious leaders did. Because of his claims, they were almost as afraid of Jesus after his death as when he was alive. They tried to take every precaution that his body would remain in the tomb. The tomb was sealed by stringing a cord across the stone that had been rolled over

The tomb where Jesus was laid was probably a man-made cave cut out of one of the many limestone hills in the area. These caves were often large enough to walk into.

the entrance. The cord was sealed at each end with clay. But the religious leaders took a further precaution, asking that guards be placed at the tomb's entrance. With such precautions, the only way the tomb could be empty would be for Jesus to rise from the dead. The Pharisees failed to understand that no rock, seal, guard, or army could prevent the Son of God from rising again. Because Jesus came back to life, we know that nothing that happens to us can prevent us from rising again and enjoying eternity with our Lord.

December 17

Jesus rises from the dead
Mark 16:1-8 (also in Matthew 28:1-7; Luke 24:1-8; John 20:1)
(Harmony 239a)

*T*he next evening, when the Sabbath ended, Mary Magdalene and Salome and Mary the mother of James went out and purchased burial spices to put on Jesus' body. Very early on Sunday morning, just at sunrise, they came to the tomb. On the way they were discussing who would roll the stone away from the entrance to the tomb. But when they arrived, they looked up and saw that the stone—a very large one—had already been rolled aside. So they entered the tomb, and there on the right sat a young man clothed in a white robe. The women were startled, but the angel said, "Do not be so surprised. You are looking for Jesus, the Nazarene, who was crucified. He isn't here! He has been raised from the dead! Look, this is where they laid his body. Now go and give this message to his disciples, including Peter: Jesus is going ahead of you to Galilee. You will see him there, just as he told you before he died!" The women fled from the tomb, trembling and bewildered, saying nothing to anyone because they were too frightened to talk.

Then they reported all these instructions briefly to Peter and his companions. Afterward Jesus himself sent them out from east to west with the sacred and unfailing message of salvation that gives eternal life. Amen.

RESURRECTION REALITY
The Resurrection is vitally important for many reasons: (1) Jesus kept his promise to rise from the dead, so we can believe that he will keep all his other promises. (2) The Resurrection ensures that the ruler of God's eternal Kingdom will be the living Christ, not just an idea, hope, or dream. (3) Christ's resurrection gives us the assurance that we also will be resurrected (1 Corinthians 15:12-19). (4) The

The women purchased the spices on Saturday evening after the Sabbath had ended so they could go to the tomb early the next morning and anoint Jesus' body as a sign of love, devotion, and respect. Bringing spices to the tomb was like bringing flowers to a grave today.

power of God that brought Christ's body back from the dead is available to us to bring our morally and spiritually dead selves back to life so that we can change and grow. (5) The Resurrection provides the substance of the church's witness to the world. We do not merely tell lessons from the life of a good teacher; we proclaim the reality of the resurrection of Jesus Christ.

December 18

Jesus rises from the dead
John 20:1-10 (also in Luke 24:9-12) *(Harmony 239b)*

*S*he ran and found Simon Peter and the other disciple, the one whom Jesus loved. She said, "They have taken the Lord's body out of the tomb, and I don't know where they have put him!"

Peter and the other disciple ran to the tomb to see. The other disciple outran Peter and got there first. He stooped and looked in and saw the linen cloth lying there, but he didn't go in. Then Simon Peter arrived and went inside. He also noticed the linen wrappings lying there, while the cloth that had covered Jesus' head was folded up and lying to the side. Then the other disciple also went in, and he saw and believed—for until then they hadn't realized that the Scriptures said he would rise from the dead.

STAGES OF BELIEF

People who hear about the Resurrection for the first time may need time before they can comprehend this amazing story. Like Mary and the disciples, they may pass through four stages of belief. (1) At first, they may think the story is a fabrication, impossible to believe (20:2). (2) Like Peter, they may check out the facts and still be puzzled about what happened (20:6). (3) Only when they encounter Jesus personally will they be able to accept the fact of the Resurrection (20:16).

The linen cloth that had been wrapped around Jesus' body was left as if Jesus had passed right through it. The cloth that had covered Jesus' head was folded up and lying to one side. A grave robber couldn't possibly have made off with Jesus' body and left the linens as if they were still shaped around it.

(4) Then, as they commit themselves to the risen Lord and devote their lives to serving him, they will begin to understand fully the reality of his presence with them (20:28). If people don't understand when you tell them about Jesus' resurrection, give them time. Even the disciples didn't believe it at first!

Jesus appears to Mary Magdalene
John 20:11-18 (also in Mark 16:9-11) *(Harmony 240)*

*T*hen they went home.

Mary was standing outside the tomb crying, and as she wept, she stooped and looked in. She saw two white-robed angels sitting at the head and foot of the place where the body of Jesus had been lying. "Why are you crying?" the angels asked her.

"Because they have taken away my Lord," she replied, "and I don't know where they have put him."

She glanced over her shoulder and saw someone standing behind her. It was Jesus, but she didn't recognize him. "Why are you crying?" Jesus asked her. "Who are you looking for?"

She thought he was the gardener. "Sir," she said, "if you have taken him away, tell me where you have put him, and I will go and get him."

"Mary!" Jesus said.

She turned toward him and exclaimed, "Teacher!"

"Don't cling to me," Jesus said, "for I haven't yet ascended to the Father. But go find my brothers and tell them that I am ascending to my Father and your Father, my God and your God."

Mary Magdalene found the disciples and told them, "I have seen the Lord!" Then she gave them his message.

HE IS NEAR

Mary didn't recognize Jesus at first. Her grief had blinded her; she couldn't see him because she didn't expect to see him. Then Jesus spoke her name, and immediately she recognized him. Imagine the love that flooded her heart when she heard her Savior say her name. Jesus

Jesus did not want to be detained at the tomb. If he did not ascend to heaven, the Holy Spirit could not come. Both he and Mary had important work to do.

is near you, and he is calling your name. Can you, like Mary, regard him as your Lord? Are you filled with joy by this good news, and do you share it with others?

December 20

Jesus appears to the women
Matthew 28:8-10 *(Harmony 241)*

The women ran quickly from the tomb. They were very frightened but also filled with great joy, and they rushed to find the disciples to give them the angel's message. And as they went, Jesus met them. "Greetings!" he said. And they ran to him, held his feet, and worshiped him. Then Jesus said to them, "Don't be afraid! Go tell my brothers to leave for Galilee, and they will see me there."

HE WON'T GIVE UP

Jesus told the women to pass a message on to the disciples—that he would meet them in Galilee, as he had previously told them (Mark 14:28). But the disciples, afraid of the religious leaders, stayed hidden behind locked doors in Jerusalem (John 20:19). The disciples had already run away from Jesus at the time of his greatest need; one of them had betrayed Jesus to his death and another had denied ever knowing him. Imagine the sorry group they must have been as they sat hidden and locked away. But Jesus did not give up on them. He met them first right in their secret room in Jerusalem (Luke 24:36) and then later in Galilee (John 21). Jesus gives second chances—and more! No matter how bad your sin, he is ready to forgive. He has great work for you to do!

By "my brothers," Jesus meant his disciples. This showed that he had forgiven them, even after they had deserted him. Their relationship would now be even stronger than before.

December 21

Religious leaders bribe the guards
Matthew 28:11-15 *(Harmony 242)*

As the women were on their way into the city, some of the men who had been guarding the tomb went to the leading priests and told them what had happened. A meeting of all the religious leaders was called, and they decided to bribe the soldiers. They told the soldiers, "You must say, 'Jesus' disciples came during the night while we were sleeping, and they stole his body.' If the governor hears about it, we'll stand up for you and everything will be all right." So the guards accepted the bribe and said what they were told to say. Their story spread widely among the Jews, and they still tell it today.

Jesus' resurrection was already causing a great stir in Jerusalem. A group of women was moving quickly through the streets, looking for the disciples to tell them the amazing news that Jesus was alive. At the same time, a group of religious leaders was plotting how to cover up the Resurrection. Today there is still a great stir over the Resurrection, and there are still only two choices: to believe that Jesus rose from the dead, or to be closed to the truth—denying it, ignoring it, or trying to explain it away. Which choice have you made?

The problem with the council's story that the disciples stole the body is that these same disciples later suffered greatly; some were even martyred for their faith in the risen Christ. If they knew that they had stolen a dead body in order to perpetrate a hoax, it is highly doubtful that they would willingly die for that hoax.

December 22

Jesus appears to two believers traveling on the road
Luke 24:13-35 (also in Mark 16:12-13) *(Harmony 243)*

*T*hat same day two of Jesus' followers were walking to the village of Emmaus, seven miles out of Jerusalem. As they walked along they were talking about everything that had happened. Suddenly, Jesus himself came along and joined them and began walking beside them. But they didn't know who he was, because God kept them from recognizing him.

"You seem to be in a deep discussion about something," he said. "What are you so concerned about?"

They stopped short, sadness written across their faces. Then one of them, Cleopas, replied, "You must be the only person in Jerusalem who hasn't heard about all the things that have happened there the last few days."

"What things?" Jesus asked.

"The things that happened to Jesus, the man from Nazareth," they said. "He was a prophet who did wonderful miracles. He was a mighty teacher, highly regarded by both God and all the people. But our leading priests and other religious leaders arrested him and handed him over to be condemned to death, and they crucified him. We had thought he was the Messiah who had come to rescue Israel. That all happened three days ago. Then some women from our group of his followers were at his tomb early this morning, and they came back with an amazing report. They said his body was missing, and they had seen angels who told them Jesus is alive! Some of our men ran out to see, and sure enough, Jesus' body was gone, just as the women had said."

Then Jesus said to them, "You are such foolish people! You find it so hard to believe all that the prophets wrote in the Scriptures. Wasn't it clearly predicted by the prophets that the Messiah would have to suffer all these things before entering his time of glory?" Then Jesus quoted passages from the writings of Moses and all the prophets, explaining what all the Scriptures said about himself.

By this time they were nearing Emmaus and the end of their journey. Jesus would have gone on, but they begged him to stay the night with them, since it was getting late. So he went home with them. As they sat down to eat, he took a small loaf of bread, asked God's blessing on it, broke it, then gave it to them. Suddenly, their eyes were opened, and they recognized him. And at that moment he disappeared!

They said to each other, "Didn't our hearts feel strangely warm as he talked with us on the road and explained the Scriptures to us?" And within the hour they were on their way back to Jerusalem, where the eleven disciples and the other followers of Jesus were gathered. When they arrived, they were greeted with the report, "The Lord has really risen! He appeared to Peter!"

Then the two from Emmaus told their story of how Jesus had appeared to them as they were walking along the road and how they had recognized him as he was breaking the bread.

STEP OF FAITH

Why did Jesus call these followers foolish? Even though they well knew the biblical prophecies, they failed to understand that Christ's suffering was his path to glory. They could not understand why God did not intervene to save Jesus from the cross. The world has not changed its values: A suffering servant is no more popular today than two thousand years ago. But we have not only the witness of the Old Testament prophets but also the witness of the New Testament apostles and the history of the Christian church all pointing to Jesus' victory over death. Will we step outside the values of our culture and put our faith in Jesus? Or will we foolishly continue to be baffled by his good news?

Jesus' followers from Emmaus were counting on him to redeem Israel—that is, to rescue the nation from its enemies. Most Jews believed that the Old Testament prophecies pointed to a military and political Messiah; they didn't realize that the Messiah had come to redeem people from slavery to sin. When Jesus died, therefore, they lost all hope. They didn't understand that Jesus' death offered the greatest hope possible.

December 23

Jesus appears to the disciples behind locked doors
Luke 24:36-43 (also in John 20:19-23) *(Harmony 244)*

*A*nd just as they were telling about it, Jesus himself was suddenly standing there among them. He said, "Peace be with you." But the whole group was terribly frightened, thinking they were seeing a ghost! "Why are you frightened?" he asked. "Why do you doubt who I am? Look at my hands. Look at my feet. You can see that it's really me. Touch me and make sure that I am not a ghost, because ghosts don't have bodies, as you see that I do!" As he spoke, he held out his hands for them to see, and he showed them his feet.

Still they stood there doubting, filled with joy and wonder. Then he asked them, "Do you have anything here to eat?" They gave him a piece of broiled fish, and he ate it as they watched.

HIS REPRESENTATIVES

The disciples knew that the tomb was empty but didn't understand that Jesus had risen, and they were filled with fear—even when Jesus appeared to them. Despite the witness of the women and the biblical prophecies of this very event, they still didn't believe. Today the Resurrection still catches people by surprise, and many refuse to believe. What more will it take? For these disciples it took the living, breathing Jesus in their midst. For many people today, it takes the presence of living, breathing Christians. As part of Christ's body on earth, you have the responsibility to be his representative to a lost world. What do people think of Christ when they think of you?

Jesus' body wasn't just a figment of the imagination or the appearance of a ghost—the disciples touched him, and he ate food. On the other hand, his body wasn't merely a restored human body like Lazarus's (John 11)—he was able to appear and disappear. Jesus' resurrected body was immortal. This is the kind of body we will be given at the resurrection of the dead (see 1 Corinthians 15:42-50).

December 24

Jesus appears to the disciples, including Thomas
John 20:24-31 (also in Mark 16:14) *(Harmony 245)*

*O*ne of the disciples, Thomas (nicknamed the Twin), was not with the others when Jesus came. They told him, "We have seen the Lord!" But he replied, "I won't believe it unless I see the nail wounds in his hands, put my fingers into them, and place my hand into the wound in his side."

Eight days later the disciples were together again, and this time Thomas was with them. The doors were locked; but suddenly, as before, Jesus was standing among them. He said, "Peace be with you." Then he said to Thomas, "Put your finger here and see my hands. Put your hand into the wound in my side. Don't be faithless any longer. Believe!"

"My Lord and my God!" Thomas exclaimed.

Then Jesus told him, "You believe because you have seen me. Blessed are those who haven't seen me and believe anyway."

Jesus' disciples saw him do many other miraculous signs besides the ones recorded in this book. But these are written so that you may believe that Jesus is the Messiah, the Son of God, and that by believing in him you will have life.

GOOD DOUBTS

Jesus wasn't hard on Thomas for his doubts. Despite his skepticism, Thomas was still loyal to the believers and to Jesus himself. Some people need to doubt before they believe. If doubt leads to questions, questions lead to answers, and the answers are accepted, then doubt has done good work. It is when doubt becomes stubbornness and stubbornness becomes a lifestyle that doubt harms faith. When you doubt, don't stop there. Let your doubt deepen your faith as you continue to search for the answer.

To understand the life and mission of Jesus more fully, all we need to do is study the Gospels. John tells us that his Gospel records only a few of the many events in Jesus' life on earth. But the gospel includes everything we need to know to believe that Jesus is the Christ, the Son of God, through whom we receive eternal life.

December 25

Jesus appears to the disciples while fishing
John 21:1-6 *(Harmony 246a)*

*L*ater Jesus appeared again to the disciples beside the Sea of Galilee. This is how it happened. Several of the disciples were there—Simon Peter, Thomas (nicknamed the Twin), Nathanael from Cana in Galilee, the sons of Zebedee, and two other disciples.

Simon Peter said, "I'm going fishing."

"We'll come, too," they all said. So they went out in the boat, but they caught nothing all night.

At dawn the disciples saw Jesus standing on the beach, but they couldn't see who he was. He called out, "Friends, have you caught any fish?"

"No," they replied.

Then he said, "Throw out your net on the right-hand side of the boat, and you'll get plenty of fish!" So they did, and they couldn't draw in the net because there were so many fish in it.

A CALL FROM THE BEACH

Jesus reminded his disciples of his power and called them once again to be his followers.

Jesus had performed a similar miracle for the disciples before. Luke 5:1-11 records how the disciples had experienced an unsuccessful night of fishing, only to have a record-breaking catch on Jesus' instructions. At the time, the disciples had been amazed to see that not only did Jesus teach, heal, and cast out demons, but he also cared about their day-to-day routine. Here the disciples had gone back to what they knew best—fishing. And Jesus came to them right where they were, performing another miracle to demonstrate his great love for them. Jesus meets us where we are, gently showing us where he wants us to be. Is he standing on the beach calling to you? Pull in your boat and listen!

December 26

Jesus appears to the disciples while fishing
John 21:7-14 *(Harmony 246b)*

*T*hen the disciple whom Jesus loved said to Peter, "It is the Lord!" When Simon Peter heard that it was the Lord, he put on his tunic (for he had stripped for work), jumped into the water, and swam ashore. The others stayed with the boat and pulled the loaded net to the shore, for they were only out about three hundred feet. When they got there, they saw that a charcoal fire was burning and fish were frying over it, and there was bread.

"Bring some of the fish you've just caught," Jesus said. So Simon Peter went aboard and dragged the net to the shore. There were 153 large fish, and yet the net hadn't torn.

"Now come and have some breakfast!" Jesus said. And no one dared ask him if he really was the Lord because they were sure of it. Then Jesus served them the bread and the fish. This was the third time Jesus had appeared to his disciples since he had been raised from the dead.

WILLINGNESS TO SERVE

Simon Peter must have felt pretty worthless. He had run away when Jesus was arrested, and then he had denied he even knew his Lord. Only a few hours before that happened Peter had told Jesus, "Not even if I have to die with you! I will never deny you!" (Matthew 26:35). But then Jesus gave himself up without a fight, and Peter's courage gave out. He had failed his Lord.

Impetuous Peter jumped out of the boat and swam to the shore when he realized that it was Jesus on the beach. Clearly he wanted to talk to Jesus and to experience Jesus' forgiveness.

Although the Lord had already visited the gathered disciples twice before this fishing scene, Peter's guilt and failure were unrelieved. He had decided to do something he could be successful at—fishing. But he failed at that, too.

Then the Lord appeared and gave him success—so many fish that "they couldn't draw in the net"! Peter swam to the Lord as fast as he could, and then hurried to bring the catch of fish when the Lord asked. Jesus had begun to restore Peter. He can restore each of us when we fail.

December 27

Jesus talks with Peter
John 21:15-19 *(Harmony 247a)*

After breakfast Jesus said to Simon Peter, "Simon son of John, do you love me more than these?"

"Yes, Lord," Peter replied, "you know I love you."

"Then feed my lambs," Jesus told him.

Jesus repeated the question: "Simon son of John, do you love me?"

"Yes, Lord," Peter said, "you know I love you."

"Then take care of my sheep," Jesus said.

Once more he asked him, "Simon son of John, do you love me?"

Peter was grieved that Jesus asked the question a third time. He said, "Lord, you know everything. You know I love you."

Jesus said, "Then feed my sheep. The truth is, when you were young, you were able to do as you liked and go wherever you wanted to. But when you are old, you will stretch out your hands, and others will direct you and take you where you don't want to go." Jesus said this to let him know what kind of death he would die to glorify God. Then Jesus told him, "Follow me."

This was a prediction of Peter's death by crucifixion. Tradition indicates that Peter was crucified for his faith upside down because he did not feel worthy of dying as his Lord had died. Despite the future, Jesus told Peter to follow him.

DO YOU TRULY LOVE HIM?
Jesus asked Peter three times if he loved him. The first time Jesus said, "Do you love (Greek *agape:* volitional, self-sacrificial love) me more

than these others?" The second time, Jesus focused on Peter alone and still used the Greek word *agape*. The third time, Jesus used the Greek word *phileo* (signifying affection, affinity, or brotherly love) and asked, in effect, "Are you even my friend?" Each time Peter responded with the Greek word *phileo*. Jesus doesn't settle for quick, superficial answers. He has a way of getting to the heart of the matter. Peter had to face his true feelings and motives when Jesus confronted him. How would you respond if Jesus asked you, "Do you love me?" Do you really love Jesus? Are you even his friend?

December 28

Jesus talks with Peter
John 21:20-25 *(Harmony 247b)*

*P*eter turned around and saw the disciple Jesus loved following them—the one who had leaned over to Jesus during supper and asked, "Lord, who among us will betray you?" Peter asked Jesus, "What about him, Lord?"

Jesus replied, "If I want him to remain alive until I return, what is that to you? You follow me." So the rumor spread among the community of believers that that disciple wouldn't die. But that isn't what Jesus said at all. He only said, "If I want him to remain alive until I return, what is that to you?"

This is that disciple who saw these events and recorded them here. And we all know that his account of these things is accurate.

And I suppose that if all the other things Jesus did were written down, the whole world could not contain the books.

DON'T COMPARE
Peter asked Jesus how John would die. Jesus replied that Peter should not concern himself with that. We tend to compare our life to others, whether to rationalize our own level of devotion to Christ or to question God's justice. Jesus responds to us as he did to Peter: "What is that to you? *You* follow me." When you follow Christ and live as he wants you to, there is no need to compare yourself with others. People make comparisons for many reasons. Some point out others' flaws in order to feel better about themselves. Others simply want reassurance that they are doing well. When you are tempted to compare, look at Jesus Christ. His example will inspire you to do your very best, and his loving acceptance will comfort you when you fall short of your expectations.

Early church history reports that after John spent several years as an exile on the island of Patmos, he returned to Ephesus, where he died as an old man, near the end of the first century.

December 29

Jesus gives the great commission
Matthew 28:16-20 (also in Mark 16:15-18) *(Harmony 248)*

*T*hen the eleven disciples left for Galilee, going to the mountain where Jesus had told them to go. When they saw him, they worshiped him—but some of them still doubted!

Jesus came and told his disciples, "I have been given complete authority in heaven and on earth. Therefore, go and make disciples of all the nations, baptizing them in the name of the Father and the Son and the Holy Spirit. Teach these new disciples to obey all the commands I have given you. And be sure of this: I am with you always, even to the end of the age."

GO AND TELL

God gave Jesus authority over heaven and earth. On the basis of that authority, Jesus told his disciples to make more disciples as they preached, baptized, and taught. With this same authority, Jesus still commands us to tell others the Good News and make them disciples for the Kingdom. We are to go—whether it is next door or to another country—and make disciples. It is not an option but a command to all who call Jesus "Lord." We are not all evangelists in the formal sense, but we have all received gifts that we can use to help fulfill the great commission. As we obey, we have comfort in the knowledge that Jesus is always with us.

Jesus' words affirm the reality of the Trinity. He did not say baptize them into the names but into the name of the Father, Son, and Holy Spirit. The word Trinity *does not occur in Scripture, but it well describes the three-in-one nature of the Father, Son, and Holy Spirit.*

December 30

Jesus appears to the disciples in Jerusalem
Luke 24:44-49 *(Harmony 249)*

*T*hen he said, "When I was with you before, I told you that everything written about me by Moses and the prophets and in the Psalms must all come true." Then he opened their minds to understand these many Scriptures. And he said, "Yes, it was written long ago that the Messiah must suffer and die and rise again from the dead on the third day. With my authority, take this message of repentance to all the nations, beginning in Jerusalem: 'There is forgiveness of sins for all who turn to me.' You are witnesses of all these things.

"And now I will send the Holy Spirit, just as my Father promised. But stay here in the city until the Holy Spirit comes and fills you with power from heaven."

STUDY GOD'S WORD

The phrase "Moses and the prophets and in the Psalms" is a way to describe the entire Old Testament. In other words, the entire Old Testament points to the Messiah. For example, Jesus' role as prophet was foretold in Deuteronomy 18:15-20; his sufferings were prophesied in Psalm 22 and Isaiah 53; his resurrection was predicted in Psalm 16:9-11 and Isaiah 53:10-11. Jesus opened these people's minds to understand the Scriptures. The Holy Spirit does this in our lives today when we study the Bible. Have you ever had trouble understanding a difficult Bible passage? Besides reading surrounding passages, asking other people, and consulting reference works, pray that the Holy Spirit will open your mind to understand, giving you the needed insight to put God's Word into action in your life.

Luke wrote to the Greek-speaking world. He wanted them to know that Christ's message of God's love and forgiveness should go to all the world. We must never ignore the worldwide scope of Christ's gospel. God wants all the world to hear the Good News of salvation.

December 31

Jesus ascends into heaven
Luke 24:50-53 (also in Mark 16:19-20; and Acts 1:1-11)
(Harmony 250)

*T*hen Jesus led them to Bethany, and lifting his hands to heaven, he blessed them. While he was blessing them, he left them and was taken up to heaven. They worshiped him and then returned to Jerusalem filled with great joy. And they spent all of their time in the Temple, praising God.

WITH YOU ALWAYS

As the disciples stood and watched, Jesus began rising into the air, and soon he disappeared into heaven. Seeing Jesus leave must have been frightening, but the disciples knew that Jesus would keep his promise to be with them through the Holy Spirit. This

Jesus' left the disciples physically when he returned to heaven (Acts 1:9), but the Holy Spirit soon came to comfort them and empower to spread the gospel of salvation (Acts 2:1-4).

same Jesus, who lived with the disciples, who died and was buried, and who rose from the dead, loves us and promises to be with us always. We can get to know him better through studying the Scriptures, praying, and allowing the Holy Spirit to make us more like Jesus.

250 EVENTS IN THE LIFE OF CHRIST:
A Harmony of the Gospels

All four books in the Bible that tell the story of Jesus Christ—Matthew, Mark, Luke, and John—stand alone, emphasizing a unique aspect of Jesus' life. But when these are blended into one complete account, or harmonized, we gain new insights about the life of Christ.

This harmony combines the four Gospels into a single chronological account of Christ's life on earth. It includes every chapter and verse of each Gospel, leaving nothing out.

The harmony is divided into 250 events. The title of each event is identical to the title found in the corresponding Gospel. Parallel passages found in more than one Gospel have identical titles, helping you to identify them quickly.

Each of the 250 events in the harmony is numbered. The number of the event corresponds to the number next to the title in the Bible text. When reading one of the Gospel accounts, you will notice, at times, that some numbers are missing or out of sequence. The easiest way to locate these events is to refer to the harmony.

In addition, if you are looking for a particular event in the life of Christ, the harmony can help you locate it more rapidly than paging through all four Gospels. Each of the 250 events has a distinctive title keyed to the main emphasis of the passage to help you locate and remember the events.

This harmony will help you to better visualize the travels of Jesus, study the four Gospels comparatively, and appreciate the unity of their message.

I. BIRTH AND PREPARATION OF JESUS CHRIST

	Matthew	Mark	Luke	John
1. Luke's purpose in writing			1:1-4	
2. God became a human being				1:1-18
3. The ancestors of Jesus	1:1-17		3:23-38	
4. An angel promises the birth of John to Zechariah			1:5-25	
5. An angel promises the birth of Jesus to Mary			1:26-38	
6. Mary visits Elizabeth			1:39-56	
7. John the Baptist is born			1:57-80	
8. An angel appears to Joseph	1:18-25			
9. Jesus is born in Bethlehem			2:1-7	
10. Shepherds visit Jesus			2:8-20	

II. MESSAGE AND MINISTRY OF JESUS CHRIST

	Matthew	Mark	Luke	John
38. Jesus heals a man with leprosy	8:1-4	1:40-45	5:12-16	
39. Jesus heals a paralyzed man	9:1-8	2:1-12	5:17-26	
40. Jesus eats with sinners at Matthew's house	9:9-13	2:13-17	5:27-32	
41. Religious leaders ask Jesus about fasting	9:14-17	2:18-22	5:33-39	
42. Jesus heals a lame man by the pool				5:1-15
43. Jesus claims to be God's Son				5:16-30
44. Jesus supports his claim				5:31-47
45. The disciples pick wheat on the Sabbath	12:1-8	2:23-28	6:1-5	
46. Jesus heals a man's hand on the Sabbath	12:9-14	3:1-6	6:6-11	
47. Large crowds follow Jesus	12:15-21	3:7-12		
48. Jesus selects the twelve disciples		3:13-19	6:12-16	
49. Jesus gives the Beatitudes	5:1-12		6:17-26	
50. Jesus teaches about salt and light	5:13-16			
51. Jesus teaches about the Law	5:17-20			
52. Jesus teaches about anger	5:21-26			
53. Jesus teaches about lust	5:27-30			
54. Jesus teaches about divorce	5:31-32			
55. Jesus teaches about vows	5:33-37			
56. Jesus teaches about retaliation	5:38-42			
57. Jesus teaches about loving enemies	5:43-48		6:27-36	
58. Jesus teaches about giving to the needy	6:1-4			
59. Jesus teaches about prayer	6:5-15			
60. Jesus teaches about fasting	6:16-18			
61. Jesus teaches about money	6:19-24			
62. Jesus teaches about worry	6:25-34			
63. Jesus teaches about criticizing others	7:1-6		6:37-42	
64. Jesus teaches about asking, seeking, knocking	7:7-12			
65. Jesus teaches about the way to heaven	7:13-14			
66. Jesus teaches about fruit in people's lives	7:15-20		6:43-45	
67. Jesus teaches about those who build houses on rock and sand	7:21-29		6:46-49	
68. A Roman soldier demonstrates faith	8:5-13		7:1-10	

	Matthew	Mark	Luke	John
94. Jesus prepares the disciples for persecution	10:16-42			
95. Herod kills John the Baptist	14:1-12	6:14-29	9:7-9	
96. Jesus feeds five thousand	14:13-21	6:30-44	9:10-17	6:1-15
97. Jesus walks on water	14:22-33	6:45-52		6:16-21
98. Jesus heals all who touch him	14:34-36	6:53-56		
99. Jesus is the true bread from heaven				6:22-40
100. The Jews disagree that Jesus is from heaven				6:41-59
101. Many disciples desert Jesus				6:60-71
102. Jesus teaches about inner purity	15:1-20	7:1-23		
103. Jesus sends a demon out of a girl	15:21-28	7:24-30		
104. The crowd marvels at Jesus' healings	15:29-31	7:31-37		
105. Jesus feeds four thousand	15:32-39	8:1-9		
106. Religious leaders ask for a sign in the sky	16:1-4	8:10-12		
107. Jesus warns against wrong teaching	16:5-12	8:13-21		
108. Jesus restores sight to a blind man		8:22-26		
109. Peter says Jesus is the Messiah	16:13-20	8:27-30	9:18-20	
110. Jesus predicts his death the first time	16:21-28	8:31-9:1	9:21-27	
111. Jesus is transfigured on the mountain	17:1-13	9:2-13	9:28-36	
112. Jesus heals a demon-possessed boy	17:14-21	9:14-29	9:37-43	
113. Jesus predicts his death the second time	17:22-23	9:30-32	9:44-45	
114. Peter finds the coin in the fish's mouth	17:24-27			
115. The disciples argue about who would be the greatest	18:1-6	9:33-37	9:46-48	
116. The disciples forbid another to use Jesus' name		9:38-42	9:49-50	
117. Jesus warns against temptation	18:7-9	9:43-50		
118. Jesus warns against looking down on others	18:10-14			
119. Jesus teaches how to treat a believer who sins	18:15-20			
120. Jesus tells the parable of the unforgiving debtor	18:21-35			
121. Jesus' brothers ridicule him				7:1-9

	Matthew	Mark	Luke	John
151. Jesus is the good shepherd				10:1-21
152. Religious leaders surround Jesus at the Temple				10:22-42
153. Jesus teaches about entering the Kingdom			13:22-30	
154. Jesus grieves over Jerusalem			13:31-35	
155. Jesus heals a man with dropsy			14:1-6	
156. Jesus teaches about seeking honor			14:7-14	
157. Jesus tells the parable of the great feast			14:15-24	
158. Jesus teaches about the cost of being a disciple			14:25-35	
159. Jesus tells the parable of the lost sheep			15:1-7	
160. Jesus tells the parable of the lost coin			15:8-10	
161. Jesus tells the parable of the lost son			15:11-32	
162. Jesus tells the parable of the shrewd accountant			16:1-18	
163. Jesus tells about the rich man and the beggar			16:19-31	
164. Jesus tells about forgiveness and faith			17:1-10	
165. Lazarus becomes ill and dies				11:1-16
166. Jesus comforts Mary and Martha				11:17-37
167. Jesus raises Lazarus from the dead				11:37-44
168. Religious leaders plot to kill Jesus				11:45-57
169. Jesus heals ten men with leprosy			17:11-19	
170. Jesus teaches about the coming of the Kingdom of God			17:20-37	
171. Jesus tells the parable of the persistent widow			18:1-8	
172. Jesus tells the parable of two men who prayed			18:9-14	
173. Jesus teaches about marriage and divorce	19:1-12	10:1-12		
174. Jesus blesses little children	19:13-15	10:13-16	18:15-17	
175. Jesus speaks to the rich young man	19:16-30	10:17-31	18:18-30	

III. DEATH AND RESURRECTION OF JESUS CHRIST

	Matthew	Mark	Luke	John
229. Judas kills himself	27:3-10			
230. Jesus stands trial before Pilate	27:11-14	15:2-5	23:1-5	18:28-38
231. Jesus stands trial before Herod			23:6-12	
232. Pilate hands Jesus over to be crucified	27:15-26	15:6-15	23:13-25	18:39–19:16
233. Roman soldiers mock Jesus	27:27-31	15:16-20		
234. Jesus is led away to be crucified	27:32-34	15:21-24	23:26-31	19:17
235. Jesus is placed on the cross	27:35-44	15:25-32	23:32-43	19:18-27
236. Jesus dies on the cross	27:45-56	15:33-41	23:44-49	19:28-37
237. Jesus is laid in the tomb	27:57-61	15:42-47	23:50-56	19:38-42
238. Guards are posted at the tomb	27:62-66			
239. Jesus rises from the dead	28:1-7	16:1-8	24:1-12	20:1-9
240. Jesus appears to Mary Magdalene		16:9-11		20:10-18
241. Jesus appears to the women	28:8-10			
242. Religious leaders bribe the guards	28:11-15			
243. Jesus appears to two believers traveling on the road		16:12-13	24:13-35	
244. Jesus appears to the disciples behind locked doors			24:36-43	20:19-23
245. Jesus appears to the disciples, including Thomas		16:14		20:24-31
246. Jesus appears to the disciples while fishing				21:1-14
247. Jesus talks with Peter				21:15-25
248. Jesus gives the great commission	28:16-20	16:15-18		
249. Jesus appears to the disciples in Jerusalem			24:44-49	
250. Jesus ascends into heaven		16:19-20	24:50-53